Seeing the Light

Seeing the Light

The Social Logic
of Personal Discovery

THOMAS DeGLOMA

The University of Chicago Press   Chicago and London

THOMAS DeGLOMA is assistant professor of sociology at Hunter College, City University of New York.

The University of Chicago Press, Chicago 60637
The University of Chicago Press, Ltd., London
© 2014 by The University of Chicago
All rights reserved. Published 2014.
Printed in the United States of America

23 22 21 20 19 18 17 16 15 14   1 2 3 4 5

ISBN-13: 978-0-226-17574-4 (cloth)
ISBN-13: 978-0-226-17588-1 (paper)
ISBN-13: 978-0-226-17591-1 (e-book)
DOI: 10.7208/chicago/9780226175911.001.0001

Library of Congress Cataloging-in-Publication Data

DeGloma, Thomas, author.
   Seeing the light : the social logic of personal discovery /
Thomas DeGloma.
        pages cm
   Includes bibliographical references and index.
   ISBN 978-0-226-17574-4 (cloth : alk. paper) — ISBN 978-0-226-17588-1
(pbk. : alk. paper) — ISBN 978-0-226-17591-1 (e-book) 1. Autonomy
(Psychology) 2. Self-actualization (Psychology) 3. Religious awakening.
I. Title.
   BF575.A88D46 2014
   158.1—dc23   2014012388

♾ This paper meets the requirements of ANSI/NISO Z39.48-1992
(Permanence of Paper).

Contents

Illustrations

Acknowledgments

No book is possible without the vital support of one's community of colleagues, friends, and family. I am fortunate to have received insightful comments and suggestions from several people. Most significantly, I owe an extraordinary debt of gratitude to Eviatar Zerubavel, who has been a truly giving and inspirational mentor and friend. In addition to providing an immeasurable amount of constructive guidance and intellectual direction, Eviatar always encouraged me to stick with this project and to take intellectual risks with my work in general. He has shown me, by example, how to follow my passion in an academic world that often punishes intellectual risk taking and marginalizes those who choose to take one of the (unfortunately) many paths less traveled. My sociological imagination has been deeply influenced by Eviatar's remarkable ability to see social patterns and explore the fascinating social dimensions of mental life. A special word of thanks also goes to Allan Horwitz, Ann Mische, Arlene Stein, and Robin Wagner-Pacifici for reading past drafts of the manuscript in its entirety and providing invaluable insight. Each of them provided comments that helped me, in different ways, to hone my analysis of the cultural and symbolic dimensions of the narratives and images that grace these pages. I am also very grateful for helpful discussions with several people, including (in alphabetical order) Rachel Brekhus, Wayne Brekhus, Yael Bromberg, Andrea Catone, Karen Cerulo, Dan Chambliss, Lynn Chancer, Karen Danna, Audrey Devine-Eller, Jeffrey K. Dowd, Asia Friedman, Judith Gerson, Daina Cheyenne

Harvey, Jennifer Hemler, Jenna Howard, Erin Johnston, Christena Nippert-Eng, Carol Rambo, Dan Ryan, and Ruth Simpson.

Doug Mitchell was a phenomenal editor. We first spoke about this project years ago and every conversation we have had since has been a pleasure. His enthusiastic support, editorial guidance, and intellectual perspective have been invaluable throughout this process. I am also grateful to Tim McGovern, Kelly Finefrock-Creed, and the rest of the Chicago team for all of their assistance as well as to two excellent anonymous readers who provided careful and constructive comments.

In addition, I am fortunate to have had the caring support of family and friends, including my parents, Thomas DeGloma Sr. and Cathi DeGloma, along with Izzy Posner, Sharon Posner, and Spiro Trupos, my siblings Michael, Melanie, Peter, Paul, Angela, Jake, Brian, and Adrianna, as well as friends Michael Bacchione, Blair Brown, Elena Callahan, Nelson Downend, Amanda Geraci, Thomas "Toast" Hansen, Xavier Hansen, Kelly Hoffman, Jennifer Huttenberger, Katinka Locascio, Thomas "Ziggy" McMullen, Kris Miller, Avianna Perez, Julie Poulos, Chrissie Reyes, Joe Valentine, and way too many other good friends and comrades to list.

Finally, with affection and sincerity, I owe a special word of thanks and loving recognition to my wife, Lena DeGloma, a true soul mate, partner, and friend who, in addition to providing multiple astute comments over several drafts, accompanied me every step of the way along this journey. Through storms and discoveries, times of excitement and grief, moves to Ithaca and then Brooklyn, and crazy adventures with Maya and Rio, Lena has helped me to truly know the meaning of heart space. Her love and support have been and continue to be a refuge. She is a gift in a challenging world. She helps me to be the best person I can be.

Certain small sections of this text, along with much earlier versions of some ideas, have appeared in the journals *Sociological Forum* (vol. 25, no. 3 [2010]: 519–40) and the *Hedgehog Review* (vol. 12, no. 2 [2010]: 74–84). A few of the cases specifically pertaining to those individuals who recover memories of child sexual abuse and those who retract memories of child sexual abuse previously appeared in the journal *Symbolic Interaction* (vol. 30, no. 4 [2007]: 543–65). Support for the final stages of this project was provided by a PSC-CUNY Award, jointly funded by the Professional Staff Congress and the City University of New York.

ONE

Discovering "Truth"

I once was lost, but now am found,

Was blind, but now I see.

JOHN NEWTON, "AMAZING GRACE"

Awakenings

The first verse of the popular Christian song widely known as "Amazing Grace," partially reproduced in the epigraph above, is one of the most recognizable articulations of religious conversion in the Western world. The hymn was composed by John Newton when he was serving as an Anglican priest in Buckinghamshire, England, and published with a collection of hymns in 1779 under its original title, "Faith's Review and Expectation." It is also an autobiographical account. Prior to serving the Christian ministry, Newton worked as a slave trader. He tells us that on March 10, 1748, at the age of twenty-three, a violent storm threatened to sink the ship he worked while en route from West Africa to England. According to his own account, the young Newton cried out in deep and profound fear for his life and begged God for mercy.[1] Nearly four weeks and several storms later, his badly damaged vessel reached land. Newton later interpreted his escape from this near-death experience as an act of divine intervention, writing, "[. . .] [T]he Lord of heaven delivered me out of deep waters. [. . .] About this time I began to know that there is a God who hears and answers prayer."[2] This experience, John Newton tells us, was a major moment in a more protracted awakening that ultimately led him to embrace a newfound Christian worldview and strive for a way of life grounded in Christian morality. Decades later, Newton became a vocal abolitionist,[3] taking a stand in marked contrast to his earlier profession. It was not until this later period of his life when he began working in the priesthood that he composed "Amazing Grace." In just a few words, the poet-priest captured the tension between a life of despair marked by wretched "blasphemy and profaneness"[4] and the joy of salvation and virtue. Using his own life story as a template, he produced a popular story model that his parishioners and the public at large could use to account for their own personal discoveries.

For centuries individuals have told stories about discovering truth in their lives. Such storytellers describe having once held false beliefs about the world and consequently having lived a significant part of their lives "blind" to reality. Simultaneously, they tell of "seeing the light" or "waking up" to discover the "truth" about themselves and the "reality" of the world in which they live.[5] Some, like Newton, tell stories about discovering a religious "truth," typically to explain their conversion to a new faith or their rejection of a religion in which they once believed. Yet others describe discovering a political "truth" as they work to promote an ideological agenda they once actively opposed. More, some individuals account for a newfound psychological "truth," often finding causes for their psychological troubles in newly discovered childhood experiences. Others describe discovering a sexual "truth," commonly to account for their embrace of a newly acquired sexual orientation or identity. Still others describe coming to a newfound scientific "truth" that leads them to reject long-held beliefs about the universe. Despite the notable differences among their concerns, all such individuals tell autobiographical stories about awakening to a "truth" that pertains to some personally and socially significant issue.[6]

In this book, I explore the distinctly social logic of such *awakening narratives*—stories people tell about having once been contained in a world of darkness and ignorance and subsequently awakening to an enlightened understanding of their experiences and situations. Such stories do not concern relatively mundane or minor developments in the storyteller's life. Rather, individuals tell awakening stories to explain a radical transformation of consciousness, a fundamental change in their perception of their lives and their orientation to the world around them.[7] People tell such stories in order to account for a major change of heart and mind—to convey what Peter Berger describes as an "alternation . . . between varying and sometimes contradictory systems of meaning."[8] As opposed to relatively localized discoveries (such as discovering the cause of an ongoing problem at work) or accounts of a particular misperception (such as realizing a friend or lover is not the person you thought they were), awakening stories involve a narrated substitution of one worldview—what David A. Snow and Richard Machalek call a "master attribution scheme"[9]—for another. Individuals use such accounts to justify their embrace of new attitudes, beliefs, perceptions, and actions. As we will see, awakening stories are quite prevalent; they pertain to many different subject matters and span a wide variety of social and historical contexts.

There are various ways that we might understand the stories people tell about discovering truth, each of which also represents an established scholarly approach to questions about personal discovery and transformation. One way would be to view awakenings as experiences in which individuals actually discover an objectively "real" yet previously hidden truth or reality. Such a rationalist approach, inherited from Enlightenment models of scientific reasoning, lies at the core of methodological positivism in the social and natural sciences today. This view relies on the idea that our minds—and our stories—are separate from the world in which we live. Our task, then, is to use our mental capacity to discover some objective and universal truth that resides "out there."[10]

Contrary to the rationalist position, I am not interested in measuring the objective character of truth and falsehood. Nor do I take a position on the issue of what *really* happened in an individual's life and what did not. I know nothing of the many individuals I reference in this book except the stories they tell, and further, I do not take their accounts at face value. Instead, I am interested in the ways such awakenings involve conceptions of truth that rely on and take shape around the worldview—the beliefs, values, perceptions, ideas, feelings, and moral evaluations—of the community to which one belongs. That is to say, rather than a representational view of truth (one that involves judging claims about truth based on whether or how well they represent the "real" world), I advance a social and interrelational view (one that involves treating truth as a function of the social situation or cultural vantage point of the individual making claims).[11] Thus, the stories people tell are the "reality" I am analyzing. I treat them as events in and of themselves. Further, building on Norman K. Denzin's discussion of the "major epiphany,"[12] I am interested in how individuals use these awakening stories to give meaning to their lives.

Alternatively, proponents of a psychological position view the stories we tell about our lives as primarily idiosyncratic and inherently personal phenomena. According to this view, awakenings involve discovering a subjective truth that is fundamentally and uniquely our own. Proponents of such an approach often acknowledge culture as a secondary variable yet treat our autobiographical stories as principally personal. For example, while recognizing culture as a factor in the shaping of one's "personal myth," psychologist Dan P. McAdams argues that our stories are ultimately experienced as a truth residing "inside of us . . . in the secrecy of our own minds . . . and for our own psychological discovery and enjoyment."[13] Cultural anthropologist Peter G. Stromberg, while identifying common themes in Christian conversion narratives, argues that conversion accounts are manifestations of unresolved personal emotional conflicts.[14] For Stromberg, "the self-transformation associated with the conversion occurs as a result of changing embodied aims into articulable intentions,"[15] thus moving something inside the individual toward outer expression. These scholars provide important insight into the value of studying narrative but ultimately see our stories as reflecting something internal.

Contrary to the tenets of psychological individualism, I am interested in the social foundations of awakenings. I explore the ways individuals and communities draw on shared sociomental norms[16] and deep-seated cultural and emotion codes[17] to frame the relationship between the "true" and the "false" as they tell their seemingly personal awakening stories. Telling stories about discovering "truth" involves seeing the world through a new "community's distinctive mental lenses."[18] As opposed to viewing such stories "as a manifestation of the underlying personality" of a few individuals or "as a key to understanding the personality of the teller,"[19] I intentionally bring a sociological view of knowledge, cognition, and memory to bear on an analysis of awakenings in an effort to better understand how culture provides individuals with resources they use to experience a sense of discovery.[20]

Further, while individuals tell awakening stories to convey a personally relevant discovery, they also wield their stories as cultural tools in a broader social context. As opposed to individuals who express an ambivalent or multifaceted outlook,[21] such storytellers articulate new and definite worldviews. They use such seemingly personal narratives to do cultural work as they defend one version of truth and reality while undermining and debunking others. Thus, I highlight the ways individuals and communities use these stories to weigh in on cultural disputes over meaning. The cultural meaning-making work of these stories illuminates a link between our autobiographical accounts and the intersubjective, "impersonal social mindscapes that we *share in common*"[22] with some but also *hold in contrast* to others. Awakening stories tell us something about the tensions and conflicts between different groups in the world. However, as opposed to conventional conflict theory, which stresses the interest-based struggle for material domination and power, I focus on the struggle to establish and assert cultural and *cognitive authority*[23]—the authority to define important events, experiences, issues, relationships, and situations in the world.[24]

In order to elucidate the central role of culture in shaping both the form and content of our personal discoveries, the robust cultural meaning-making work individuals and communities do with stories of this type, and the communicative activity at the heart of the awakening story, I examine the striking similarities among a wide variety of stories dealing with an eclectic range of topics that are typically not compared or analyzed in relation to one another. Deliberately downplaying the nuances that set these topics apart from one another and intentionally tuning in to the underlying patterns that tie them together, I analyze a variety of political, religious, sexual, psychological, scientific, and philosophical stories from various times and places. I thus present the social foundations of our seemingly personal discoveries of "truth."

Three Dimensions of Autobiographical Work

In order to fully appreciate the distinctly social significance of awakening stories, we need to be aware of three interrelated dimensions of autobiographical work[25]—the self-reflexive, the dialogical, and the performative. By using the concept of autobiographical work, I mean to emphasize the social consequences of autobiographical storytelling, especially insofar as autobiographical stories have an impact at the levels of cognition and emotion. Together, these three dimensions will help us to understand how people who tell stories about discovering truth use those stories to situate themselves in relation to others in a broad social environment.

Stories are "autobiographical" whenever they are identity-shaping narratives that reflect back on the storyteller as the subject of the story and, more, as one who seeks to explain something about his or her arrival at the standpoint from which he or she tells the story. All of the stories people tell about awakening to "truth" involve this self-reflexive dimension. Autobiographical stories can be general and expansive or partial and focused; they can chronicle a storyteller's life or detail a particular defining moment.[26] They are, "in the broad sense of an interpretive self-history produced by the individual concerned, whether written down or not . . . actually at the core of self-identity in modern social life."[27] They are, in the more focused sense of a testimony pertaining to a specific issue, particular "accounts of identity, narratives of the self"[28] in which one connects oneself to an occasion or situation of concern. In either case, the self is a continually evolving "reflexive project,"[29] and what we experience as, and feel about, ourselves manifests in story form. When I use the term *autobiographical* to describe a story, I mean what Anthony Paul Kerby refers to as "acts of *self-narration*" that are "not only . . . descriptive of the self but, more importantly, [are] *fundamental to the emergence and reality*" of the storytelling human subject.[30] From this perspective, the self is "the implied subject of a narrated history."[31] Autobiographical stories are the media individuals use to facilitate "personal becoming" and the process of "shaping oneself as a human being."[32] In other words, the way we conceive of and represent who we are is inseparable from the stories we tell about ourselves.

Beyond the self-reflexive dimension, autobiographical stories are also a means by which individuals connect their lives to others and to the world in which they live. As Vered Vinitzky-Seroussi argues, "Autobiographies may appear to be personal matters, life stories that people tell themselves. In practice, however, autobiographies are social acts" that can never "be detached from the audience before whom the story of one's life is told."[33] Thus, autobiographical stories are created and circulated within social environments in which people negotiate shared definitions of their situation with an audience that, by virtue of the dynamic between storyteller and interlocutor, becomes part of the autobiographical story itself.[34] Such an audience can be physically present or at large. Either way, telling an autobiographical story involves engaging in a conversation—and sometimes multiple conversations— and the story absorbs something of that communicative activity. From this perspective, "there is no such thing as a self-story if that term is taken literally; only self-other-stories."[35] Autobiographical stories, however personal they seem, contain the social relationships within which the storyteller is situated. Following Arthur W. Frank, I consider "autobiographical work as dialogue" and "the tension of this dialogue is to include the voices of others without assimilating these voices to one's own."[36] Awakening stories are parts of broader conversations and deliberations over meaning in the world. They also contain and express those conversations and deliberations; they have a dialogical character. Well beyond showing us something about the individual storyteller, awakening narratives give us insight into the dynamics of culture and the meanings people attribute to their lives in relation to others and to the concerns of the world around them.

The stories people tell about discovering truth typically involve descriptions of various events and experiences that are crucial to the meaning-making work in which the teller is engaged. However, an awakening story is also an event in and of itself.[37] Such a distinction calls our attention to the diegetic and nondiegetic levels of performance.[38] The diegetic level refers to the story as a contained world of social drama (focusing on story content and highlighting the definition of situations and events internal to the narrative). By analyzing the diegetic characteristics of awakening narratives, I am building on the tradition established by the literary theorist Kenneth Burke. Burke proposes a pentadic schema—what he calls "the five key terms of dramatism"—to show how we can interpret narratives as worlds of meaning involving actions, scenes, agents, agency, and purpose.[39] Taking a related view and claiming that explanatory narratives are an important subject matter of sociology, C. Wright Mills argues that social actors use "vocabularies of motive" to explain and account for their actions and the actions of others.[40] Developing such an approach to narrative in order to highlight the ways agents synch their stories with entrenched properties of culture to make effective claims, Philip Smith argues that "narratives allocate causal responsibility for action, define actors and give them motivation, indicate the trajectory of past episodes and predict consequences of future choices, suggest courses of action, confer and withdraw legitimacy, and provide social approval by aligning events with normative cultural codes."[41] Alternatively, attending to the nondiegetic level means seeing the *act* of storytelling as a dramatic performance (external to and framing the content of the narrative). As Erving Goffman has shown with regard to the analysis of everyday interaction,[42] nondiegetic dramaturgical devices are fundamental to the meanings storytellers work to convey. Actors ground their stories in certain contexts and use various props and literary devices (such as voice and emotional expression) to frame the content of their stories and reinforce their intended meanings.

We must pay attention to both levels of performance to understand how people who tell awakening stories work at impression management and use various dramaturgical devices, including settings, characters, affect (or manner), and descriptive intentionality. With both of these levels in mind, I view autobiographical stories as performative speech acts.[43] I am interested in both the tactics (logistics and means) and strategies (mobilization and goals) of storytelling as meaning-making work and highlight the fact that agents often hope their autobiographical narratives will have "some illocutionary force or performative impact."[44] Building on these perspectives, we can interpret awakening stories as social dramas with which storytellers define important relationships, events, situations, and experiences, as well as attribute motives to various characters, when engaging their audiences and general surroundings.

Taking these three interrelated dimensions of autobiographical work into account, we can begin to see how the stories we tell about our lives are inseparable from our experience of self and identity and our position in a web of social relationships. We use our autobiographical stories to establish our moral orientation in a world marked by competing viewpoints and multiple ideas about "truth." As Charles Taylor argues, "To know who you are is to be oriented in moral space, a space in which questions arise about what is good or bad, what is worth doing and what not, what has meaning and importance for you and what is trivial and secondary. . . . Our identity . . . is what makes possible these discriminations. . . . Our identities define the space of qualitative distinctions within which we live and choose."[45] When people tell awakening stories, they make use of a generic story formula to resolve such questions and make such qualitative discriminations as they orient themselves in a complex world. In the process, they give life to feelings and give meaning to events and experiences as they advance strong evaluative claims about the distinction between "falsehood" and "truth."

The Awakening-Story Formula

Writing to an audience of fellow ex-Mormons, an individual who goes by the name Moonshine comments, "Like many of you, I have spent the last several years trying to make sense out of the most extraordinary experience of my life—my evolution through and beyond traditional Mormon beliefs. [. . .] [I now have] an acute awareness of the [. . .] fear and dependence the church fosters in its faithful members [. . .]. What a trip! [. . .] The cognitive dissonance I felt set in motion a chain of events that led to some painful conclusions."[46] Using phrases like "evolution through and beyond," "a chain of events," and "What a trip!" Moonshine lays out a rudimentary temporal map of her life with just a few words. She uses the general metaphors of evolution and a journey[47] to shape her life along a formulaic *plotline*. As she goes on to fill in more detail, her audience is already given a sense of her personal awakening. We are aware of a sharp distinction between her former mindset (defined by her "traditional Mormon beliefs") and her present world-view (as an apostate who has moved "beyond" Mormonism). From her current storytelling standpoint, Moonshine sees things very differently than she used to.

Awakenings are stories that adhere to a common, socially patterned story formula and consequently share the same generic plot.[48] When I refer to the plot of a story, I mean to highlight the patterned succession of episodes, as well as the projective implications, that provide a structural foundation for the meaning of the account conveyed by the storyteller. Focusing on the plot of a story calls our attention to the form in which we recount our experiences as we regularly "reduce highly complex event sequences to inevitably simplistic, one dimensional visions"[49] of our lives. As Joseph E. Davis argues, the plot structure of our stories allows us to portray select events "as a meaningful sequence unfolding from the beginning event toward a valued endpoint or 'moral' the story anticipates."[50] Thus, the structural organization of the story is what gives us a sense of change over time. In the case of our autobiographical narratives, emplotment allows for our sense of a distinction between past, present, and future in our lives, or *autobiographical time*. As Paul Ricoeur demonstrates, "What is ultimately at stake in the case of the structural identity of the narrative function as well as that of the truth claim of every narrative work, is the temporal character of human experience. The world unfolded by every narrative work is always a temporal world. . . . Time becomes human time to the extent that it is organized after the manner of narrative; narrative, in turn, is meaningful to the extent that it portrays the features of temporal experience."[51] In other words, our experience of time (and therefore change) and the structural organization of narrative are two sides of the same phenomenon; "Human time is a storied affair."[52] Whereas chronometric time refers to a standardized unit of temporal measurement and developmental time refers to an organism's physiological or psychological growth and eventual decline, autobiographical time refers to the way that storytellers arrange their life stories as an ordered course of events, perceptions, and feelings,[53] situating themselves in the world by giving their lives "historicity and relationality"[54] in the process.

Focusing on plot structure and the awakening-narrative formula, I advance several interrelated arguments. First, individuals who are in otherwise different situations use the same story formula to emplot their lives around a transformative realization of "truth," whatever the storyteller understands truth to be at the time the story is told. Thus, focusing on the story formula allows us to see the prevalence of awakening stories across time and context and regardless of subject matter. Second, individuals use the same story formula despite making divergent or oppositional claims and advancing disparate agendas. Often storytellers who are conventionally said to be in opposing camps tell stories that follow the same pattern. With regard to the content and orientation of their stories, they have "reverse" narratives. Structurally, however, they are the same. Third, the awakening formula is constructed from a foundational pool of cultural resources, which includes a "remarkably durable set of binary oppositions"[55] that we use to make the types of qualitative distinctions necessary to establish our orientation in the world. The defining character of the awakening narrative is a temporally situated, binary distinction between "falsehood" and "truth." Individuals and communities use this epistemic distinction to classify the world into negatively and positively charged moral realms, giving meaning to experiences, events, and relationships in the process.[56] Such a sociomental organization of the world, facilitated by a stock of tropes in the form of "conventional metaphors and imagery,"[57] also provides a general structure of feeling[58] that storytellers use to ascribe emotions to particular events and issues. The awakening formula allows storytellers to mobilize "emotion codes which encourage audience members to feel in particular ways"[59] given the antithetical visions of falsehood and truth, notions of evil and good, and experiences of loss and discovery intrinsic to the narrative formula.

I first took interest in awakenings while studying trauma narratives. In particular, as I was researching "recovered" memories of child sexual abuse, I began to notice that the process of recovering memories involves a formulaic discovery of "truth" (in this case, the memory of abuse) and a consequent formulaic account of the narrator's "false" belief (the prior, mistaken perception that the abuse wasn't there). Such self-identified survivors of child sexual abuse tell scripted stories about awakening to the truth about their lives.[60] Philip's account, for example, was published in a therapeutic volume. Philip recalls, "When I was 14 my mother used to come into my bed in the early hours of the morning, arouse me sexually, and sexual intercourse would take place. Until recently (I am now 52) I thought I had dreamed those sessions, because I must have never been fully awake [. . .]. [. . .] I can't tell you how I felt when this dawned on me."[61] Philip is telling us that what he used to believe was a dream, he now—quite suddenly at the age of fifty-two—knows was sexual abuse. As he tells us this story, he is describing his prior state of "false" consciousness ("I thought I had dreamed those sessions") while testifying to the "truth" (intercourse, sexual abuse) and radically redefining his relationship with his mother. In remarkably few words, he describes a major transformation of consciousness—a discovery of "truth" and "reality" that is accompanied by profound feelings and has significant implications for his future attitudes, behaviors, and relationships.

Philip's story is certainly very personal. His "dawning" or awakening, however, is far from unique. With regard to this particular issue, many other individuals use this psychological version of the awakening story to describe recovering memories of child sexual abuse in therapeutic or support group–like settings.[62] However, at a transcontextual level, such stories are formally similar to stories told in other settings about different topics. For example, Eleonai "Eli" Israel, an Army National Guard specialist and member of the social movement organization Iraq Veterans Against the War, describes a major transformation of consciousness with regard to an explicitly political subject matter. Eli recounts,

Like many after September 11th I wanted to serve, again. I felt I owed something more to my country after my years of training. I trusted my president and my leadership to tell me the truth. I also trusted my own integrity. I knew that I would never willingly do anything that I knew to be immoral or wrong. [. . .] I reasoned that my actions during these missions were justified in the name of "self-defense." However, I came to realize my perception was wrong. I was in a country that I had no right to be in, violating the lives of people, and doing so without regard to the same standards of dignity and respect that we as Americans hold our own homes and our own lives to. [. . .] I have taken and/or destroyed the lives of people who were defending their families from being the "collateral damage" of the day.[63]

Like Philip, Eli describes a significant personal discovery, a dawning in which he realized his old perceptions and beliefs were "false" while coming to understand the "true" nature of his actions, experiences, and relationships. Despite using their autobiographical stories to address very different subject matters, Moonshine, Philip, and Eli all juxtapose a past state of *cognitive constraint* (a false or deluded mental state) with a more current state of *cognitive emancipation* (a newly enlightened mental state). Their stories conform to this common social pattern and formula of storytelling.

By focusing on the formal properties shared by these three stories at the expense of their otherwise significant differences, we can begin to see how this story formula has a generic social logic that Moonshine, Philip, and Eli each use to give meaning to their lives and justify their current beliefs and perceptions. When individuals tell such a story, they make use of a strong cultural doctrine that truth emerges from the debunking of false belief and is therefore temporally situated in binary opposition to some falsehood.[64] In other words, the properties of the story formula allow individuals to justify a major change of mind by positioning a newfound "truth" in diametric contrast to their previous mindset. They thereby emplot their life course as a testimony to that newfound "truth." Despite their variant concerns, they each justify one way of seeing by negating another.[65] In the process such individuals use their autobiographical accounts to corroborate particular—and often controversial—knowledge claims in the world.

The generic properties of the awakening-story formula are evident in the following example in which conservative activist David Horowitz describes realizing that his long-held Marxist worldview was in fact "false." Horowitz writes,

One evening [. . .] I had a sudden shock of recognition. [. . .] I had always [. . .] visualized a pyramid whose apex was Marxism, which was my life's work and which provided the key to all other knowledge. [. . .] But in that very moment a previously unthinkable possibility also entered my head: The Marxist idea, to which I had devoted my entire intellectual life and work, was *false*. All around me, the room went black. In the engulfing dark, the pyramid flattened and a desert appeared in its place, cold and infinite, and myself an invisible speck within it. [. . .] For the first time in my conscious life I was looking at myself in my human nakedness, without the support of revolutionary hopes, without the faith in a revolutionary future [. . .].[66]

Horowitz goes on to describe his realization of political "truth" as he rejects his prior, left-wing beliefs in favor of a conservative worldview. However, regardless of the particular political details of his autobiographical account, Horowitz uses a generic awakening-story formula to depict his life and engage in an ongoing social dispute over truth and meaning. The generic character of his account can be seen when we eliminate a mere four words (just over 3 percent of the selected passage) and replace them with others. The account becomes generic when the stricken words below are ignored. If we were to replace them with either *Catholicism/Catholic* or *conservatism/conservative*, for example, we would completely change the meaning of the story, illustrating the remarkable flexibility of the story formula.

One evening [. . .] I had a sudden shock of recognition. [. . .] I had always [. . .] visualized a pyramid whose apex was ~~Marxism~~, which was my life's work and which provided the key to all other knowledge. [. . .] But in that very moment a previously unthinkable possibility also entered my head: The ~~Marxist~~ idea, to which I had devoted my entire intellectual life and work, was *false*. All around me, the room went black. In the engulfing dark, the pyramid flattened and a desert appeared in its place, cold and infinite, and myself an invisible speck within it. [. . .] For the first time in my conscious life I was looking at myself in my human nakedness, without the support of ~~revolutionary~~ hopes, without the faith in a ~~revolutionary~~ future [. . .].

As a result of changing just a few words, we can use Horowitz's rendition of the awakening narrative to create an entirely different meaning. By replacing the stricken words with the words *Catholicism/Catholic*, we make the story about religion as opposed to political revolution. By using the words *conservatism/conservative*, we turn the story into its ideological "opposite." Further, we could continue to replace the same four words and apply the story to any of a wide variety of subject matters and moral or political positions (e.g., we might use psychoanalysis, nationalism, or any other system of thought in place of Marxism, and the adapted narrative would be just as plausible as the original). The versatility of the basic story framework and the generic character of its moral and emotional symbolism are exactly what make the narrative *formulaic*. With slight changes, the narrative formula can be used to undermine and reject any one system of meaning and pave the way to justify and defend any newly acquired worldview.

Figure 1 is a map of the awakening-narrative formula.[67] The x axis represents autobiographical time. To move leftward is to move into the past; to move rightward is to advance into the present and future. Alternatively, the y axis represents the storyteller's distinction between "falsehood" (structurally represented by the lower plane) and "truth" (structurally represented by the higher plane). The starburst in the center of the figure symbolizes the narrated awakening experience—an event or process that is required to jump the border marking the dichotomy of ignorance and enlightenment. The dashed line represents the way that such storytellers plot their autobiographical accounts in relation to this two-dimensional narrative map.

Stories that follow this formulaic awakening plot involve several core components. First, storytellers account for a past state of "darkness," which usually involves conveying a sense of reaching a low point in one's life as an inevitable consequence of one's commitment to a worldview or belief system from which one is now estranged. Second, storytellers describe their experience of discovery and personal transformation.

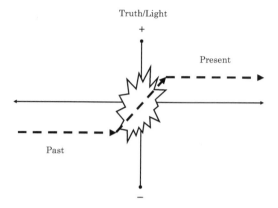

Truth/Light

+

Present

Past

−

Falsehood/Darkness

> X Axis = Autobiographical Time
>
> Y Axis = A Moral and Epistemic Dichotomy
>
> Dashed Line = The Autobiographical Account

1   The structure of an awakening narrative

Third, storytellers account for a current state of "light" and commonly describe having found their true place in the world. Here, they "redeem the past,"[68] making up for self-ascribed failures, mistakes, and misbeliefs by casting their current worldview as a positive moral contrast to their former worldview. Advancing an explicit "social geometry"[69] of awakening stories, I elucidate these general narrative features and social patterns that transcend any one particular story, case, or substantive realm of focus.

The Semiotic Structure of Awakening Stories

When telling awakening stories, individuals draw from a stock of conventional metaphors to strike a moral contrast between their now-rejected and newly embraced worldviews. Generally speaking, this moral contrast is reinforced by the widespread practice of depicting "falsehood" and "truth" as situated on different *epistemic planes*, linking downward or lower with falsehood/ignorance/bad and upward or higher with truth/knowledge/good.[70] As Barry Schwartz has shown, such a vertical classification scheme is an entrenched feature of Western culture that provides semiotic and cultural "codes by which social divisions themselves find meaning."[71] Social representations of awakening typically reiterate this vertical organization of enlightenment in various ways.

Such a vertical organization of cognitive emancipation is evident in William Holman Hunt's *The Awakening Conscience* (1853) (see fig. 2). In this mid-nineteenth-century painting, Hunt, known for portraying religious themes, depicts a young woman's moment of awakening. As she (who is the man's mistress or perhaps a prostitute) "sees the light" emanating from a window (perceptible to the viewer only through its reflection in a mirror behind the characters), she rises upward and away from her dark-suited lover, who is left sitting and reclining behind her. The young, now-illuminated woman is symbolically dressed in white. Her "conscience," a concept that in the Durkheimian sense is inseparable from the concept of "consciousness,"[72] is awakened. Given the

2   William Holman Hunt's *The Awakening Conscience* (1853)

momentum of her body, she leaves her sexual affair behind and below as she moves upward and outward toward the light (a vertical organization of experience that is also captured in the common phrase "take the moral *high* ground"). Her gaze is directed up and away from her immoral lifestyle (if she were moving to sit, she would be looking down). In the bottom, back left corner of the scene, a cat paws at a captured bird, a symbolic portrayal of the young woman's prior entrapment in the clutches of cognitive constraint and moral peril. Like the bird, she longs to escape up and out to the light (and freedom) emanating though the window. Hunt's painting captures the sociomental structure of the awakening-narrative formula in a visual representation of spiritual transformation.

Individuals who tell awakening stories use four interrelated metaphoric contrasts to depict these morally polarized epistemic planes and to describe the experiences, environments, conditions, and interpersonal consequences central to their awakenings.[73] Each family of metaphors captures a different facet of the diametric contrast between falsehood/evil and truth/good that is central to the awakening-narrative formula. However, as Arthur W. Frank notes, an individual's reliance on "culturally conventional rhetorics" does not mean that his or her lived experiences are any less real.[74] Rather, storytellers use these cultural codes as a framework with which to organize, define, and articulate their personal experiences while sharing their stories with others and situating themselves in the world.

Individuals who tell awakening stories use the metaphoric contrast of *asleep* versus *awake* to define the experience of "falsehood" and the discovery of "truth" from a first-person perspective. Sleeping and dreaming involve an intense personal isolation, a solipsistic mental experience. Alternatively, being awake involves and typically requires intersubjective cooperation with others (this is also the realm of dream interpretation). The act of waking up (note the vertical implication) is culturally linked to a social time of consciousness and interaction. Using metaphors of sleep (including symbolic "illusion" as well as various depictions of the process of dreaming or the condition of being deluded, brainwashed, or contained within a world of fantasy) and waking up (including variants of the phrase *eye opening* as well as various ways of detailing the process of emerging from containment in a fantasy world), individuals account for their prior lack and more recent attainment of the "consciousness" of "truth" in the world.

Related to the asleep-versus-awake family of metaphors, *darkness-versus-light* metaphors are used to characterize various environments of falsehood and truth by people who tell awakening stories. They use "darkness" to define the contexts and conditions of cognitive constraint and "light" (including the related concepts of enlightenment, fire, illumination, elucidation, dawning, and more) to define the contexts and conditions of cognitive emancipation. Darkness is commonly associated with a narrow, submerged, and confining space, while light is associated with a free and open environment. Further, light also carries a positive moral connotation, as in the Old Testament's book of Genesis where it is written, "God said, 'Let there be light,'" followed soon after by the comment, "God saw that light was *good*, and he separated the light from the darkness."[75] Historically, light and the sun are typically associated with truth, knowledge, and discovery or creation. The Egyptian sun god, Ra, is associated with vision, creation, and, given his connection to the Bennu bird (similar to the Greek phoenix), fire and rebirth. The Greek god Apollo is associated with the sun as well as truth and prophecy. The light bulb is a contemporary symbol of a new idea, vision, or awareness. Using metaphors of darkness and light, individuals who tell awakening stories account for their prior lack and more recent attainment of the social and environmental conditions necessary to see and know "truth" in the world.

When individuals use the *blindness*-versus-*sight* family of metaphors, they combine the themes inherent in the asleep/awake and darkness/light metaphoric contrasts to portray their sense of looking at the world through a new set of eyes. They use such distinct optical metaphors to clearly express the act of taking on new "optical norms"[76] as they account for their awakenings. This metaphoric contrast is perhaps most blatantly obvious in John Newton's expression "I once [. . .] was blind, but now I see," which like the remainder of the most famous verse of the hymn is formally neutral and flexibly applicable. When storytellers use these metaphors directly, they claim their prior way of seeing was actually an inability to see.

Finally, people who tell awakening stories use the broad *lost*-versus-*found* family of metaphors (including various related concepts and themes) to define the experiences of *cognitive alienation* and *cognitive solidarity*. When one is lost, one is typically in an unfamiliar and perhaps threatening setting. When one has been found, one joins a space of comfort and familiarity, a home base where one is supposed to be. Storytellers often convey the experience of being "lost" by describing their isolation and loneliness or by depicting the inauthenticity of their "false" relationships. They often convey the experience of being "found" with metaphors of family and homecoming. Using this broad set of metaphoric contrasts, individuals account for their prior state of being without a "true" community and their more current state of finding a sociomental "family."

The metaphoric contrasts of asleep versus awake, darkness versus light, blindness versus sight, and lost versus found are certainly interrelated, but each highlights a different symbolic dimension of the moral and epistemic polarity at the heart of the awakening-narrative formula.[77] Individuals use these metaphoric contrasts to describe the process of acquiring new cognitive norms—to express a *sociomental migration* between different worldviews. Further, these binary codes are coupled with polarized emotion codes. Thus, individuals and communities use the awakening-story formula to structure feelings with regard to whatever particular issue is at hand. The moral charge associated with "falsehood" (and thus sleep, darkness, blindness, and being lost) is typically linked to the emotion codes betrayal, hurt, anger, and fear. The moral charge associated with truth (and thus consciousness, light, sight, and being found) is typically linked to the emotion codes hope, salvation, pride, and love. Using this morally and emotionally charged story formula to guide my analysis of content, I illuminate the ways that individuals and communities use autobiographical accounts to weigh in on unresolved cultural tensions or disputes over the definition of various moral and political concerns as they work to shape the cognitive norms and feeling rules of a broader environment. By studying awakening narratives at the formal level, we can learn about the most salient moral and cultural tensions of any given era.[78]

The Awakener as a Social Type of Storyteller

In addition to viewing awakenings as an autobiographical formula, I also consider the *awakener* to be a "social type" of storyteller. The notion of a social type was pioneered by Georg Simmel who sought to identify the generic characteristics of actors that stem from their dynamic position vis-à-vis others—their place and part in the social structure. Simmel coined the notion of a social type to identify the generic actor positions that give rise to various "forms of sociation" or "particular kinds of reciprocal attitude and behavior"[79] that exist despite the particularities of any given interaction. He identified several examples of such social types, including the "stranger," the "mediator," the "dude," and the "poor."[80]

As Lewis A. Coser notes, "Simmel conceives of each particular social type as being cast by the specifiable reactions and expectations of others. The type becomes what he is through his relations with others who assign him a particular position and expect him to behave in specific ways. His characteristics are seen as attributes of the social structure."[81] Thus, social types exist because of their relationally situated position in the social world, regardless of the personal, idiosyncratic characteristics of any individual who stands in that position.[82]

Adapting the notion of social types to a narrative perspective, I argue that one is an awakener because one uses a patterned story formula to account for discovering truth in one's life and thereby assumes a *discursively situated* position in relation to others. Despite any given storyteller's personality, psyche, or particular situation, all individuals who use this story formula share a generic type of position in a multifarious "network of social communication and praxis."[83] Their position in this network involves four main *dialogical orientations* that characterize awakeners as a social type of storyteller.

When I use the concept of dialogical orientations, I stress the ways that awakeners formulate their autobiographical accounts with multiple audiences in mind. Despite the content of their stories, awakeners speak or write in anticipation of the different ways that separate groups of people will hear and react to their accounts. These multiple audiences are inherent in the story formula and, therefore, in each particular version of the story, giving such autobiographical accounts a distinct polyphonic character.[84] Thus, the awakener's situation in the social structure manifests in narrative (autobiographical) form. As Mikhail Bakhtin argues, "The utterance occupies a particular *definite* position in a given sphere of communication. It is impossible to determine its position without correlating it with other positions. Therefore, each utterance is filled with various kinds of responsive reactions to other utterances of the given sphere of speech communication."[85] Like "utterances" more generally, awakening stories contain "responsive reactions" and "evaluative tones"[86] situated in relation to multiple parties in a broader sphere of communication. Further, such spheres of communication contain both contemporaneous and temporally situated links (communicative relationships) and channels of influence. The particular constellation of dialogical orientations inherent in the awakening-story formula can be used to define the awakener as a social type of storyteller.

First, the awakener takes a contentious dialogical orientation toward the proponents of a rejected worldview (one that the awakener has left

in the past). This contentious and antagonistic orientation, typically im-
bued with feelings related to betrayal, loss, and anger, is not necessarily directed against the members of the awakener's former community
(for whom the awakener may feel sympathy) but toward the cognitive
authority figures and other advocates who uphold the worldview that
the awakener is working to undermine. Second, the awakener takes a
harmonious dialogical orientation toward the proponents of a newly
embraced worldview. These include cognitive authority figures and con-
federates that make up a new community of like-minded others with
whom the awakener expresses sentiments of solidarity, such as love, ap-
preciation, comfort, or security. Third, the awakener takes a proselytizing dialogical orientation toward individuals in the world at large (who
are often conceived to be the "sleeping" or the "blind") as the act of telling the story inherently involves an invitation to share in or sympathize
with the awakening. Finally, the awakener takes a critical-deprecating
dialogical orientation toward his or her past self. The awakener portrays
and symbolically engages his or her past persona in order to facilitate
the contentious, harmonious, and proselytizing orientations mentioned
above.

From a narrative perspective, these dialogical orientations are storied forms of social interaction. By taking them into account, we can
illustrate how awakeners enact their social-relational situations as they
strategically portray their lives and utilize their autobiographical stories, establishing their position in what Charles Taylor refers to as "webs
of interlocution."[87] By telling their stories, awakeners are both converts
and apostates—sociomental conformists and deviants.[88] On the one
hand, like religious testimonials, their stories "provide [a] collectivity
with evidence that its beliefs are efficacious."[89] On the other hand, their
testimonies also repudiate countertestimonies and thereby undermine
the beliefs and values of other groups. Thus, interest groups and thought
communities spotlight their awakeners as role models that others can
emulate to "see the light." These groups wield awakening narratives to
legitimate their worldview in the face of competition. Treating awakeners as a social type of storyteller allows me to link my formal analysis
of these autobiographical stories to a discussion of the patterned ways
various individuals use their stories in dialogic relation to others within
a broader social context. Despite a variety of idiosyncratic differences
among the individuals whose stories grace the pages of this book, it
is their common formulaic pattern of storytelling that makes them all
awakeners.

Autobiographical Communities and Autobiographical Fields

In March 2008, over 100 veterans of the US-led wars in the Middle East gathered in Silver Spring, Maryland, "to testify about their experiences in Iraq and Afghanistan" and provide "eyewitness accounts of the occupations" in order to give "an accurate account of what is *really happening* day in and day out, on the ground."[90] Organized by the social movement organization Iraq Veterans Against the War (IVAW), this event was scheduled to commemorate the fifth anniversary of the invasion of Iraq by US-led forces. The event's title, "Winter Soldier: Iraq and Afghanistan," was chosen to pay tribute to a three-day public testimonial organized by Vietnam Veterans Against the War in 1971 at which 109 veterans and 16 civilians testified to their knowledge of war crimes in Vietnam.[91] The Vietnam-era event signaled a movement of veterans out of the semipublic "safe spaces" of political meetings and "rap groups"[92] into the public sphere so that their stories might spur a collective discovery of the "true" character of the war. Now, over thirty-seven years later, another diverse group of veterans testified to civilians and news media about the atrocities of war. Over the course of four days, they made powerful claims about a range of issues—from the devastation and dehumanization of Iraqi and Afghani civilians to the lack of adequate health care for returning soldiers.

While working to expose the political and moral atrocities of war, these "winter soldiers" were able to assert a unique authoritative perspective because they drew on their own personal experiences to show what was "really happening." As with testimony more generally, these veterans derived their authority to speak about and define a controversial social issue from the details of their autobiographical accounts.[93] However, beyond the issue of autobiographical presence, many of these speakers claimed further authority to define the wars at hand (and US politics more generally) because they once wholeheartedly believed in the rationales or ideological justifications for the wars they were now condemning. Many described voluntarily joining the military and/or entering the war effort after donning a patriotic worldview in the wake of the September 11th attacks on the World Trade Center and Pentagon buildings in New York and Washington, DC. Others claimed they once had a more ambivalent or less defined outlook and later became committed to an antiwar worldview. These veterans are awakeners who convey what psychiatrist Robert Jay Lifton describes, with reference to

Vietnam veterans, as a shift from the paradigm of John Wayne to the paradigm of Country Joe and the Fish.[94] Their testimonies thus combine two seemingly contradictory points of view—they are both insiders who carry the experience of war and outsiders who no longer share the mindset or embrace the ideology of the once-embodied insider.[95]

The particular circumstances and content of these veterans' testimonies are historically and contextually situated in the post-9/11 US political sphere. As Joseph E. Davis states, "Stories are always produced and told under particular social conditions."[96] However, these veterans expressed their particular concerns by creatively using a story formula that has existed for thousands of years. The conditions and issues particular to this case are relatively new, but the narrative pattern is well established. What these storytellers did, then, was articulate a *situated version* of the awakening-story formula. They used a tried-and-true narrative model and artfully infused it with the situated moral, cognitive, and emotional outlook associated with their particular social context and conditions. Thus, their awakening stories tell us something about the sociomental and emotional norms of their community. Further, because the awakening-narrative formula is a means of engaging in dialogue with various audiences, their stories also tell us something about relations between communities in the broader discursive environment. While these veterans creatively advanced a situated version of "truth," they also worked to undermine competing claims and ideas; they conveyed a partisan view of a cultural and political tension in autobiographical form.

In order to understand the relationship between the transcontextual and transhistorical awakening-narrative formula, on the one hand, and the more-particular contexts in which individuals put them to use, on the other, we need to consider the relationship between the foundational and contextual levels of culture—between culture as a durable, overarching phenomenon and the cultural worlds of more "concrete and bounded" spheres of locally situated "beliefs and practices."[97] Therefore, while I outline the formal similarities common to a variety of substantively different stories, I also illuminate the ways that individuals and communities use this autobiographical formula for different purposes. In other words, while the awakening formula transcends time and context, individuals and communities tell different versions of the story to suit their particular situations and objectives as they compete with each other in a broader social arena. The tension between community norms and this broader competitive field gives life to these stories, allowing agents to animate the story formula with content. Therefore, when individuals tell such awakening stories, they clue us in to deep moral and cultural fissures in the world around them. They also take a stand, using their personal testimonies to mark their place within a contested social terrain.

Generally speaking, people tell stories about their lives during various "autobiographical occasions"[98] and in a variety of social contexts that affirm particular types of accounts and privilege "institutionally preferred themes, plots, and characters."[99] Such institutional contexts also compel certain perceptions and enforce particular definitions of reality.[100] Social movement meetings, therapeutic support groups,[101] high school reunions,[102] Alcoholics Anonymous meetings,[103] religious rituals,[104] and other social contexts serve as "narrative environments"[105] where individuals adopt shared autobiographical scripts and construct personal accounts in accordance with (often unacknowledged) social norms of storytelling, cognitive conventions, and feeling rules. Participants face social pressures (from other individuals, from the group as a whole, and from the context itself) to accentuate certain details of their lives while ignoring others. Further, institutions often have homogeneous goals and work to shape personal accounts and particular types of identities so that they are in line with those goals.[106] However, even given the impact of contextual norms, individuals are typically adept at conveying a feeling of personal experience with their stories. This is in part because "how we come to understand ourselves and narrate our experience" does not involve blind compliance to expectation but is "an artful and interactional process."[107] Individuals creatively fashion their experiences and sentiments with socially approved scripts in order to convey personal information.

The concepts of "autobiographical occasion" and "narrative environment" have served to enhance our understanding of how specific times, spaces, and group processes influence the ways individuals account for their lives. However, like IVAW, many of the groups that affirm particular autobiographical scripts and enforce social rules of personal storytelling transcend the temporal and spatial boundaries that define particular occasions and environments. Such *autobiographical communities* sometimes cohere in one particular social setting at one particular time, but like other communities, they typically transcend these geographical and temporal constraints. They are relatively durable associations that serve as foundational reference groups in their members' lives.

When individuals identify with an autobiographical community, they situate themselves in the world and emplot themselves in relation to various others. The autobiographical community, in turn, becomes a referential locus of situated perceptions, beliefs, values, and feelings as members share community-based cognitive, epistemic, moral, and affective frameworks for understanding the world. As Tamotsu Shibutani notes with regard to reference groups more generally, such communities shape their members' orientation to the world as "one comes to perceive the world from [the group's] standpoint."[108] In the process, adherents use community norms to shape stories about their lives.[109] An autobiographical community can be a formal organization (like an established religion or social movement organization) or a less formal, more diffuse reference group (like communities of ex-Mormons or self-identified survivors of child sexual abuse). In either case such communities are "autobiographical" because they privilege particular scripts and conventions that individuals use to construct stories about their lives for specific purposes.

In addition to being a locus for situated norms, autobiographical communities are a type of carrier movement[110] in that their members articulate and disseminate morally laden truth claims in order to define the world according to their particular cognitive orientations.[111] While in many cases not all members of a given autobiographical community tell awakening stories, awakeners are often crucial to the sociomental and emotional work such communities do. Looking outward to a broader social environment, awakeners perform their situated versions of truth, advancing their particular community's cognitive norms and emotion codes in an effort to change the way others see and feel.[112] In short, they act with their stories. As awakeners undermine one worldview and embrace another, they distinguish between their autobiographical community and other groups that are not like their own—specifically whatever autobiographical community (or communities) to which they used to belong. "Truth," then, is a narrative claim that takes form both *within* such communities and as a function of the relations *between* them.[113] Our social environment is less a homogenous space of collective agreement and much more a heterogeneous space of competition between various interested parties who engage in contests over the correct definition of important situations and experiences.[114] Competition between communities then often further reinforces the norms of each group.[115] Just as awakeners give story form to their situated community norms, they also express these intercommunity cultural and cognitive tensions in their stories. Therefore, by examining the various situated manifestations of the awakening-story formula, we can outline the contours of a broad *autobiographical field* where individuals and communities use self-stories to wage cultural contests over meaning.

In November 2008, Christine Bakke appeared at a public press conference in Denver, Colorado, in order to tell the story of her personal "journey" to accept her homosexuality after years of corrective therapy intended to "cure" her of her homosexual attractions. Her account was especially relevant because she was speaking to oppose the annual convention of the National Association for Research and Therapy of Homosexuality (NARTH), one of the largest and most-vocal organizations promoting "sexual reparative therapy" and advancing the view that homosexuality is a pathological condition. Like other self-identified "ex-gay survivors," Christine described once accepting the tenets of sexual reparative therapy and believing the psychological professionals who defined her homosexuality as a mental disorder while promising a therapeutic remedy. Now wholeheartedly rejecting that position and defending the authenticity of her homosexuality, Christine told the public, "I've spent the past five years in recovery from the ex-gay treatments I received. [. . .] I have also met hundreds of others negatively affected by ex-gay theories and treatments, and together we have helped each other in moving beyond this troubled time in our lives."[116] Like the war veterans previously described, such ex-gay survivors derive their authority to define sexual reparative therapy because they once subscribed to it but, they claim, have since come to see what it "truly" means.

While sharing her personal story, Christine undermines the core vision, ideas, and values expressed by NARTH and its advocates. Like the many other members and affiliates of the "Beyond Ex-Gay" community[117] or the "Truth Wins Out"[118] movement, her autobiographical account reveals the contours of a cultural conflict over the "truth" concerning the nature of human sexuality. In this battle over scientific and sexual "truth," the awakening stories told by members of the gay pride community, an autobiographical community that includes ex-gay survivors like Christine, are socially situated in opposition to the awakenings of those individuals who embrace sexual reparative therapy—those who describe awakening to discover their "true" heterosexuality after years of leading a homosexual lifestyle.

In the introduction to his book *Healing Homosexuality: Case Stories of Reparative Therapy*, psychologist Joseph Nicolosi undermines the gay pride community's standpoint and articulates the sexual reparative community's position in this cultural and epistemic conflict when he writes, "[. . .] [W]e are offering *the opposite sort of personal testimony*, that of homosexual men who have tried to accept a gay identity but were dissatisfied and then benefited from psychotherapy *to help free them* of the gender identity conflict that lies behind most homosexuality."[119] In order to reinforce the sexual reparative community's authority in this contest, Nicolosi then deploys a collection of biographical sketches (testimony in the form of psychotherapeutic case studies) that detail the lives of individuals who have discovered the "truth" about their sexuality as they rejected homosexuality and embraced a heterosexual lifestyle. The awakening stories published in Nicolosi's collection, as well as the first-person accounts of "repaired" heterosexuals published elsewhere, are oppositionally situated in relation to the awakening stories of those who "come out" as gay as well as those who, like Christine Bakke, identify as "ex-gay survivors." Their life stories are in dialogical contrast—"counternarratives"[120] mobilized in competition with one another in a broader autobiographical field. Despite expressing antithetical versions of truth, these dueling autobiographical communities both use the awakening-story formula to wage this cultural battle over the nature of sexuality. Further, both autobiographical communities offer the awakening stories of their members as evidence, providing autobiographical models that those who are committed to the opposing sexual orientation can (and, from each perspective, *should*) use to jump ship and switch sociomental camps.

Likewise, in his foreword to the 2001 edition of Richard Crossman's *The God That Failed*—a collection of autobiographical stories written by former communists originally published in the wake of World War II— historian David C. Engerman outlines the contours of a different cultural contest. He argues that "[w]hile the essays here are deeply personal, they also represent the close intertwining of private lives with national and international politics," and that this collection of autobiographical stories served "as a how-to manual for transforming interwar radicals into Cold-War liberals."[121] Thus, Crossman's collection of awakening narratives is to communists what Nicolosi's is to homosexuals. Both editors pit their community of awakeners against another group in order to weigh in on broadly important (yet very different) topics of moral and political concern. In each case, dueling camps vie for the cognitive authority to define the moral parameters of a contested issue (in one case, the nature of human sexuality; in the other case, the international politics of the Cold War). Both wield patterned, formally similar awakening narratives as ammunition in these broader cultural contests.

Building on Robert Wuthnow's notion of a "discursive field,"[122] I use the concept of autobiographical field to mean a broad, multifarious cultural arena where individuals construct and deploy autobiographical stories in mutual relation to one another for strategic purposes. As they tell their personal stories, awakeners establish their *sociomental standpoint* in a community that is situated in a pluralistic and contentious world.[123] The act of writing or telling an awakening story involves adopting that autobiographical community's distinctive "mental lenses"[124] and particular "group style"[125] of storytelling. From this standpoint, awakeners formulate (as narrative) and deploy (as social action) their situated autobiographical accounts in dialogic relation to other actors who use "different repertoires of meanings and values"[126] to produce alternative autobiographical accounts in the broader cultural arena. Thus, their autobiographical stories are "part of an interlocking set of narratives."[127] However, structurally speaking, the relations of the autobiographical field often take form as a "matrix of oppositions"[128] in that many autobiographical communities are situated against or in direct competition with other communities within the broader field. In another sense, the competition between autobiographical communities exists less directly, as a function of the diversity of communities, each with their own cognitive orientation, populating the social landscape.[129] The dialogical relations between different autobiographical communities "commonly determine our experience of meaning and value"[130] by providing a discursive framework for individuals to construct meaningful stories about their lives. Agents use the generic awakening formula, one that involves founding a truth claim on the declaration of "false" belief, to fit their stories within this discursive framework. In the process, they mark the social distinction between those they claim to be awake and those they deem asleep. Therefore, just as social discourses in general "both reflect and reproduce power relations that 'live' in social structures,"[131] autobiographical stories can reflect and reproduce cultural contests over the cognitive authority to define ongoing and past issues of significant moral and political concern.

Methods and Data

Methodologically, I approach my study of awakening narratives from the perspective of social pattern analysis.[132] In the tradition of Georg Simmel, social pattern analysts "distill generic social patterns from [multiple] cultural, situational, and historical contexts" in an effort to identify cross-contextual similarities, "thereby making their essentially decontextualized findings more generalizable."[133] By focusing on the common formal characteristics of several substantively different narratives, we can identify cultural similarities among otherwise different communities, variant discourses, and diverse spheres of social life.[134]

Social pattern analysis requires a strict analytic focus. Rather than commit to one particular case or setting, I elucidate common themes in the stories I analyze.[135] Following Eviatar Zerubavel, I consider my "deliberate effort to view" my cases "*selectively* as a methodological virtue, a necessary precondition for staying analytically focused."[136] Further, in order to hone my focus on shared themes, I carefully foreground specific parts of those narratives that serve to illustrate the theme at hand. I use bracketed ellipses—[. . .]—to signify the parts of the story that I have removed for the purpose of focus and brevity.[137] I then focus my interpretation of each quotation in order to signify its empirical and theoretical relevance to the current theme-based discussion. Providing several substantively distinct autobiographical clips to illustrate each theme while actively pointing out what one story has in common with others allows me to highlight structural generalities that would otherwise be less clear. In other words, the interpretive payoff of the analysis only emerges over the course of several illuminating examples. Each story is only relevant insofar as it adds to my building discussion of a common theme.

While I emphasize the structural commonalities among otherwise different narratives, I also interpret the cultural meanings and implications of the stories I put forth.[138] Such a structural hermeneutics[139] involves exploring the ways that social actors bring culturally ingrained binary oppositions (such as truth and falsehood, good and evil) and the temporal structure of story plots together to make meaning in the world. As Philip Smith argues, "In the paradigmatic dimension binary codes are responsible for classifying the world and so doing according to moral criteria, detailing the qualities and attributes of the sacred and profane, polluted and pure. Along the syntagmatic axis, however, narrative structures place actors and events into plots, allocate moral responsibility, causality, and agency, shape outcome expectations and in some cases provide exemplary models for action. Binary codes provide building blocks, but narratives add subtlety to our understandings of the world and convert situations into scenarios."[140] Rather than commit myself to interpreting the depths of meaning associated with a single case—what Clifford Geertz called "thick description"[141]—I focus my interpretive lens on the narrative formula as a sense-making device. Applying such a mode of cultural interpretation to a theme-based study allows us to see how actors use the same social formulas to make claims that are quite diverse, and even antithetical, with regard to content.[142] I have chosen particular cases that represent different value spheres, and my diverse collection of narratives allows me to present a thorough picture of the broad cultural and cognitive significance of the awakening-narrative formula. Only when seen collectively and relationally, through a broad-angle lens, can the autobiographical field be understood as a matrix of interconnected and dynamic autobiographical narratives. Applying the methodological lens of social pattern analysis and a structural herme-neutics to the study of autobiographical stories, I bridge the concerns of cultural sociology and social psychology. I aim to illuminate broadly relevant and durable aspects of culture and show how they serve as meaning-making resources for individuals who are constructing identi-ties and situating themselves in a complex and combative world.

Given this approach, and given my commitment to showing the role of autobiographical stories in public contests over the meaning of mor-ally and politically salient issues, I analyze narrative data published in a variety of formats and rooted in multiple social and historical settings. These include what I call *foundational awakening narratives*—historical or theoretical manifestations of the awakening-story formula that are held to be iconic or sacred by particular communities. They also include *pop-ular awakening narratives*—published autobiographical memoirs of no-table figures, biographical sketches, fictional stories, films, and visual art that portray the themes of awakening.[143] Such narratives, whether they pertain to individual or collective discovery, provide story templates, convey ideologies, and contain symbolic codes that modern individu-als use to construct their self-stories. Despite their myriad substantive differences, various formats, and diverse social and historical origins, all such foundational and popular narratives employ the same generic story formula.

In addition to a wide array of foundational and popular awakening narratives, during my research I examined hundreds of autobiographi-cal stories that were published online at any one of various public sites where individuals share their stories with the world.[144] Each of these sites is an expressive vehicle used by a broader autobiographical commu-nity (see table 1). I view the Internet as a virtual narrative environment and an evolving manifestation of the public sphere where individuals and communities direct their stories to other users and "to the unseen generalized others of public opinion."[145] Notably, some of these sites host individuals who would not coalesce in one narrative environment without the Internet. Others host groups that hold regular meetings or annual conferences offline. In some cases, as with the Iraq Veterans Against the War site, not all individuals who share autobiographical sto-ries are awakeners. In other cases, as with those sites dedicated to reli-gious conversion, posters are awakeners by definition. All of these sites

Table 1 Online storytelling spaces

Website	Description
Iraq Veterans Against the War (http://ivaw.org)	A site hosted by an organization of veterans who oppose the US-led wars in Iraq and Afghanistan
Susan Smiles—Surviving Childhood Sexual Abuse http://www.susansmiles.com/	A site for survivors of child sexual abuse
Safeguarding Our Children—Uniting Mothers http://www.healthyplace.com/abuse/soc-um /about-safeguarding-our-children-united -mothers/menu-id-821/	A child abuse awareness and resource site
The False Memory Syndrome Foundation http://fmsonline.org/	A site hosted by an organization focused on "false memories" of child sexual abuse
Precious-Testimonies http://www.precious-testimonies.com/	A born-again Christian site
Faith-Travels http://www.faith-travels.org/	A born-again Christian site
ExChristian http://new.exchristian.net/	A site for those who have left Christianity
Mormon Converts http://www.mormonconverts.com/	A Mormon conversion site
Recovery from Mormonism http://www.exmormon.org/	A site with resources for ex-Mormons
Postmormon http://www.postmormon.org/exp_e/index.php /home	A site with resources for ex-Mormons
People Can Change http://www.peoplecanchange.com	A "sexual reparative" site for men "struggling with unwanted homosexual feelings"
Courage http://couragerc.net/	A faith-based sexual reparative site
Beyond Ex-Gay http://www.beyondexgay.com/	"An online community for those who have survived ex-gay experiences"

contain public storytelling contexts where individuals work at "writing the self into existence" and "create personally meaningful identities in electronic space"[146] as they share stories and make claims about social problems.[147] Their stories are "snapshots of cultural performances"[148] that are dialogically situated in relation to various audiences. Further, each site also contains other data, such as collective statements and other forms of information about the broader community and various resources for the public at large.

Due to the rise of Internet technology, the act of writing, publishing, and sharing autobiographical stories has radically expanded. In addition to the fact that countless sites invite individuals to share their stories, the medium allows individuals to complement their narratives with self-selected links, photographs, videos, and other graphics. Compared to traditional storytelling environments, these online spaces are more portable,[149] perpetually accessible, and publicly exposed. However, because they are published by interested parties and "moral entrepreneurs,"[150] these sites are monitored and edited. They change over time and allow for a mechanism of formal editorial control that often goes beyond the social control characteristic of traditional narrative contexts. The sites listed in table 1 range in style from public message boards (where individuals or members freely post stories) to controlled publications (where interest groups publish submitted personal stories for specific purposes).[151] Storytelling patterns primarily arise due to social pressures in the former and are enforced by editorial traditions in the latter. Despite these differences, all of these sites provide a platform for autobiographical communities that stress story sharing and promote socially rooted rules of storytelling.

When individuals post personal accounts about discovering "truth" on these sites, they work to broaden social support for their community's positions and objectives. Thus, the World Wide Web becomes a medium that facilitates the transmission of epistemic claims, cognitive norms, and feeling rules. By reading such stories, users gain access to a community's version of the truth with regard to some important issue. In the process, they are prompted to adopt new ways of seeing and to identify with the transformative experiences that are recounted and displayed there. These sites consequently serve as virtual base camps of meaning production and contestation. However, because of this strategic utility, and because each site is relatively self-contained, the Internet may actually serve to inhibit the type of intergroup communicative dialogue that would lead to the resolution of cultural tensions and disputes between autobiographical communities.[152]

Analytically speaking, Internet technology allows us to more easily see how the increasingly diverse and multifarious "going concerns" of the late modern world manifest as multiple contexts of storytelling.[153] Because these spaces are "virtual" in the technological sense, I am able to compare many different narrative venues and observe the formal social patterns common to the accounts produced in each. From a Weberian perspective, the Internet hosts a multiplicity of "orders and values."[154] As a research site, it is ideally suited for gathering multicontextual evidence, comparing different autobiographical communities in general, and analyzing the various manifestations of awakening stories in particular.

Despite their differences, I view all of these foundational, popular, and varied public awakening narratives as actions that are directed to impact the world by changing hearts and minds. In addition to this diverse collection of narrative data, I examined during my research a wide variety of primary source materials related to the communities and conflicts central to this study. These include newsletters, collective statements, campaign materials, video documentaries and clips, and foundational texts. As demonstrated earlier in this chapter, I contextualize each community and the conflicts between them as I interpret their members' stories about discovering "truth."

Outline of the Book

In this book, I contribute to important discussions in the interrelated areas of cultural and cognitive sociology, social psychology/symbolic interaction, and social memory studies. While I address a variety of themes and issues, I am primarily concerned with detailing the cultural and distinctly sociomental dimensions of the stories individuals tell about discovering truth. In the process, I outline the contours of a more general sociology of autobiographical stories. Because I use story formula to drive my analysis, the cases I discuss pertain to quite different subject matters. Therefore, I also explore issues that are relevant to the sociological analysis of trauma and mental health, religion, nationalism and patriotism, social movements, sexuality and gender, emotion, knowledge and ideology, and the body.

In chapter 2, which is uniquely historical in comparison to subsequent chapters, I outline the rich cultural history of the awakening-narrative formula. Looking back to roughly the ninth century BCE, I explore the ways that awakening narratives have evolved and proliferated over time. I examine a select group of cases—from the ancient religious and philosophical camps of the Axial Age to the new social movements and sectarian communities of the late modern world—in order to show how awakening stories emerged in various historical eras to mark the prominent cultural and moral tensions of those periods. In each case cultural entrepreneurs used the awakening-narrative formula to advance new ideas about falsehood and truth in order to challenge the entrenched moral frameworks of their day. I also explore what these foundational awakening narratives tell us about the general properties of the awakening-story formula.

In order to tell a story about discovering truth, individuals must account for the time they spent upholding a false belief. In chapter 3, I explore the mnemonic dimensions of awakening. Specifically, this chapter deals with the way awakeners resolve the tension between multiple versions and interpretations of the past. I introduce the concept of *mnemonic authority* and discuss the ways that awakeners use autobiographical memory to weigh in on cultural disputes concerning the definition of morally and politically salient issues and situations. Exploring the connection between autobiographical memory and collective memory, I argue that a cultural and cognitive sociology of autobiographical narrative offers new insights into the social dynamics of collective memory and commemoration.

How do awakeners explain their motivation to make such a radical transition in their lives? How do they account for such life-changing discoveries and drastic changes of mind? In chapter 4, I explore the ways individuals describe having a transformative awakening experience. Distinguishing between two ideal-typical *vocabularies of liminality*, I explore the relationship between autobiographical time, agency, emotion, and transformation in awakening narratives. Guided by the theories of Victor Turner, Kenneth Burke, and Erving Goffman, I show how awakeners use various dramaturgical conventions and employ props, characters, and settings to convey their sociomental discoveries and transformations.

While in chapter 3 I explore the ways awakeners use autobiographical memory to define events and issues, in chapter 5 I focus on the ways they portray and perform their contrasting, temporally divided selves. How do individuals account for the otherwise contradictory dynamic between two radically different identities in their lives? Developing a narrative theory of identity that reconciles the themes of self-interaction, social context, plot and temporality, the performance of self, and what I refer to as *self-character schemes*, I consider how awakeners mobilize depictions of lifestyle, emotionality, manner, taste, perception, values, and embodiment as they distinguish between different conceptions of the self in order to classify the world into morally and epistemologically contentious camps. If, as George Herbert Mead has argued, the self is a product of our social relationships, what does it mean when our past and present communities of reference are in conflict? In this chapter, I consider the sociocognitive and cultural implications of such a divided self.

I conclude this book by considering how awakeners work to resolve cultural contradictions while simultaneously reinforcing social divisions and exacerbating cultural conflict. Bringing together several themes that I introduced in prior chapters, I then propose seven interrelated principles for a sociological—and specifically cultural and cognitive—approach to autobiographical narrative more generally.

TWO

Awakenings:
A Cultural History

If a man can control his mind he can find the way to Enlightenment, and all wisdom and virtue will naturally come to him.   THE BUDDHA[1]

Reason is natural revelation.
JOHN LOCKE, "AN ESSAY CONCERNING HUMAN UNDERSTANDING"[2]

As the poet brings the guilt of Oedipus to light by his investigation, he forces us to become aware of our own inner selves [. . .].
SIGMUND FREUD, THE INTERPRETATION OF DREAMS[3]

When individuals tell awakening stories, they weigh in on cultural disputes over truth and meaning that have emerged during various historical eras and evolved through time. In this chapter I sketch a cultural history of the awakening-narrative formula. I show how awakening narratives proliferated over time with the emergence of different and contentious "spheres of values,"[4] and the rise of various "communities of discourse,"[5] each with their own ideas about the nature of truth and discovery. By using the term *cultural history*, I mean to stress how the emergence of new versions of truth and awakening signifies the rise of cultural challenges to an existing moral order and consequently affects the transformation of social relations and institutions.

For centuries before the modern era, religious worldviews were culturally predominant. The origins of the world's foremost religious ideologies can be traced to what Karl Jaspers refers to as the Axial Period, an era extending from approximately 800 BCE to 200 BCE marked by the rise of world-transforming philosophical and spiritual traditions in the Middle East, Greece, India, and China.[6] These Axial Age "breakthroughs," however, were preceded by a profound experience of moral and cultural "breakdown" that was due to increasing tensions between communities with different views on how to ascribe meaning to the human condition.[7] The great thinkers of the Axial Age, including Zarathustra, Siddhārtha Gautama, Plato, Confucius, the early Jewish authorities, and others, advanced their doctrines in competition with many others in an effort to define and bring about moral order amid a new and pronounced cultural uncertainty and political unrest.[8]

Axial Age thinkers were the first to articulate a sharp distinction between "mundane" and "transcendental" orders.[9] "In the wake of . . . clashing alternatives . . . followed [by] an almost unbearable tension threatening to break up the fabric of society" they began to engage in a new type of critical second-order theoretical reflection that involved, in each case, postulating the nature of, and path to, ultimate truth.[10] In other words, as the Axial Age thinkers conceived of new ways to bridge the divide between day-to-day life and some higher moral order, they developed and promoted various positively charged visions of a future toward which humankind, individually and collectively, ought to strive. They combined "criticism of the existing order" with "utopian projections of a good [and joyous] society."[11] By laying out various paths to transcendence, this "new type of intellectual elite" also formulated a morally charged distinction between past, present, and future.[12] Such a perception of the distinction between temporal dimensions facilitated a new type of autobiographical and collective emplotment. Further, because the Axial elites of each region were competing with others over the proper conception of truth and moral order, their newly articulated divisions between day-to-day life and the realm of truth also became a way to distinguish between contentious camps in the world. Falsehood came to be associated with suffering and truth with joy, and for the first time, individuals and communities began to use the contrast between these realms of experience as a way of coding and comprehending the distinction between "them" and "us."[13] Thus, while Axial Age ideas "were made possible by a previous shaking of the 'taken-for-granted,'" they also opened the door for a general ethos of reflexivity and new competing views on how to live correctly and "how to relate to the world in the most general sense."[14] The awakening-narrative formula was born within this tumultuous epoch as a means to achieve that newly desired yet practically elusive moral order.

Centuries later, challenges to religious notions of truth, initially sparked by classical Greek philosophy, became culturally entrenched with the rise of modern philosophy and the Age of Enlightenment. Subsequently, various contentious notions and discourses of truth emerged, including multiple and divergent political, scientific, psychological, and sexual discourses. This fractioning of different and contentious discourses of truth has led us to a late modern cultural milieu marked by heightened sociomental pluralism and a multiplicity of autobiographical communities that contend for the allegiance of individuals. Such a cultural milieu affords late modern individuals the potential to repeatedly and reflexively reconstitute themselves by abandoning one "truth" in favor of another.[15] However, despite this historically "emerging multiplicity in perspectives"[16] on the content and character of truth, and despite an increase in cultural emphasis on "expressive individualism,"[17] individuals and communities continue to articulate patterned, formally similar awakening narratives as they use their life stories to express cultural tensions over truth and meaning.

The historical proliferation of autobiographical communities, from the Axial Period to the present era, was accompanied by the concurrent rise of various foundational awakening narratives that, although not all purely autobiographical, provided a cultural and theoretical basis for the general idea that one can be mentally unaware of a "truth" or "reality" and subsequently awaken to grasp that reality. These foundational narratives expressed various worldviews and ideologies. The historical emergence of each new ideology signaled "changes in the moral order—in public definitions of moral obligations—that make room for or necessitate new efforts to dramatize the nature of social relations."[18] Beginning with the various responses to the legitimation crisis of the Axial Period, each presented a cultural challenge to existing social dynamics by introducing a moral imperative couched in a new articulation of the contrast between the realms of falsehood/darkness and truth/light. As such, each of these foundational accounts created new cognitive opportunities and, as Anthony Paul Kerby argues with regard to the impact of twentieth-century literary developments, each allowed for "the broadening," and I would add reorganization, "of affective experience."[19] Further, each provided a general story template and a set of cultural tools that individuals used to construct their personal awakening stories. Such entrenched story models continue to serve as social referents for individual awakeners and consequently illuminate some of the central themes and vocabularies that reoccur throughout lay or popular versions of the story today.

In this cultural history I briefly discuss several important foundational awakening narratives. These stories span different social contexts, belief systems, and historical periods. They variously express philosophical, religious, political, scientific, psychological, and sexual worldviews. They also span different levels of analysis, from the micro, or individual, to the macro, or collective. First, I focus my attention on seven cases. These include the story of Zarathustra, Plato's allegory of the cave, the Buddhist story of Siddhārtha Gautama, the Christian story of the apostle Paul, the Western Enlightenment narrative, the Marxist account of false consciousness and class consciousness, and Freud's theory of psychoanalysis and the psychoanalytic case study. Then I discuss the proliferation of sectarian awakening stories that accompanied the rise of identity politics and New Age religious movements in the 1970s and 1980s. I have chosen to focus on these cases because each exemplifies an important historical manifestation of the awakening-narrative formula; they are pivotal moments in the development of the various truth claims and disputes that populate the contemporary cultural landscape.[20] Because these story models accrue rather than supplant one another, in combination they show how notions of truth have evolved and proliferated over time. While my purpose limits my treatment of each case, I focus my analysis on the specific characteristics of each story that serve to illuminate my subsequent discussion of the awakening-narrative formula. What follows, then, is a brief cultural history of this story type.

Zarathustra

The story of Zarathustra, the ancient Iranian philosopher, poet, and founding prophet of the Zoroastrian religion,[21] provides one of the earliest articulations of the idea that the universe is divided into a dichotomous conflict between falsehood and truth.[22] Notably, the Hellenic translation of the prophet's name (Zoroaster) has been variously linked to "stars" and "gold."[23] As described throughout various Zoroastrian scriptures, especially the Gathas which consist of seventeen hymns attributed to Zarathustra himself,[24] the ancient prophet is said to have "sought a revelation of the purpose of man's troubled days on earth."[25] As Mary Boyce describes, Zoroastrian tradition upholds that the prophet-priest "spent years in a wandering quest for truth" while repeatedly witnessing evils, violence, and social conflict and yearning for moral order. One day during a spring festival, Zarathustra, at the age of thirty, was at a river and—"in a state of ritual purity, emerging from the pure element, water, in the freshness of a spring dawn—he had a vision" of several "radiant figures," most importantly the god Ahura Mazda, who bestowed upon him a revelation.[26] Upon this awakening, Zarathustra asserted that the universe is defined by a conflict between the forces of good (*aša* or *asha*, meaning "order," "truth," and "justice") and evil (*druj*, meaning both "disturbance" and "lie" or "deception").[27] Further, he discovered that the god Ahura Mazda is the omnipotent and eternal creator of all other gods, mankind, and life in general, as well as the primary force of order, truth, and goodness in the world. According to this doctrinal awakening story, Ahura Mazda is opposed by an adversary, Angra Mainyu, who is "equally uncreated, but ignorant and wholly malign,"[28] and the two (god and anti-god) are locked in a struggle for supremacy.

The division of the universe into two diametric, mutually exclusive, and antagonistic morally charged realms is the central drama of Zarathustra's story. In the Gathas, Zarathustra states,

Now I will proclaim to those who will hear the things that the understanding man should remember, for hymns unto Ahura and prayers to Good Thought; also the felicity that is with the heavenly lights, which through Right shall be beheld by him who wisely thinks. Hear with your ears the best things; *look upon them with clear-seeing thought*, for *decision between the two Beliefs*, each man for himself before the Great consummation, bethinking you that it be accomplished to our pleasure. Now the *two primal Spirits*, who reveal themselves in vision as *Twins*, are *the Better and the Bad*, in thought and word and action. And between these two *the wise ones chose aright, the foolish not so*. And when these twain Spirits came together in the beginning, they created *Life and Not-Life*, and that at *the last Worst Existence shall be to the followers of the Lie, but the Best Existence to him that follows Right*. Of these twain Spirits *he that followed the Lie chose doing the worst things; the holiest Spirit chose Right*, he that clothes him with the massy heavens as a garment. So likewise they that are fain to please Ahura Mazda *by dutiful actions*.[29]

By portraying this binary coding of the universe (good god and anti-god, truth/Right and falsehood/Lie, Life and Not-Life, light and darkness), the story of Zarathustra signals the emergence of an autobiographical field marked by cultural antagonism between two contentious camps— "the followers of the Lie" and any "that follows Right."[30] Further, by asserting his revelation that the universe is defined by conflict between the forces of good/truth/light and the forces of evil/falsehood/darkness, Zarathustra established himself as a prophetic figure and articulated a destiny for humankind. At the core of this destiny is a moral imperative: people ought to devote themselves to upholding *aša* by living a good life so that evil and darkness may be defeated and eternal peace may be achieved.[31] The conflict between Ahura Mazda and Angra Mainyu established a storied framework for a "choice which every man must make for himself in this life."[32] The binary coding inherent to the story then became mapped to thoughts, actions, and loyalties in the world. Further, as with other Axial teachers, Zarathustra linked suffering to ignorance and happiness to overcoming ignorance.[33] With the emergence of various foundational awakening narratives in other contexts and subsequent eras, this basic duality remains, but individuals and communities use the diametric division of the world in different ways. The basic structure of the semiotic system stays the same, but truth/good/light and false/bad/darkness come to signify different things.[34]

Zarathustra, followed by the Athravans and other Zoroastrian priests of various eras, used his awakening to emplot the progress of humanity beyond a state of darkness. Simultaneously, he established that emplotment as a structural framework that individuals could use to shape their own autobiographical awakenings. As Zarathustra's awakening symbolized a new beginning—a dawning for humanity—movement through time took on new meaning at both the individual and collective levels. Somewhat satirically, Friedrich Nietzsche mimicked this prophetic aspect of Zarathustra's awakening in his philosophical story *Thus Spake Zarathustra* in order to proclaim that "God is dead," undermine traditional conceptions of moral authority, and theorize human evolution beyond a religious moral framework to the era of the Übermensch (theoretically and symbolically heightening—*Über*—man *over* God).[35] Nietzsche used the Zoroastrian formula to undermine its content, inspiring German composer Richard Strauss in 1896 to write a symphonic movement by the same name, a piece that was adapted for Stanly Kubrick's 1968 film *2001: A Space Odyssey*. Like Nietzsche, Kubrick deals with the theme of human evolution, in this case from "the Dawn of Man" (the film's opening scene) through the age of modern/future technology and "Beyond the Infinite" (the final scene) to rebirth. Following this tradition first set forth in Zarathustra's foundational and influential awakening narrative, awakeners use their personal stories to establish a moral imperative and set a future course of action for others, a theme that will reemerge in subsequent chapters.

Plato's Allegory of the Cave

Plato's allegory of the cave is the archetypical philosophical version of the awakening story. Plato used this allegory, dated to roughly 380 BCE, to illustrate how individuals can become enlightened and acquire knowledge of the "essential Form of Goodness," arguing that goodness "is itself sovereign in the intelligible world and the parent of intelligence and truth."[36] Plato produced this allegorical awakening story in the midst of an ongoing debate among Greek thinkers over the nature of philosophical and political truth. Within this competitive context, Plato's account can be seen as an allegorical expression of a key notion—that ultimate knowledge and philosophical insight stem from the practice of *theoria*.[37] In Greece during the fourth century BCE the practice of *theoria* often involved an individual (*theoros*) traveling to another land to witness some sort of dramatic event, usually a religious ritual, and then returning home to report his observations. As Andrea Wilson Nightingale argues, "*theoria* encompassed the entire journey, including detachment from home, the spectating, and the final reentry," and "this sacralized mode of spectating . . . offered a powerful model for the philosophic notion of 'seeing' divine truths."[38] Further, the experience of *theoria* (the origin of our contemporary notion of theory) gave the philosopher a place of exception that ultimately, according to Plato, justified his political rule. After giving a brief summary of Plato's allegory, I will highlight several aspects of this foundational awakening narrative and the broader notion of *theoria* that are central to my purposes here.

In this allegorical lesson Plato described a cave where several prisoners are confined by chains that are attached to their legs and necks, prohibiting them from leaving and from turning their heads to see anything but the wall in front of them. On this wall there are several shadows cast from artificial objects that are moved along a roadway behind them, between the prisoners' backs and a fire that casts the shadows on the wall. As several have noted, a modern version of Plato's cave might look more like a movie theater, where the fire is replaced by a projector. Given their situation, the prisoners in the allegory have very limited knowledge of the world. Plato wrote, "In every way, then, such prisoners would recognize as reality nothing but the shadows of those artificial objects."[39] Plato thus made a sharp distinction between mere sensory perception (appearance) and the ability to contemplate perception, a distinction that informed his analysis of the division between the darkness of ignorance and enlightened knowledge.

After describing the cave world, Plato then hypothesized about the plight of a prisoner who is freed from captivity and ascends to the surface world where, for the first time in his life, he sees sunlight. The prisoner's ascent is a symbolic representation of philosophical enlightenment. However, the process of ascent is marked by notable pain that is associated with seeing an illuminated world for the first time—with the rise to a new state of knowledge and awareness. The newly emancipated prisoner, Plato commented, would be disoriented as his eyes are burned by the newly experienced sun. His eyes, Plato said, would be "so full of its radiance that he could not see a single one of the things that he was now told were real." He would be tempted to "turn back to the things that he could see distinctly, convinced that they really were clearer than these other objects now being shown to him."[40] Plato then argued that a freed prisoner would eventually grow accustomed to the "upper world." If, however, he were to return to free his former bondsmen,

[. . .] [H]is eyes would be filled with darkness. He might be required once more to deliver his opinion on those shadows, *in competition with the prisoners who had never been released,* while his eyesight was still dim and unsteady; and it might take some time to become used to the darkness. They would laugh at him and say that he had gone up only to come back with his sight ruined; it was worth no one's while even to attempt the ascent. If they could lay hands on the man who was trying to set them free and lead them up, they would kill him.[41]

Plato's cave metaphor contains important figurative dimensions that illustrate central features of awakening narratives in general. First, Plato depicted personal enlightenment by describing a freed prisoner's ascent from a cave (contained belowground) to the surface of the earth (aboveground, the open space of sunlight), portraying a culturally significant vertical organization of moral and cognitive authority.[42] The lower realm is the space of ignorance and illusion; the upper realm is the space of truth and clarity. The freed prisoner makes this journey through a tunnel, a liminal space between the two worlds that, although hardly discussed in Plato's account, is absolutely necessary to the transition. Notably, the structure of Plato's allegorical setting closely resembles the structure of autobiographical awakening stories as displayed in chapter 1 (see fig. 1).[43] Similar to the function of the antagonism between antigod and god in Zarathustra's account, the structural distinction between the cave and the upper world mirrors the autobiographical distinction between the prisoner's past mental state and his more current outlook. Further, this structural division also reflects the *social* distinction between those who reside in the cave and those who live in the upper world, a relationship that is played out in the frustrating interaction between the freed prisoner and his former bondsmen.[44] Thus, Plato used the biography of his hypothetical prisoner to illustrate the sociomental tension between those who are blind and those who have come to see the light, a tension rooted in their discrepant understandings of reality. The generic character of the allegory is evident when one considers that it can be interpreted from religious, intellectual, political, artistic, and other perspectives.[45]

Second, Plato represented ignorance with both physical constraint (leg chains) and perceptual constraint (neck chains), metaphorically associating access to truth and knowledge with freedom of movement and perceptual flexibility. Leg chains prevent physical escape by restricting bodily movement. Neck chains, however, prevent *mental* escape by restricting perceptual mobility, constraining the *cognitive options* of the prisoners. From a sociological perspective, these neck chains symbolize socially enforced rules of seeing and social constraints on perception that often exist without material fetters. For example, as Gordon J. Horwitz shows, Austrian locals during the Nazi Holocaust commonly obeyed unwritten yet strict social conventions to avoid turning their heads to see the events of local concentration camps.[46] Plato thus directly associated truth with sight and, more importantly, the ability (freedom) to see from different angles *despite* conventions. Darkness and ignorance are symptomatic of a narrow perceptual repertoire. This perspective on truth is central to Plato's argument and the more general idea that the process of *theoria* affords the philosopher a place of exception in the world as "the philosopher is altered and transformed by the journey of *theoria* and the [consequent] activity of contemplation."[47] This position of exception, experienced as a profound tension between the realm of home and the foreign and "a peculiar combination of detachment and engagement" that leaves the returned *theoros* as "a sort of stranger to his own kind," affords the philosopher his claim to political rule.[48] For Plato, the philosopher-*theoros* is a central figure in the good polis, which is held up as an ideal and positively coded in contrast to other ideas about the direction of political affairs.[49] Thus, Plato linked cognitive, political, and moral authority to a relativistic awareness of multiple realities—a state of transcendence resulting from the ability to see from multiple perspectives. Further, while such a transcendent truth "is affective and emotional, . . . brings intense pleasure and happiness, [and] is erotic, even sexual,"[50] it is also perilous due to the antagonism inherent to its exceptionalism.

Notably, Plato's prisoners are not blind in a physical sense; every one of them has the capacity to see, but their sight is restricted. Plato reinforced this sense of optical restriction with his use of "shadows," which exist when light is blocked from one's view, to portray ignorance. This powerful symbolism informs Plato's position that, while every person has the capacity to "see" the "truth," most, including Plato's political opponents who are represented as the antagonistic bondsmen in the allegory, remain blind.[51] Further, the symbolism of the allegory reflects Plato's view that education involves a process of redirecting the student's "vision" to "see" what is already there. For Plato, education is "an art whose aim would be to effect [. . .] the conversion of the soul, in the readiest way; not to put the power of sight into the soul's eye, which already has it, but to ensure that, instead of looking in the wrong direction, it is turned the way it ought to be."[52] With this in mind, the unnamed hero of Plato's allegory is the emancipator, whoever it was that "set free" the prisoner and "forced" him to "walk with eyes lifted to the light."[53] Using this relationship between emancipator and emancipated prisoner, unexplained in the story but implicitly portrayed in the dialectic between Socrates and Glaucon, Plato symbolically represented cognitive authority and acknowledged that the process of enlightenment involves a social dynamic and is not an individualistic venture. Plato's figurative association of optical restriction with ignorance/falsehood and a newly experienced way of seeing with knowledge/truth underscores important aspects of what I call *cognitive constraint* and *cognitive emancipation*.

Foundational Religious Awakenings

Most, if not all, religions have foundational awakening stories. They are central to both Eastern and Western traditions. The stories of prophets, saints, gurus, and spiritual founders express religious ideologies and provide biographical models that potential adherents can use to account for awakenings in their own lives in order to join a particular religious collective and reject competing ways of life. Thus, religious awakening narratives mark the divisions between various religious sects and communities, each claiming to hold the key to universal and divine truth. These stories typically pit a utopian vision of salvation against worldly conditions, promising the way to achieve happiness, joy, and comfort while depicting a world filled with sadness, sorrow, and pain. However, while Plato believed that true philosophical enlightenment was possible only for the special few, religions are typically much more inclined toward assimilation. As Weber explains, the rise of prophetic religions involved a new ethical emphasis on a "universalist brotherhood."[54] Yet while many religions uphold the idea that everyone can achieve salvation, most also rely practically on the notion that not everyone will. The damned exist as an oppositional cultural force that increases the solidarity and status of the saved.[55]

Before briefly introducing other important cases, I focus my discussion on two foundational religious awakening stories of far-reaching significance. First, Siddhārtha Gautama, the Buddha (which literally means "the Awakened One"), achieved enlightenment at the end of a six-year journey.[56] Second, roughly six centuries later, the Christian apostle Paul awakened after being struck by lightning while traveling to Damascus in order to persecute Christians.[57] As with the awakening of Zarathustra and the story of Plato's escaped prisoner, light (whether the aura of enlightenment or a bolt of lightning) is associated with truth in both accounts. However, each of these stories conveys a different idea about how individuals access or acquire "truth." Further, each story represents an alternative strategy of cultural contention and change. As we will see in chapter 4, each exemplifies a variant mode of awakening that individuals use to account for major discoveries pertaining to concerns outside the realm of religion.

The story of Siddhārtha Gautama is dated to the sixth or fifth century BCE. This account was passed down orally for at least three generations before it was recorded, and several versions of the story exist today. What follows is a sketch of the account that accentuates the basic elements while avoiding many nuances and controversies.

Siddhārtha Gautama was the son of a king (or lord) who was committed to protecting the young prince from any awareness of the human condition, especially suffering and death. Destined to be a great king, Siddhārtha was provided a life of privilege and power, a life that he ultimately rejected. While Siddhārtha's palace life was certainly more comfortable than the conditions defining the life of Plato's prisoner in the allegory of the cave, both characters suffered from an intellectual and philosophical "confinement." The young prince's luxurious palace is the allegorical equivalent of Plato's cave and, as Karen Armstrong notes, "a striking image of a mind in denial."[58] When he was twenty-nine years old, Siddhārtha left his palace for the first time, against his father's wishes. During this initial expedition, he encountered a very elderly man and perceived the realities of death. Shortly after, Siddhārtha encountered a sickly man, a corpse, and an ascetic monk who, along with the elderly man, are said to have been holy "messengers" who introduced the sheltered prince to the realities of the human condition.

These initial excursions mark Siddhārtha's first awareness of human suffering and the starting point of a protracted quest in which the prince, now in somewhat of an existential crisis, struggled to understand and transcend this condition. Following these eye-opening experiences, Siddhārtha fled his father's palace and rejected his life of privilege and power. He intended to live the life of an ascetic in hopes of avoiding the otherwise inevitable state of old age and death. He studied with various teachers, each time moving on after becoming frustrated with the limits of their teachings. He then went deeper into an ascetic life looking for answers as "he practiced severe extremities that gravely damaged his health,"[59] eventually rejecting this course as well. Toward the end of his quest, Siddhārtha began meditating under a Bodhi tree for weeks until, it is told, he attained enlightenment. He became aware of the "Truth" and, consequently, realized that human suffering is caused by ignorance (delusion).

After achieving enlightenment, the Buddha initially rejected the idea of teaching others. He feared it was impossible for anyone to grasp what he now comprehended. Fortunately, according to the story, the god Brahmā Sahampati appeared on earth to implore the Buddha to share his newly achieved awakening, promising that, while many will fail to see the Buddha's truth, *some* will understand. This aspect of the Buddha's story marks the truth associated with enlightenment as elusive and prestigious (thus increasing its allure). Further, casting the Buddha as a reluctant teacher pressures students to prove their worthiness and work for answers. Thus, one of the main objectives of Buddhism is to emphasize the process of "attaining liberation by one's own efforts."[60] Further, the notion that the god Brahmā Sahampati begged the Buddha to share his wisdom expresses the deep cultural tension inherent in the story and "suggests that the gods remained subject to the cycle of rebirth from which the Buddha was now free; they depended on him to show them the path to liberation. The incident also shows the way in which Buddhism subordinated the Indian gods to the authority of the Buddha."[61] In other words, the story of the Buddha's awakening is also a radical critique of the predominant moral order of his day. After achieving a new form of nirvāna, a peace only possible with the overcoming of worldly delusions, the Buddha established a separatist alternative to entrenched Brahmanic traditions. By rejecting his royal birthright, he renounced the predominant kingly justice and wordly morality and embraced a new transcendent *dhamma* and emergent moral order.[62] By grounding this new moral order outside the boundaries of mainstream society, the Buddha and his followers built a parallel monastic social world that ultimately served to undermine the previously established and more-entrenched cultural authorities, a world separate and distinct yet in competition for the allegiance of the population.

Turning our attention now to the story of Paul, we are given a foundational religious awakening that involves an alternative type of transformative experience linked to a variant strategy of cultural contention. The story of Paul, a Pharisee also known as Saul of Tarsus, is primarily recounted in the New Testament's book of Acts. Paul, who accounted for his "previous way of life" by describing "how intensely [he] persecuted the church of God and tried to destroy it,"[63] was traveling with a band of men on the road to Damascus with the intention of arresting Christians—many of whom, it is presumed, would have been put to death. According to the book of Acts, "As he neared Damascus on his journey, suddenly a light from heaven flashed around him. He fell to the ground and heard a voice say to him, 'Saul, Saul, why do you persecute me? [. . .] I am Jesus, whom you are persecuting. [. . .] Now get up and go into the city and you will be told what you must do."[64] Later, in his defense to King Agrippa, Paul recalled that "the Lord replied, 'I will rescue you from your own people and from the Gentiles. I am sending you to them to *open their eyes* and turn them *from darkness to light*, and from the power of Satan to God, so that they may receive forgiveness of sins and a place among those who are sanctified by faith in me.'"[65] Because Paul was first blinded by his awakening experience (a symbolic representation of the ultimate "darkness" in his life), he had to be led by his compatriots into the city of Damascus, where, after three days of blindness and abstinence from food and drink, he was visited by the Christian disciple Ananias. Ananias, who was already aware of Paul's reputation for persecuting Christians, was fearful at first: "But the Lord said to Ananias, 'Go! This man is my chosen instrument to carry my name before the Gentiles and their kings and before the people of Israel. I will show him how much he must suffer for my name.'"[66] Ananias went to Paul and touched him. Immediately, scales fell from Paul's eyes and he regained his sight (thus, symbolically seeing through new or reborn eyes). Paul was then baptized and soon became an ardent proselytizer for the Christian sect who repeatedly recounted his road to Damascus experience to justify his Christian faith to others as he worked to "open their eyes and turn them from darkness to light."

The stories of the Buddha and Paul illustrate two very different awakening experiences. Both stories emerged as a means for agents to vie for cognitive and moral authority in the face of cultural and political instability, yet they portray alternative strategies of cultural contention. Siddhārtha's quest began with his renunciation of his royal birthright and led him to remain "permanently homeless"—a model that encouraged followers to critique "established society from the outside."[67] This foundational awakening story captures the monastic character of the early Buddhist community. However, unlike the Buddhist monists who retreated from the structures of traditional authority, the early Christians lived among the Jews and Romans so that apostles did not "confront the community" from the outside "but arose from its midst."[68] In addition to competing with various non-Christian Jewish sects,[69] the Christians after Paul refused to take part in the most visible cultural practices and rituals, notably the consumption of sacrificial meat, that would designate them members of the Roman community.[70] The Christian sectarian movement, a project that eventually led to the rise of feudal Christian Europe, confronted the Roman state and traditional laws of the time (*patrioi nomoi*) from within. Christian proselytizers used the story of Paul not only to provide an efficient model of conversion but to passionately admonish those who persecuted Christians (as Paul once did) while whittling away at both Roman and Jewish cultural (and political) authority. Using quite different strategies, both the early Buddhists and Christians created parallel societies as critical alternatives to the existing moral order. Their respective foundational awakening stories express something of their discrepant strategies and thus the different character of their parallel worlds. Siddhārtha's extended travels brought him well outside the geographic boundaries of his former community. Paul's expeditious and electric experience allowed for a transformation of mental allegiance without leaving his home setting.

Many of the general themes evident in the stories of the Buddha and the apostle Paul also occur in other foundational religious awakening narratives. Muhammad, the founding prophet of Islam, awoke to his destiny and discovered the tenets of the Islamic faith after being visited by the angel Gabriel in a cave on Mount Hira.[71] Saint Augustine of Hippo spent years searching for theological truth until one day, after a child's voice led him to read Saint Paul's Epistle to the Romans, he converted to Christianity.[72] Joseph Smith founded Mormonism after two visions.

The first vision was of two radiant figures—said to be God and his son, Jesus—who appeared before the fourteen-year-old Smith in a wooded grove and informed him that all existing religions are "false." The second, years later, was of the angel Moroni who led Smith to the source material for the Book of Mormon (and thus revealed the "truth").[73] Some religious awakenings (e.g., Paul, Augustine) highlight the protagonist's conversion to a preexisting faith. Others (e.g., Siddhārtha, Muhammad, Smith) portray an initial "revelation" or the protagonist's "discovery" of a new religious ideology. In all cases such quests, visions, revelations, voices, spiritual visits, and divine interventions provide narrative models that others, emulating these iconic religious figures, use to account for their own awakenings. Various religious communities deploy these foundational awakening narratives to defend their particular visions of divine truth and repudiate all other antagonistic worldviews.

Foundational Political Awakenings

Foundational political awakening narratives are stories about collective political progress that impel the transformation of society. I focus on two cases: the story of the Western Enlightenment and the Marxist account of revolutionary class consciousness. Each of these collective-level awakening stories was advanced by a community of discourse that arose to challenge the predominant moral order of its day.[74] Further, each functions as a "master frame"[75] that individuals use to construct autobiographical awakening accounts grounded in the modern political sphere. Given my focus, I center my discussion on three broad and related points. First, both the Western Enlightenment and Marxism link the discovery of truth to sharable *worldly experiences*. In doing so, they advance the notion that human beings have an inherent capacity to discover truth via their reasoned or scientific interaction with the natural world. Second, both foundational narratives promote a radical new separation of the thinking subject from the embodied subject, of the mind from the natural world, a distinction that opened the door for newly conceived ideas about the self as well as new ideas about false consciousness and alienation. Third, these foundational political narratives bind the notion of truth and discovery to the idea of *collective progress* and emancipation. For the Enlightenment thinkers, the principal unit of awakening was the civil society or nation. For Marx and the Marxists, the principal unit of awakening was the socially and economically constituted class. In both cases an individual's discovery of truth is conceived to be inseparable from the historically plotted progress of humanity (the direction or outcome of which, proponents claimed, could also be determined by the scientific study of worldly conditions).

Like the Axial Age, the era of Western Enlightenment was both a period of profound cultural uncertainty and a great pivotal moment in the historical evolution and proliferation of awakenings narratives.[76] Addressing an increasing "domestic and international disorder wrought by wars of religion"[77] and, later, civil wars between emergent liberal forces and entrenched feudal regimes, various factions of Enlightenment thinkers worked to undermine religious authority by advancing the notion that human beings could access truth by means of their reason-driven interactions with the world. From the motives of human behavior to the motion of inanimate objects, the world was said to operate by a set of universal and knowable *natural* laws that, if discovered and mastered, would be the key to humanity's collective emancipation. Whereas light was previously linked to divine providence while darkness was associated with the mundane world, the modern philosophers now equated light (as in the En*light*enment) with the use of reason to escape the intellectual confines of a religious worldview. In contrast to religion's emphasis on the transcendence of worldly activity, the empiricists stressed the role of earthly experience in the acquisition of truth and knowledge.[78] In his *Critique of Pure Reason*, Immanuel Kant attempted to synthesize Enlightenment empiricism and the tenets of philosophical rationalism, arguing that human beings are endowed with the innate mental capacity to make sense of the world.[79] Defending "the light of the intellect" and rational thought from the "ridiculous mysteries" of religious dogma, Benedict de Spinoza argued that religion prevents individuals from "distinguishing truth from falsehood."[80] While advancing the notion that the laws of nature could be "unearthed by the special techniques of scientific investigation and mathematical observation,"[81] these Enlightenment-era thinkers reformulated the binary contrast between good/truth and bad/falsehood (or illusion) and launched a revolution that would radically transform the world.

While redefining the essence of truth, these modern philosophers also theorized about humanity's collective progress from a "state of nature" to "civil society."[82] For Hobbes, the state of nature was a state of war marked by "continual fear, and danger of violent death;"[83] for Rousseau, life in the state of nature was organically simple and human beings were ignorant and animallike.[84] Despite a variety of differences, however, the Enlightenment thinkers argued that human beings possessed the mental capacity to progress out of a precivil state of ignorance and unrealized potential to establish the social and legal framework of a modern secular civil society. Such precivil states of nature served as both theoretical constructs used to justify particular courses of civil development and proxies for the religious states of feudal Europe. Armed with the capacity to reason, the philosophers argued, nations (and humanity in general) would awaken from the ignorance of the "Dark Ages" and subsequently progress into "the century of light."[85]

By formulating such a collective story of human advancement, the modern philosophers established the Enlightenment as a cultural framework for individuals to awaken to scientific and political truths in their own lives.[86] Personal discovery became inseparably intertwined with the notion of collective progress, as is perhaps most evident in the work of Nicolas de Condorcet, who established the "progress of the human mind" as a condition for the progress of society toward an ideal state.[87] More generally, the idea of progress must be seen in relation to the newly conceived "division that emerged in this period between private selves and public roles"[88] as well as a new subjugation of emotion to the rational utilitarian calculation deemed appropriate for the public sphere. As progress became "one of the most important modes of narration in modernity,"[89] it was a notion of progress that redefined personal discovery as a civic responsibility. Given this new civic responsibility to progress, revolution came to be seen as a both "an imperative prescription" and a legitimate mode of collective public action "in which people become capable of making a decisive break with age-old forms and structures that impede or distort the moral order."[90] These developments led to a "dynamic tension" between the social worlds of religion and politics, a tension that Weber refers to as a "mutual strangeness" to describe the evolving cultural contradiction between the two realms.[91] The Enlightenment conception of truth and progress provided the rationale for numerous social movements and political revolutions and continues to shape modern liberal thought, as well as our understanding of individuality and rational action, in the world today.

The century following the revolutions of the late Enlightenment saw its own form of upheaval given the the systematic dispossession of the European peasantry along with the rapid growth of modern industry and a new industrial workforce. In this tumultuous era, the Enlightenment promises of freedom and liberty did not sync with the experiences and observations of many, including the middle-class intellectual communities of which Karl Marx was a part. Retaining the Enlightenment emphasis on a scientific rationality and universal laws of progress, Marx and the Marxists mapped "falsehood" and "truth" to social structure in a new way, recoding and transforming the idea of political awakening.

In the Marxist version of the story, the structural conflict between classes in a given historical epoch (mode of production) is reflected in the superstructural realm of ideas, which includes everything human beings "say, imagine, conceive," or otherwise believe, including "morality, religion, metaphysics, [and] all the rest of ideology and their corresponding forms of consciousness."[92] In other words, the hierarchically organized conflict between social classes in the "material" world maps to a hierarchical conflict in the realm of consciousness, and "[t]he ideas of the ruling class are in every epoch the ruling ideas; i.e. the class, which is the ruling material force of society, is at the same time its ruling intellectual force. The class which has the means of material production at its disposal, has control at the same time over the means of mental production, so that thereby, generally speaking, the ideas of those who lack the means of mental production are subject to it."[93] Thus, Marx reformulated notions of "false" and "true" consciousness in two fundamental and interrelated ways. First, advancing a materialist critique of ideology, Marx argued that consciousness in general is a reflection of "real" human activities in the objective material world.[94] Second, advancing a dialectical approach to consciousness, he argued that "false" and "true" beliefs exist because of evolving oppressive social relationships organized around these material activities.

In the Marxist awakening narrative, it is the task of the subordinate class (emergent and positively coded) to throw off the ideological yoke of the dominant class (declining and negatively coded) and to awaken to an enlightened understanding of its role in history.[95] In the modern era, Marx argued, the proletariat at first suffers from a deluded acceptance of bourgeois consciousness; they treat bourgeois ideas as the ultimate "truth" even though these ideas are merely the expression of (outdated) bourgeois class interests (and are therefore in conflict with proletarian interests). Second, the proletariat suffers from a more amorphous ignorance that class interests and class mentalities exist at all. Thus, the proletariat needs to awaken, first, to an understanding of itself as a class and, then, to an understanding of its historically determined role—the overthrow of the bourgeoisie, the abolition of the capitalist mode of production, and the establishment of a new socialist society. Unlike Plato, who portrayed his hypothetical prisoners to be confined solely to symbolize their lack of philosophical awareness, Marx saw the unenlightened masses as exploited (robbed of the fruits of their labor), alienated (separated from the process and product of their labor as well as denied their connection to nature), and oppressed (politically dominated and disenfranchised) wage slaves. Their "false" consciousness stemmed from and reflected their economic and political subordinance. Thus, the awakening of the proletariat is the mental facet of the concurrent revolutionary transformation of society. In this new theory of historical and social progress, the proletariat "stands between the two poles of present reality and future ideal, providing a character to whom the virtues necessary for moving forward from the present to the future can be ascribed."[96] "Truth," and, more particularly, true *consciousness*, becomes something the oppressed must necessarily acquire along the path through revolutionary upheaval and to the future ideal state.[97]

The Marxist version of awakening establishes the ideological conditions for any individual to reinterpret his or her personal "past as a captivity in the 'false consciousness' of a bourgeois mentality."[98] More generally, Marxist theory provides a broad ideological framework for individuals to account for a discovery of political truth in their own lives by articulating two simultaneous processes. First, political awakeners (no matter their political orientation!) account for their personal political blindness or ignorance as a "false consciousness" caused by political power relations. Second, they explain their discovery of truth as an impetus to social conflict and change, an imperative to abolish those power relations and transform society. While Marx never explicitly used the term *false consciousness*, this dimension of Marx's work was widely influential. The term *false consciousness* was first noted by Friedrich Engels in a letter to Franz Mehring ten years after Marx's death. Engels commented, "Ideology is a process accomplished by the so-called thinker consciously, it is true, but with a false consciousness. The real motive forces impelling him remain unknown to him."[99] Such a view was elaborated by Vladimir Lenin, who later argued, "People always have been the foolish victims of deception and self-deception in politics, and they always will be until they have learnt to seek out the interests of some class or other behind all moral, religious, political and social phrases, declarations and promises."[100] The distinction between "false consciousness" and "class consciousness" was later elaborated by Georg Lukács. Lukács sought to use Marx's dialectical method "to investigate this 'false consciousness' concretely as an aspect of the historical totality and as a stage in the historical process."[101] Finally, this aspect of Marxist theory was central to Antonio Gramsci's elaboration of "hegemony," or the process by which a ruling class uses cultural ideas to secure the "spontaneous consent" of oppressed groups to the conditions of their oppression and thereby maintains the social relations of dominance and subordination.[102] This related set of ideas continues to influence revolutionary-minded social movements today.

Both the story of the Western Enlightenment and the Marxist account of revolutionary class consciousness advance the notion that the source of truth lies within collectively rooted, historically situated worldly experiences. Further, both accounts advance the idea that individual awakenings are necessary to achieve collective emancipation from the oppression of dying eras and to acquire the ability to progress toward an ideal future political and economic system. In both cases individual autobiographical accounts are conceived within a collective awakening framework. With Marxism, however, truth takes a step (albeit a small one) away from the universal character of the religious and Enlightenment conceptions that preceded it. While Marxism holds the social and historical principles of human progress to be universal, truth, and, more particularly, true consciousness, is relative to one's class position. This notion of relativity hints at the impending fractioning of the autobiographical field. It will be appropriated and transformed by the postmodernists and identity activists of the late twentieth century.

Freud and the Psychoanalytic Case Study

While Western Enlightenment thinkers valued universal truth and declared the process of its discovery to involve a rational engagement with the external world, the accompanying separation of private life from public persona led to a growing "conflict between inner and outer worlds of human experience."[103] As personal life was becoming an increasingly distinct realm of experience in the late nineteenth and early twentieth centuries, Freud moved the locus of truth to the interiority of the individual and established a new "ethic of personal self-exploration."[104] By establishing the theory of psychoanalysis, Freud provided a cultural framework for individuals to tell awakening stories about discovering hidden "truths" buried deep within the recesses of "the mind and latent in consciousness."[105] Pre-Freud notions of awakening certainly allowed for individuals to tell stories about personal awakening experiences. However, each relied on the idea that one can discover an external, universal truth. Further, although ideas about a "subconscious" (a term introduced by Pierre Janet) were fairly prevalent in early dynamic psychiatry, non-Freudian notions of hidden mental content posited the internal storage of socially shared (impersonal) meanings. Freud, however, conceived the unconscious to be a deeply personal inner world of symbolism and encoded meanings. As Eli Zaretsky so eloquently notes,

The founding idea of psychoanalysis, the idea of a dynamic or *personal unconscious*, reflected this new experience of personal life. According to that idea, stimuli that came to the individual from the society or culture were not directly registered but were first dissolved and internally reconstituted in such a way as to give them personal, even idiosyncratic, meanings. Thus, there was no direct or necessary connection between one's social condition and one's subjectivity. Equally important, Freud's idea of the unconscious signaled the absence, under modern conditions, of any pregiven fit or harmony between larger, public patterns of cultural symbolism and the private, inner symbolic worlds of individuals. The idea of the unconscious marked a lived sense of disjuncture between the public and the private, the outer and the inner, the sociocultural and the personal.[106]

Thus, the Freudian version of awakening, as typically elaborated in the psychoanalytic case study,[107] is based on the notion that "truth" must be found via the dynamic exploration of the personal unconscious and is only knowable through the interpretive process of psychoanalysis.

Given this foundational tenet, the goal of psychoanalysis (and many of the various subsequent forms of psychotherapy influenced by Freud) is often to rescue "truth" from the depths of oblivion. Freud symbolically and metaphorically located personal truths below the surface of our explicit awareness where they are waiting to be brought to light by the analyst.[108] The personal inner world of the self became a frontier. The idiosyncratic self (an idea that was itself a cultural construction) became the core unit of analysis. Personal and emotional deliberation was accentuated over impersonal and rational calculation. As Nancy Chodorow comments, the psychoanalytic "encounter illuminates the power of feelings" and "tells us why we feel deeply about certain things, certain experiences, and certain people and why these powerful feelings are part of a meaningful life."[109] Emotion was now seen as a necessary part of truth in a way that was previously unimaginable.

Freud's theory launched a revolution in the field of psychiatry. As the earlier asylum psychiatry was replaced with Freud's more modern, dynamic version, aberrant psychological states and neuroses were now understood to be linked to relatively normal childhood experiences.[110] Impulses, feelings, and behaviors operated like clues or codes that needed to be deciphered. Even when an individual's behavior was unexceptional, the unconscious was said to be operating behind the scenes, lying in wait of realization. In the psychoanalytic relationship, analyst and patient cooperate to discover unconscious drives and motivations, allowing the patient to awaken into a new, "healthier" self-awareness. Thus, Freud established a cultural framework with which any individual could conceive of his or her awakening story as "a healing narrative of the self,"[111] one that typically involved acquiring access to long-repressed memories.

Throughout his work, Freud stressed that truth could be revealed by unveiling repressed memories, typically of early childhood experiences, that would provide clues to more "primal scenes" that are at the core of the psychological symptoms and unexplained behaviors of concern. Take as an example Freud's analysis of the "Wolf Man"[112] in which he explained the patient's fears and anxieties by working through layers of memory recovered from the unconscious. He wrote,

It thus became clear that *behind* the *screen-memory* of the hunted butterfly the memory of the nursery-maid lay *concealed*. [. . .] Very soon after this *there came the recollection of a scene*, incomplete, but, so far as it was preserved, definite. Grusha [the nursery-maid] was kneeling on the floor, and beside her a pail and short broom made of a bundle of twigs; he was also there, and she was teasing him or scolding him. [. . .] When he saw the girl scrubbing the floor he had urinated in the room and she had rejoined, no doubt jokingly, with a threat of castration. [. . .] By means of the accompanying associations and the inferences that followed from them, *it was possible with certainty to supply this significant element which was lacking in the patient's memory.*[113]

Freud then used this recovered memory of the nursery-maid to suggest a bridge between a more primal and repressed scene in the patient's even earlier childhood (specifically having to do with the patient at a young age witnessing his parents engage in sexual intercourse) and his current neuroses in adulthood. By highlighting the unconscious dimensions of our memories of childhood experiences in this way, psychoanalysis provided a foundational awakening model that allowed individuals to discover personal truths by delving into their minds and reinterpreting their past experiences in light of their present psychological "symptoms."

In addition to positing such powerful and personal inner realities, Freud also introduced the related concepts of "resistance" and "defense" to account for our motivation to avoid memory. Both are central to psychoanalytic theory and inseparably connected to the idea that individuals can repress, and later recover, their memories of particular experiences. Defining repression as a "striving against the acceptance of a painful piece of reality" and an idea that is "the pillar upon which the edifice of psychoanalysis rests," Freud went on to comment that the psychoanalyst is "confronted with a resistance which opposes and blocks the analytic work by causing failures of memory. [. . .] The theoretical value of the fact, that this resistance is connected with amnesia, leads unavoidably to that concept of unconscious psychic activity which is peculiar to psychoanalysis, and distinguishes it markedly from the philosophical speculations about the unconscious."[114] Further, Freud normalizes the phenomenon when he argues "that even in healthy, not neurotic persons, resistances are found against the memory of disagreeable impressions and the idea of painful thoughts."[115] Like the light of Plato's sun, truth itself was defined as painful yet necessary to achieve a positive, transcendent state of well-being.

The theory of resistance provided three significant and interrelated dimensions of the Freudian conception of awakening. First, the idea of resistance firmly granted a particular type of cognitive authority—an authority to interpret and define the client's inner self—to the psychoanalyst. From the perspective of psychoanalysis, not only are certain memories "defensively driven into the unconscious"; this process also involves "an active symbolic transformation of them."[116] Thus, the analyst is granted the authority not only to decipher memories when they are present but more importantly to find and interpret them when they are not present. In the process, the analyst solicits the patient's subordinate participation in the act of making that patient's personal truths.[117] Second, this notion of resistance provided a cultural framework for individuals to believe that they likely have memories of which they are not yet aware and which might explain their present psychological problems. Third, exploration of the inner world was focused on unearthing the negative, for by the logic of resistance, there is no need for one to defend against the positive or pleasant experiences in one's life. Thus, the notion of resistance posits reluctant, self-protective individuals who defend themselves against painful realities and thus somewhat willfully embrace a false worldview. Even, and especially, when an individual defies the authoritative analyst's interpretation, his or her defiance could now be seen, like the religious shaman who is reluctant to embrace his holy destiny, as an avoidance of a necessary truth.

Freud elaborated and defended his theories through the careful presentation of psychological cases. From the self-analysis at the core of his

Interpretation of Dreams[118] to the famous cases of Dora and the Wolf Man, Freud established the psychoanalytic method of presenting biographical sketches of individuals for whom the process of psychoanalysis revealed the personal and unconscious causes of their neurotic thoughts and behaviors. In the process, Freud established a new cultural paradigm that allowed anyone to explain present-day feelings and behaviors as psychological "symptoms" by discovering previously unconscious "truths" rooted in the personal past.

Late Modern Awakenings

The latter half of the twentieth century was marked by the proliferation of various sectarian communities as the cultural landscape became defined by a new "pluralistic relativism."[119] While they have a wide variety of objectives and locally situated concerns,[120] many of these groups have been deemed "new social movements" by scholars calling attention to the characteristics that set them apart from the predominant interest groups of previous eras. In general, new social movements "tend to focus on cultural and symbolic issues" and "are associated with a set of beliefs, symbols, values, and meanings, related to sentiments of belonging" to a community that works to set itself apart by the particular way its adherents ascribe meaning to everyday life.[121] While the term *new social movements* is quite broadly conceived, the concept fits with a vision of the late modern world as a highly fragmented arena in which multifarious groups engage in a new "politics of identity"[122] and work to advance competing cultural interests.

The rise of these new social movement communities was accompanied by a mounting sense of existential uncertainty.[123] While sentiments of uncertainty spurred the rise of new epistemological visions in past eras, such an ethos now became a more pervasive part of the human experience, providing ample opportunity "for new definitions of the situation to be articulated."[124] The fragmentation of the cultural landscape and consequent "saturation of society by multiple [and competing] voices"[125] was matched by a reformulated impetus to search for truth and, consequently, a proliferation of new awakening stories. Various communities used the well-established awakening-narrative formula to reclassify the world by advancing new versions of falsehood and truth and new ideas about the tension between darkness and light. Just as elites arose to lead "protest movements" against the prevailing moral orders of the Axial Age,[126] new cognitive authority figures formed the sectarian communities of late modernity, carving out cultural niches from which they challenged entrenched moral codes and provoked cultural disputes.[127] However, the emergent voices of this era did not supersede the voices of the Axial religions, the dogma of the Christian missionary project, the rationalism of the Enlightenment, the revolutionary politics of Marxism, or the promises of psychoanalytic introspection. Rather, they had a cumulative impact, increasing the complexity of the field of contenders vying for our cognitive allegiance.

In order to highlight the ways such new social movement communities engage in cultural battles over the definition of morally and politically salient issues and situations, I focus on three principal types. The first two, trauma carrier groups[128] and sexual identity movements, vie for cultural and political recognition of what members see as their shared experiences and misrecognized identities.[129] The third type, "New Age" communities, blends late modern concerns with ancient religious themes to offer adherents new paths to personal well-being and shared ethical visions.[130] All three types are autobiographical communities that combine various historical themes with new ideas about individual voice and authenticity to provide adherents with a sense of social location in a world where, for many, modernist assumptions about rational universal knowledge have eroded.[131]

Trauma carrier groups are new social movement communities that played a central role in the development of our modern psychological concept of trauma and the advent of the posttraumatic stress disorder (PTSD) diagnosis. Such movements linked the personal discovery of psychological "truth" to the collective discovery of psychologically relevant social problems, raising public criticisms with a clinical vocabulary. Before the American Psychiatric Association (APA) included the PTSD diagnosis in the 1980 revision of the *Diagnostic and Statistical Manual of Mental Disorders* (*DSM*), this new notion of traumatic stress took nascent form in the "rap groups" organized by Vietnam Veterans Against the War.[132] As Vietnam veterans gathered to share stories, they began to link their current psychological troubles to their shared war experiences. Around the same time, the feminist community was organizing "consciousness-raising groups" and, later, began launching public campaigns to highlight the prevalence and psychological consequences of sexual assault in general and child sexual abuse in particular.[133] As the Holocaust was being redefined as trauma,[134] these and other groups told powerful stories about discovering the meaning of their psychological suffering in past external experiences, often awakening to the "truth" about their current situations in the process. For example, link-ing his former isolation and suffering to his prior lack of understanding about the impact of his war experiences, Vietnam veteran David Cline reflected,

I would wake up suddenly, soaked in sweat and afraid. I couldn't forgive myself for having taken other people's lives and for being naive enough to believe the US govern-ment's lies and winding up in the war zone to begin with. I thought that if others knew my story, they would shun me as a murderer. Sometimes when I was alone I would cry and I never talked to anyone about what was going on inside my head. I heard about Post-Vietnam Syndrome (now called Post-Traumatic Stress Disorder, or PTSD) but *didn't understand that I was experiencing it*.[135]

The personal and emotional exploration that is central to the psychoan-alytic framework was still valued over impersonal rational calculation, but shared external experience was stressed over idiosyncratic, internal processes. Further, "the personal immediacy and pain of the victim nar-ratives" lent moral authority to new collective ideas about the psycho-logical harm resulting from certain types of experiences.[136]

Using this new psychosocial paradigm, trauma carrier groups assigned a positive moral authority to public emotional testimony and enacted a sentiment expressed by the popular feminist mantra "the personal is po-litical."[137] They advanced a "therapeutic culture"[138] in which one's per-sonal story of suffering served as an expression of one's solidarity with a group of sufferers. Further, the process of story *sharing* was deemed nec-essary to each individual's personal awakening. Laura Davis exemplifies this cultural emphasis on such a communally emergent awareness in her personal statement for the preface to the self-help book for survivors of child sexual abuse, *The Courage to Heal*. Reflecting on her personal re-alization that occurred while conducting interviews for the book, Davis wrote, "[. . .] [T]here were tremendous similarities in the stories. The Black ex-nun from Boston and the ambassador's daughter from Manila described the stages of their healing process the same way. A pattern started to emerge. *What I was going through made sense*."[139] Like Davis, such new voices of protest stressed commonality over idiosyncrasy as they shared the process of awakening and personal discovery. More, they used the moral polarization of falsehood and truth at the heart of their awakening narratives to typify and polarize perpetrators and victims/survivors, whatever the particular experience at issue.[140] They depicted the trauma "survivor" as a phoenix figure, rising up from the ashes of traumatic victimization to wield testimony as a political tool, and associated this new moral champion with light and transcendence. In opposition, they cast the act of perpetration and those responsible as an unambiguous darkness and evil.

Around the same time, adherents of a diverse and growing gay pride movement brought about a proliferation of stories concerning sexual discovery. Like trauma carrier groups, these sexual identity movements overruled the subjugation of personal feelings (characteristic of both liberalism and Marxism) as participants began cooperating to tell highly emotional stories of a sexual nature in the public sphere. They articulated new sexual worldviews in the process. As Ken Plummer notes, in this era sexual stories went "from being insignificant to being widespread [and] have prefigured major social changes as a result of being told."[141] While many of these sexual stories were about "coming out" and "breaking the silence,"[142] gay pride activists linked the public act of coming out to the personal and cultural discovery of sexual "truth." They then used such awakening narratives to wage public battles over the "true" nature of sexuality. As with the case of trauma carrier groups, the act of autobiographical storytelling became inseparable from the collective claims-making work of the community. Autobiographical storytelling was at once both a personal and collective act oriented in opposition to the prevailing ideas of the time.

The issue of the true nature of sexuality was at the heart of the dispute between the gay pride movement and the APA over the classification of homosexuality as a mental disorder. During this dispute, gay pride groups used passionate stories of sexual discovery salted with the moral language of inequality and discrimination to recode heteronormativity as a morally corrupt social evil. Simultaneously, they linked the personal and social acceptance of homosexuality and the social diversity of sexual orientation to truth and goodness. This issue came to a head at the May 1973 convention of the APA, where nearly one thousand people gathered for a panel discussion organized by Robert Spitzer, an active member of the association's Committee on Nomenclature.[143] As Ronald Bayer notes, when the APA eventually sided with the gay pride movement (at the subsequent December 15th meeting of the APA Board of Trustees) and voted to remove homosexuality from the *Diagnostic and Statistical Manual of Mental Disorders*, the organization "not only placed itself in opposition to the systematic pattern of formal and informal exclusions that precluded the full integration of homosexuals into American social life, but deprived secular society, increasingly dependent upon 'health' as a moral category, of the ideological justification for many of its discriminatory practices."[144] Thus, the gay pride community deemed homosexuality "a sexual orientation fully compatible with a [positive] moral standpoint" and psychiatry "a regressive social institution."[145] Notably, the very concept of "gay pride" frames the affective dimension of homosexual identity and experience in this cultural and political contest. Pride is implicitly contrasted to the "shame" activists assert stems from the failure to realize and accept the true nature of one's sexuality. Shame, according to the voices of gay pride, is both wrongfully imposed on homosexuals by the entrenched forces of science and religion and justly due to those who fan the flames of that intolerance.[146] The inverse of this moral coding is advanced by countermovements that promote sexual "reconversion" or "reparative" stories.[147] Such stories have become increasingly common as part of a cultural backlash, one that combines conservative psychoanalytic and religious themes, against gay pride and queer-identity movements seeking cultural acceptance of non-heteronormative lifestyles.

Finally, in the same era, various "New Age" communities emerged, encompassing interrelated "practices and philosophies as diverse as shamanism, neopaganism, aura reading, goddess worship, channeling, crystal healing, past life regression therapy, and the performance of rituals inspired by American Indian traditions."[148] They include institutions as diverse as zen meditation centers, retreats associated with the human potential movement, and Pagan festivals.[149] Despite many substantial differences among them, such New Age movements commonly combine a post-1960s vision of transcendent well-being with various ancient religious beliefs in order to promise adherents a "path to spiritual awakening."[150] The emergence of this multitude of New Age projects signified a widespread longing for moral order and happiness in response to an experienced sense of alienation stemming from the perceived failures of Enlightenment rationalism and the modernist drive to subjugate the natural world. New Age awakeners look back to pre-Axial rural paganism, early Egyptian and Celtic polytheism, Eastern mysticism, and other premodern religious traditions as they tell stories about discovering long-forgotten truths and authentic ways of being in the world. In general, they "see the world as imperiled and understand their" enlightened worldviews and spiritual activities "as contributing to its salvation."[151]

Take Neopaganism as an illustrative case. Adherents typically embrace a blend of earth-based naturalism (often associated with magic and wisdom), egalitarianism (also characteristic of other new social movement communities), and heterogeneous coexistence (consistent with their polytheistic worldview).[152] Neopagan communities typically combine spiritual and therapeutic realms of experience while rejecting modern bureaucratic instrumentalism (especially the more exploitative and alienating aspects of technology and consumerism) and challenging hierarchical forms of social organization. These pervasive elements of late modern life, they claim, have historically disrupted the natural moral order, leading to a condition of widespread imbalance and unhappiness. Further, Neopagans actively undermine the core tenets of entrenched religious institutions, especially "the monolithic truths of Western Christianity."[153] In opposition to the prophetic religions of Weber's concern, Neopagans deny that true religion rejects the world. "Reclaiming" pagan spiritualism and a premodern connection to nature, practitioners believe, will ultimately have a cumulative impact, bringing light and balance to an increasingly dark world and leading to "spiritual rebirth on a global scale."[154]

Given the fact that (a) Neopaganism typically allows for a much greater flexibility of individual belief than most mainstream religions, and (b) adherents often claim that their discovery of Paganism entailed finding a home for spiritual beliefs they have always held in some way, some claim that Neopaganism is "a religion without converts."[155] However, much like self-described atheists,[156] when one identifies as Neopagan, one adopts a shared epistemological vision and common cultural orientation while also committing to the notion that other adherents travel "along similar paths" to enlightenment.[157] Further, shared rituals also unite practitioners into a group.[158] In other words, identifying as Neopagan entails joining an autobiographical community with its own discursive logic and rules of storytelling. Reflecting the community's core desire to distance itself from Christianity in particular, many Pagan awakening narratives take form in reaction to it, often more closely resembling the story of Siddhārtha Gautama rather than the story of the apostle Paul. More, when Neopagans claim to have connected to something that has always been there and yet remained unfulfilled, they model their particular autobiographical awakenings on this community's historical view that Christianity interrupted humanity's natural way of living and worshiping. In this historical vision, the Christian doctrine of human superiority over nature and the subsequent developments of modernity served as a veil that obscured fundamental cosmological and natural truths, truths that never disappeared but were simply clouded by a concerted renunciation.[159] Despite claims to the contrary, Neopagans tell stories about discovering, or more accurately *re*discovering, these long-forgotten truths as they work to transform the world while distancing themselves from the predominant institutions and normal day-to-day routines of late modernity.[160]

Conclusion

The foundational awakening narratives I outlined in this chapter span different social settings and historical periods. Some take form as biographical stories about an iconic figure. Others take form as a theoretical elaboration of falsehood and the process of discovering of truth. Some of these narratives posit a universal truth rooted in collective life, yet others posit more particular—even idiosyncratic—truths rooted in an individual's personal life. While there are certainly other cases that might be added to this discussion, these are "bifurcations that mark the road that, looking backward, we see as meaningful."[161] Despite their significant differences, it is their adherence to a common underlying narrative formula that ties this eclectic set of stories together.

Today, these formulaic narratives serve as cultural resources that individuals use to give their lives meaning and moral purpose by defining and rejecting forces of illusion, darkness, uncertainty, and moral disorder. They are established storytelling models that actors adapt and recombine in various ways to ally themselves with an autobiographical community by affirming that community's worldview while undermining competing versions of truth. Awakeners thereby situate themselves in a complex and contentious cultural arena and weigh in on disputes over the definition of salient moral and political concerns. As I will show, this story formula continues to play a determining role in the cultural tensions and epistemic disputes of the world.

THREE

Mnemonic Revisions and Cultural Contentions

Neither the life of an individual nor the history of a society can be understood without understanding both.

C. WRIGHT MILLS, *THE SOCIOLOGICAL IMAGINATION*[1]

On August 7, 1993, Jennifer J. Freyd, a professor of psychology at the University of Oregon, addressed an audience at an academic mental health conference in Ann Arbor, Michigan. Freyd is currently well-known for her research pertaining to the reasons victims of child sexual abuse might remain unaware of their abuse experiences for some time, only to recover their memories later in life. However, this particular conference address centered on a more personal matter. A few years earlier, Freyd claimed to have recovered her own memories of abuse and subsequently accused her father, a mathematician at the University of Pennsylvania, of sexually abusing her when she was a child. Her parents repudiated her claims, first anonymously[2] and later openly, prompting Freyd to address the situation publicly at the conference. "This private meeting of the personal and professional," she would later reflect, "was to play a role in touching off a heated public and political reaction."[3]

The notion that victims of child sexual abuse can lack conscious awareness of their abuse for years, even decades, and then "recover" those memories later in life emerged in the 1970s and 1980s with the convergence of a "child protection" movement, feminist campaigns against sexual assault, and a newly formulated psychological trauma model.[4] At this time, a growing community of psychological professionals, self-help authors, and self-identified survivors worked to popularize the notion that the harmful nature of such abuse leads self-protective individuals to dissociate from the experience in order to shield themselves from its devastating consequences.[5] To support their claims, they circulated theories and shared stories about abuse victims who awakened to discover their childhood abuse. By arguing that memories of abuse can lay dormant for an extended period of time, this diffuse social movement community provided a theoretical mechanism that therapists and their clients could use to interpret undesirable psychological experiences as *symptoms* of abuse and, consequently, to explore the clients' pasts in search of it. Self-identified victims began to tell these awakening stories in various public venues and forums, from "Take Back the Night" rallies[6] to, later, websites dedicated to sharing stories of sexual victimization.[7]

With the 1996 publication of her book *Betrayal Trauma: The Logic of Forgetting Childhood Abuse*, Freyd synthesized clinical evidence for the psychological phenomenon of "dissociative amnesia" and presented a theory that linked the act of "forgetting" abuse to a profound betrayal at the core of the relationship between perpetrator and victim. Because children depend on the adult figures in their lives (especially parents) for protection and survival, she argued, the traumatic impact of such abuse is likely to be suppressed by the child at the time of abuse, only to return with overwhelming force in the victim's adulthood. As both a self-identified survivor and scholar, Freyd established herself as a central authority figure in the recovered memory movement. By advancing a theoretical account of the mechanisms that cause individuals to forget and later remember their experiences of abuse, Freyd and other recovered memory advocates also argued that child sexual abuse is a prevalent but widely *unseen* social problem. The notion that individuals are awakening to discover their abuse was coupled with the notion that these awakeners have a moral responsibility to "break the silence"[8] so that society might awaken to see the "truth" about the problem. New cultural ideas about the pervasive and traumatic nature of adult-child sexual contact allowed for, indeed spurred, new awakening stories to proliferate, and these personal stories, in turn, reinforced the claims of this new autobiographical community.[9] These storytellers used a situated version of the awakening narrative to establish their authority to define a morally charged issue and, more, to challenge entrenched assumptions about sex/gender relations and the nature of modern domestic life.[10]

In the wake of their daughter's accusation and in light of the increasing popularity of claims about recovered memories, Jennifer Freyd's parents, Peter and Pamela Freyd, founded the False Memory Syndrome Foundation (FMSF) in 1992 with a small number of others facing similar accusations. This foundation has redefined recovered memories as "false memories," has pathologized the condition of believing that one has recovered memories of sexual abuse, and has been highly critical of psychotherapists and other authority figures who claim that such recovered memories are legitimate. According to its stated goals, the organization has attempted "to seek the reasons for the spread of FMS that is so devastating families, to work for ways to prevent it," and "to aid those who were affected by it and to bring their families into reconciliation."[11] While activists, scholars, and allied psychological professionals in the broad recovered memory community were highlighting stories individuals told about awakening to discover memories of abuse, FMSF members began circulating stories of individuals who once recovered and later retracted such memories. Such "retractors" were awakening to discover they were suffering because of a "false" belief. While stressing different kinds of mnemonic errors, both communities have used the same awakening-narrative formula despite making antithetical claims. They are situated in opposition to one another in a broader autobiographical field. While this cultural debate was sparked by one particular intrafamilial dispute over truth, it grew to define the contentious dynamics of many more families as it became one of the most publicly contested psychological issues of the twentieth century.

The ongoing dispute between the recovered memory movement and the False Memory Syndrome Foundation shows the central significance of memory in the stories we tell about awakening and discovering truth. Because such major changes of mind need to be explained, and because the rejection of long-held beliefs is typically "subjected to valuative inquiry,"[12] all awakenings require memory work. When awakeners account for their lives, they explicitly redefine important experiences, events, perceptions, and relationships of the past. They *negate* or "nihilate"[13] their prior beliefs and perceptions as they cast a figurative shadow of darkness on the worldview and optical norms of an autobiographical community to which they previously belonged. By revising the past, awakeners build a sharp, temporally structured cognitive discontinuity into their life stories.[14] They reinvent and mobilize their autobiographical memories as they contrast their current and former worldviews to describe a personal discovery of "truth."

While such mnemonic revisions are seemingly very personal, they take on particular meaning according to the recounting norms of an awakener's newly embraced autobiographical community. These auto-biographical communities are also "mnemonic communities"[15] with shared conventions and "traditions"[16] of remembering. Thus, various individuals use the generic awakening-narrative formula to express *mnemonic solidarity* with a group of others who define the past (i.e., who remember) in similar ways. They exhibit the "capacity to think and remember as a member of the group" and "place [themselves] in its viewpoint and employ the conceptions shared by its members."[17] As awakeners revise important events, experiences, perceptions, and rela-tionships of the past, they commit their memories to one situated ver-sion of truth while undermining others. They use their autobiographical memories to take a stand in a contentious dialogue between contempo-raneous autobiographical communities with different (and competing) ways of seeing the past.

Awakeners use two ideal-typical strategies to revise the past: *mnemonic transformation* and *mnemonic formation*. These strategies correspond to two ideal-typical vocabularies of cognitive constraint—the *illusion* and the *void*—which are culturally established forms of ignorance. In the case of mnemonic transformation, awakeners typically work to describe, undermine, and replace a specific illusory belief, perception, or world-view that they once erroneously took for granted. This subtype of mne-monic revision takes the form of a *liberation narrative*. As such awakeners replace one version of the past with another, they typically describe being freed from a specific oppressive, confining, or evil worldview.[18] In the case of mnemonic formation, awakeners account for a prior void of understanding in their lives, emphasizing their previous state of obliv-ion, lack of awareness, or emptiness. This subtype of mnemonic revi-sion takes the form of a *creation narrative*. As such awakeners fill the past with meaning, they typically describe their new worldview as if it were born to take the place of a previous absence of perspective—they account for something coming into being where nothing previously existed.[19] Awakeners use both transformation and formation strategies, at times in combination, to redefine past experiences and relationships while accounting for their prior commitment to beliefs and perceptions they now deem to be false.

In addition to their "backward" reach, awakening stories also have a distinct "forward" reach. Mnemonic revisions imply future projections; they carry major implications for awakeners' future attitudes, beliefs,

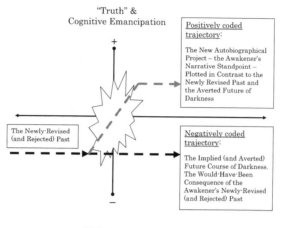

"Truth" &
Cognitive Emancipation

<u>Positively coded trajectory</u>:

The New Autobiographical Project – the Awakener's Narrative Standpoint – Plotted in Contrast to the Newly Revised Past and the Averted Future of Darkness

The Newly-Revised (and Rejected) Past

<u>Negatively coded trajectory</u>:

The Implied (and Averted) Future Course of Darkness. The Would-Have-Been Consequence of the Awakener's Newly-Revised (and Rejected) Past

"Falsehood" &
Cognitive Constraint

3   Autobiographical revisions reveal alternative autobiographical trajectories and contending projects in an autobiographical field.

relationships, and courses of action.[20] Awakeners revise the past in order to distance themselves from it and replot their future lives *in reaction* to their newly constructed memories. While such future projections can be explicit or implicit, they are a necessary consequence of the awakener's reinterpretation of the past.[21] Not only do awakeners contrast their new positively coded future-oriented autobiographical projects to newly revised and now negatively coded pasts but also to the potential future courses of "darkness" that are implied by their past "false" states of mind. Further, as they replot their personal trajectories (sometimes, as in the case of most religious conversions, beyond the point of death), awakeners advance culturally relevant *truth projects*; their stories contain moral imperatives that are more broadly relevant than their personal situations. As they reroute their autobiographical timelines, awakeners work to shape collective visions, values, and actions.[22] As with other forms of autobiographical reflection and testimony more generally, "recalling the personal past" becomes a way of "actively creating the public future."[23] As they contrast their new life trajectories with implied could-have-happened futures of "darkness," awakeners express a *projective solidarity* with others who share a common moral agenda and distinguish the objectives of their current communities from the objectives of their former communities. They use their autobiographical accounts to mark the boundaries between contending projects in a broad autobiographical field (see fig. 3).

Formulaic Mnemonic Revisions

Despite a variety of differences among the following cases, all of the storytellers describe and redefine their past perceptions, experiences, and relationships in order to account for a discovery of "truth." In each case, the individual's mnemonic revisions carry significant implications for his or her future life. By telling personal awakening stories, all of these awakeners conform to the recounting norms of some autobiographical community, be it a socially diffuse thought collective or well-defined organization. Despite the fact that they use their stories to lend credence to different situated versions of truth, they practice a common "ethic of recollection"[24] and share a formulaic style of memory work.

Melissa, a self-identified survivor of child sexual abuse, writes,

I have been remembering more, more details. [. . .] [T]he pieces started coming together [. . .]. My own father. He SA [sexually assaulted] me for all of my toddler years, and more. We were "married" he had given me a "special ring," he told me I was special and this was just between him and I, not to be shared with Mommy. I remember the downstairs bathroom and how he "washed" me, I remembered how he "dried" me when I was naked by our pool at night, I remember our "cloth game," the cloth was my "blankie." I remember how my mother commented when I was an adult, that I was inseparable from my father, that she was jealous of me.[25]

Notice how Melissa uses quotation marks to describe, discredit, and reinterpret her prior perceptions of certain childhood experiences. Her quotation marks serve as a framing device that she uses to transform the meaning of the activity at issue.[26] She rejects her previously held understanding (the "marriage," "washing," "drying," and "games" that correspond to the way the perpetrator in her story allegedly defined the situation) in favor of what she now believes to be a true understanding of the sexual abuse that occurred in her childhood. In the process, Melissa redefines important family relationships and adopts a new way to account for her current psychological state, providing a prospective justification for her future needs, attitudes, behaviors, and associations. She makes a clear distinction between her past life of delusion and victimhood and her future-oriented life of awareness and survivorhood. When such self-identified survivors transform the past, they typically portray an emotional shift as well. They link new feelings and sentiments to their newly discovered experiences. In turn, those sentiments, when expressed in the present, lend credence to their mnemonic revisions. As Melissa accounts for her personal discovery and present awareness of "truth," she throws her autobiographical weight behind a community of self-identified survivors who affirm "recovered memories" in their collective effort to define child sexual abuse as a pervasive social problem.

While Melissa revises her past to describe recovering memories of sexual abuse, her approach to the past is similar in form to a variety of other accounts. Ronn, a member of Iraq Veterans Against the War (IVAW), voluntarily reenlisted in the army in 2003 in order to fight in the US-led war in Iraq. Once a gung-ho soldier, he explains, Ronn had an awakening after an incident in which he shot and killed an Iraqi civilian. Accounting for his discovery of "truth," Ronn redefines his past experiences and perceptions. He writes,

[. . .] [F]or those of us who believed in the war at first (like most of the country), we enlisted to be defenders of the American people, not storm troopers in an American-run police state [. . .]. And I believe it's the soldiers/seamen/airmen/marines who enlisted with patriotism in mind that feel the most like I feel.[27]

The more I thought about it, the more I realized that all the reasons for us going into Iraq were false. [. . .] When I first got to Iraq, I felt that the quickest way to end the war was to [. . .] just [. . .] [k]ill them all. [. . .] I bought into the fear, the hype, and the propaganda hook, line and sinker. I'm not going to waste any more time on those arguments. Anyone who speaks in absolutes like that is completely self-deluded. I'm only going to say that [. . .] the "kill them all" mentality is called genocide when other countries do it.[28]

Ronn describes awakening to the truth about the Iraq war and, more generally, the political policies of the US government. Like Melissa, Ronn redefines his personal experiences and perceptions in order to articulate a major transformation of mind. However, whereas Melissa is redefining important family relationships, Ronn is redefining national political relationships that are important to his life. Rejecting his previously held perspectives, he redefines the Iraq war as "genocide" and equates his actions overseas to "murder," conveying a sense of shame, anger, and betrayal with his story. In the process, Ronn provides a prospective justification for his future attitudes, behaviors, and relationships. He establishes a future-oriented project of bringing the war to an end—a notable contrast to the course his life would have taken without his awakening. As he redefines his past perceptions and experiences, Ronn uses his personal story to reinforce the cognitive authority of IVAW, an organization working to undermine popular justifications for war.

Similarly, Scott also reinterprets his past, but he does so in order to explain his unwanted homosexual attractions in adulthood. He writes,

[. . .] I began to reinterpret my history in a whole new light—a light that illuminated my present turmoil. I recalled a childhood of emotional turmoil and confusion. The boys who were in my class played rough-and-tumble games during recess. I never joined in. I didn't know how to play the games and was afraid of getting hurt. I felt so uncoordinated. [. . .] Now it is amazingly clear to me that the moment I first felt something like an erotic attraction to another guy was the very moment that I first identified myself as the emotional and physical opposite to that guy.[29]

As he revises his past, Scott redefines significant interpersonal and sexual relationships in his life (in particular, his relationships with other men) and establishes a future-oriented project of heterosexuality. His story serves as a selective and "corrective intervention into the past, not merely a chronicle of elapsed events."[30] He now portrays his past as an "explanatory foundation"[31] for his current choices, values, and behaviors. As he "reinterpret[s his] history in a whole new light," Scott uses his autobiographical account to weigh in on the culturally contentious issue of sexual orientation. He lends autobiographical support to the sexual reparative movement, a community that works to undermine positive definitions of homosexuality.

Despite many differences between Melissa (whose story ultimately concerns a psychological trauma), Ronn (whose story concerns an international issue and is fundamentally political in character), and Scott (whose story is primarily focused on sexual orientation), their memory work is formally similar. In each case "what was proper before is improper after . . . and what used to be one's world becomes that which must be overcome."[32] Using the same general strategy of mnemonic revision, Kristi redefines and rejects her once-embraced view that "the godless evolution of [her] science classes was Satan's way of trying to pull [her] away from [. . .] Jesus" and now embraces evolutionary theory and atheism.[33] P. J. O'Rourke, the 1960s leftwing radical turned political satirist, ridicules and rejects his youthful political ideals, perceptions, and icons.[34] The Christian saint Augustine redefines his young adulthood as a life of "sin," "evil," and "an abomination"[35] in order to establish a future-oriented theological project. While the objective details of the awakener's past experiences remain the same in each case, their perception and understanding of those experiences changes. As these awakeners reinterpret their prior experiences and relationships, they take on new social conventions of remembering and recounting and commit themselves to new future-oriented objectives.

Each of the above awakeners replaces one particular definition of some event or situation (now defined as "false") with another. These awakeners explicitly transform specific beliefs, experiences, and actions as they account for their personal discoveries. In the following account, however, Steve redefines his past by filling a void in his awareness. In his case, he finds a memory that was not previously there in any form. Reflecting on a trip he took to the New York World's Fair in 1964 with a neighborhood man who worked with children, Steve writes,

I was in my underwear, and I remember the terror that I felt when he got into the bed in his underwear, the kind of terror that makes you feel like there is no air in the room to be had. I couldn't look at him; I couldn't look at anyone or anything. At this point, my memory goes blank. The next day, I had excruciating pains [. . .]. It felt like I had a knife sticking into my insides. [. . .] I remember that I was afraid I was going to die, but I knew I couldn't tell anyone, *even though I didn't consciously remember what he had done to me.* I just knew to keep quiet. [. . .] *I didn't put the pieces together until sometime during therapy, in my forties, when I remembered how I knew to keep quiet the morning after he molested me.*[36]

Steve describes being completely unaware of something that happened in his past until, around three decades later, he "put the pieces together" in therapy. He directly links his dissociative amnesia to a strict social imperative to silence and denial.[37] Like Melissa, Steve lends autobiographical support to a community of self-identified survivors of child sexual abuse who uphold the veracity of recovered memories. However, whereas Melissa replaces a specific bogus and illusory impression of reality, Steve forms a new memory where one previously did not exist.

Like Steve, Christie, a member of IVAW, also describes filling a void in her perception and understanding. Whereas Ronn describes replacing one moral outlook ("defenders of the American people") with another (the war is "genocide"), Christie describes being completely unaware of the moral consequences of her enlistment and eventually discovering what her "contribution" to the "military machine" meant. She writes,

In 1998 at age 18, I auditioned for the Army Band and enlisted impulsively and without informed consent. I spent a year playing flute in an all-purpose band at Fort Campbell [. . .]. The position offered permanent station, schedule flexibility, and automatic E6 [the rank and pay grade of staff sergeant]. [. . .] I grew ethically and spiritually strong, over time *coming to the realization* that my contribution, however indirect, was harming mother earth and her children. To stay would compromise my morals; I was a conscientious objector. In June 2003, I left the military. [. . .] In the last year, I've finally felt ready to *bring my past out*, and I joined IVAW to seek support in speaking out about the mental destruction and emotional trauma the military imprints on all of us. Today I study the science and art of home birth midwifery as a spiritual exercise, a healing ritual, and to bring balance on both a personal and a global level.[38]

Whereas Ronn and other IVAW members "enlisted with patriotism in mind,"[39] Christie "enlisted impulsively and without informed consent." As she accounts for her awakening, she revises her past by finding and identifying something previously absent and undefined. Other stories involve the same type of memory work. Eileen Franklin-Lipsker, for example, suddenly remembers, twenty years after the event, witnessing her father murder her best friend.[40] Edna Pontellier (Kate Chopin's fictional protagonist in *The Awakening*) awakens to discover her previously unknown desires and dissatisfaction with her traditional life.[41] Siddhārtha Gautama's early mindset is defined by his sheltered, oblivious, privileged existence prior to his enlightenment. Likewise, transgender activist Leslie Feinberg describes filling the void in his consciousness with a sexual and political analysis of transgender history.[42] Like many other veterans who describe joining the military to pay for college only to later learn the "truth" about the military and war, Christie describes filling a void in her past understanding. Discovering the harm she perpetrated as a member of the military, Christie establishes a New Age future-orientated project as an antiwar activist and midwife who seeks to "bring balance on both a personal and a global level."

Despite many significant differences among self-identified survivors of child sexual abuse, antiwar veterans, "repaired" heterosexuals, creationists turned evolutionists, religious saints and prophets, former left-wing activists turned critical pundits, and transgender activists, all of the individuals I cite above use the same general autobiographical formula to revise the past and establish a future orientation in reaction to that newly revised past. Awakeners use such mnemonic revisions and future-oriented projections to emplot their life stories as a testament to "truth." In all of these cases, "darkness" and "falsehood" must necessarily be defined in retrospect. No matter what the content of the story, and regardless of whether one describes replacing an illusory worldview or filling a void in awareness, awakeners revise their personal pasts in order to define a former state of cognitive constraint and to contrast it to their newly acquired cognitive emancipation.

Autobiographical Memory and Cultural Contention

In addition to the occurrence of formal similarities across various cases, individuals moving *into* a religion, a political ideology, a scientific paradigm, a sexual orientation, or a particular victim identity engage in autobiographical memory work that is formally similar to the memory work of individuals moving *out* of these worldviews. Such oppositionally positioned individuals use the same narrative formula to revise the past while conveying contrasting ideas about the subject matter at hand. These dueling awakeners use structurally identical moral codes but ascribe them to antithetical referents. When viewed as dialogue, their stories reveal how broader cultural tensions manifest in autobiographical form.

Martin, for example, a former cocaine addict turned born-again Christian, describes having a profound awakening while fleeing arrest for bank robbery. Martin writes,

As my mind filled with the wonder and peace of nature, questions arose that I had never considered before. I wondered who was responsible for making the stars, the moon, the clouds, and all of creation. As I was pondering these questions, it was revealed to me. I realized that only God could create such beauty. It had to be God. It was God! [. . .] As I stood on the balcony gazing toward the heavens, a series of cold surges radiated throughout my body. This filled me with shivers all over. [. . .] Vivid scenes from my past began to flash before my eyes. I was being shown all the pain and hurt I had inflicted upon others. Only this time the pain was mine. And it was real! Its realness was intensifying the heaviness in my heart. I began crying for the mess I had made of my life. Suddenly I found myself talking to God.[43]

Like the awakeners cited above, Martin retrospectively redefines his past experiences, decisions, behaviors, and relationships. While describing his discovery of ontological "truth," Martin finds "all the pain and hurt" he "had inflicted upon others" along with an overall "mess." He adopts a new way to account for his personal problems and criminal behavior. Further, he establishes a future-oriented project of Christian ministry in contrast to his newly reinterpreted life of darkness, allowing him to describe his time in prison as "walking in the light" and "fulfilling God's mission."[44] As he tells his story, Martin adopts, models, and promotes the mnemonic norms of the born-again Christian community.

While Martin's story might be fairly typical of born-again Christian conversions, it is also formally quite similar to stories about rejecting a Christian religion. Fritz, a former Episcopal minister who rejected religion to become an atheist, writes,

[. . .] I was forced to confront my own inconsistencies and hypocrisies. I saw how often I put up a false front, pretended I had everything under control when I wasn't feeling very secure at all. I saw how I repressed my fears, conflicts, and insecurities, lied even when I thought I was telling the truth. [. . .] I packed my bags and left the ministry . . . At times what I experienced was amazingly religious. My new awareness that there's no built-in meaning or purpose for life, no creator and no plan, filled me with a sense of wonder over the miracle of life and the evolution of human consciousness. I had new feelings about the preciousness of a human life, short and vulnerable as it is. [. . .] The loss of the religious beliefs I had once taken for granted opened the way to a kind of spirituality I had never known before.[45]

Both Martin and Fritz reinterpret their prior beliefs and experiences. In order to account for a major ontological and spiritual revelation, both discover that they had been living a life of delusion, darkness, and deep despair (in Fritz's case, one characterized by "inconsistencies and hypocrisies," "a false front," "repressed [. . .] fears, conflicts, and insecurities," and lies). However, they use their autobiographical memories to promote antithetical versions of truth and falsehood—contrasting views about the nature of the world or universe and the purpose of humanity's existence. Martin and Fritz use the same structural duality and very similar emotional language to justify and legitimate opposing future-oriented objectives. They use their stories to occupy contentious standpoints in an autobiographical field. While formally similar, their mnemonic revisions express an ongoing cultural, moral, and epistemological tension.

The oppositionally situated awakenings of Roman emperors Constantine and Julian express a similar cultural tension, one central to the political climate of the Roman Empire during the fourth century. Flavius Claudius Julianus (who reigned as sole emperor from CE 361 to CE 363) was baptized Christian and awoke to embrace Hellenic paganism while studying philosophy in the years preceding his first stint as Caesar.[46] Julian (who is also known as "Julian the Apostate," a title that was clearly bestowed by Christians because to pagans he would be "Julian the Convert") established official sanctions against Christianity and became a public symbol of paganism throughout the Roman Empire. He has been regarded as an iconic figure by some contemporary Neopagans.[47] To understand the significance of Julian's awakening and "apostasy" to paganism, however, it must be seen in light of Constantine's conversion to Christianity decades before Julian came to power. Constantine, who is recognized as a saint by some Orthodox Christians today, reigned as sole emperor from CE 324 to CE 337. According to one legend, Constantine, Julian's uncle, is said to have awoken to Christianity after he was "commanded in a dream that his soldiers write the sign of Christ . . . on their shields."[48] He was then, by Christian accounts, shown a cross in the sky with a message assuring him victory over his rival, Maxentius, in the Battle of the Milvian Bridge (CE 312).[49] After his awakening, Constantine went on to "alter radically the existing moral order," and Christianity saw unprecedented growth under his reign,[50] a trend Julian later sought to reverse after he awoke to paganism and systematically overturned many of Constantine's reforms. The individual awakening stories of these two men, while adhering to a common narrative formula, express the historic cultural and religious tensions between pagan polytheism and Christian monotheism that for several generations spurred political conflict in the Roman Empire.

Likewise, when proponents of creationism awaken to embrace evolutionary theory and proponents of evolution awaken to embrace creationist beliefs, they revise their personal past ways of seeing to occupy antithetical scientific and political standpoints. Charles, for example, once embraced the young-earth creationist notion that God created the earth approximately six thousand years ago. To argue that "the earth is very old, and evolution is a fact," Charles rejects his past mindset and reinterprets what he once deemed "the evil indoctrination of evolution."[51] Taking an oppositional standpoint, Gary reinterprets the evolutionary theory he used to teach and now claims it to be another religion, an "evolutionary religion" that fails, when compared to creationism, to account for the facts of the fossil record.[52] Alan, a former hydro-scientist and evolutionist turned creationist, revises his personal past and rejects his former worldview by reinterpreting the details of the geological record to support the existence of the biblical worldwide flood.[53] Not only do such dueling awakeners occupy oppositional scientific standpoints regarding the natural history of humanity; they also use their mnemonic revisions to weigh in on the controversial question regarding what constitutes legitimate educational curriculum and policy. While one person's awakening is another's sleep, and one's beacon of light is another's specter of a darkness passed, dueling awakeners use the same story formula as they awaken to oppositionally situated "truths" in a broader autobiographical field. They mobilize their autobiographical memories to define widely important issues and claim the moral superiority of particular future-oriented objectives.[54]

As these contentious accounts imply, our autobiographical memories are often connected to much more broadly relevant intercommunity dynamics. In his seminal sociological analysis of memory, Maurice Halbwachs distinguishes between three types: autobiographical ("inward," "personal"), historical ("external" and official), and genuinely collective.[55] In addition to these distinctions, Halbwachs articulates two variant manifestations of collective memory. On the one hand, he focuses on the way individual memories take form in various group settings, as when he writes, "The groups to which I belong vary at different periods of my life. But it is from their viewpoint that I consider the past."[56] On the other hand, Halbwachs takes "a more radically collectivist" stance and approaches memory as a societal phenomenon sui generis.[57] In this case he treats the collective memory itself as a unit of analysis, as, for example, when he asserts that "collective memory reconstructs its various recollections to accord with contemporary ideas and preoccupations" and "evolves according to its own laws."[58] Today, some social memory researchers highlight the ways that group processes and norms shape individual memories.[59] Others focus on more macro-collective mnemonic forms and practices such as anniversaries, calendars, museums, textbooks, monuments, or various other commemorative activities.[60] However, few have explored the ways individuals draw on widely available, transcontextual cultural resources to shape their autobiographical memories.[61] Further, there is little work that elucidates the ways individuals and groups use autobiographical memories in competition to shape broader mnemonic norms. Those who stress the agency involved in defining the past typically do not address autobiographical memory as a creative cultural act.[62] Rather, such scholarship typically focuses on particularly distinctive individuals—whether deemed "agents of memory,"[63] "commemorative agents,"[64] or "moral entrepreneurs"[65]— who work alone or in concert to set the commemorative details of some past event without necessarily foregrounding or even referencing their personal experiences. In short, the interplay between autobiographical memory and collective memory remains in need of much elaboration.[66]

Broadening the notion of mnemonic agency to include the study of autobiographical storytelling while considering multiple "sets of mnemonic practices in various social sites"[67] allows us to interpret the cultural landscape as a contested terrain in which actors use autobiographical memory as they compete to define the past. By taking autobiographical memory seriously, social memory scholars need not restrict themselves to the study of events that have officially ended but rather ought to explore how public autobiographical recollections of experience shape and reshape the collective perception and definition of ongoing and past events. In this sense, "readings of events that become influential or institutionalized can change the course of events as they unfold" and "history is written as it is read."[68] Further, actors wield autobiographical memory as a strategic cultural resource in "mnemonic battles"[69] or "memory wars,"[70] where memories are commonly met with countermemories,[71] and public definitions of morally and politically salient events are often polysemic in that they have disparate meanings to different audiences.[72] Such a view highlights competition and antagonism over harmony and solidarity and advances the notion that autobiographical memories are tools that individuals use as "means of cultural production"[73] in a contentious society.

When awakeners revise the past, they use their autobiographical memories to shape the mnemonic norms of the broader society with regard to some morally or politically contentious issue. This involves two interrelated dimensions of memory work that correspond to the variant conceptions of collective memory initially articulated by Halbwachs; awakeners use autobiographical memories to shape the collective mnemonic record and they use them to shape the cultural milieu for personal memory. While many awakening stories exemplify one dimension more than the other, all awakeners engage in both mnemonic practices. Rather than contrasting them or viewing these dimensions of memory work as empirically distinct, I treat them as analytic lenses to stress the inherent interconnectedness of the collective and personal dimensions of memory.

On the one hand, awakeners use their autobiographical memories to shape the collective memory held by some broad and heterogeneous community—to make their version of the past become "an image of the past which is in accord . . . with the predominant thoughts of the society."[74] They use autobiographical memory to assert how members of the society should perceive and remember a socially relevant event or collective phenomenon, either ongoing or already passed. On the other hand, awakeners use their autobiographical memories to shape the cultural milieu for personal recollection or self-reflection. They use autobiographical memory to assert how others should remember and account for particular experiences, relationships, and issues in their own lives. In both cases, awakeners use their autobiographical accounts to model the bridge between what C. Wright Mills calls "personal troubles of milieu" and "public issues of social structure."[75] More, they use the awakening-story formula to assert *mnemonic authority* in the face of competition as they define or redefine past experiences, events, and social relationships that are more broadly relevant than the life experiences of any one individual. While fundamentally cultural and cognitive, their memory work has significant moral and emotional implications. By attending to such strategic uses of autobiographical memory, I aim to further "bring individual men and women into our understanding of collective memory"[76] and show that memory exists as a reciprocal and symbiotic exchange between autobiographical and collective accounts of the past.

Shaping the Collective Mnemonic Record

Consider Ronn—the IVAW member who rejects his previously held pro-war worldview while redefining the war as "genocide." As Ronn reinterprets his personal experiences, he also works to undermine the popular notion, prevalent in the United States at the time of his voluntary reenlistment in the army, that "the great innocent giant [the United States] was under assault, and full, legitimate revenge—without guilt or responsibility—was justified."[77] Further, he mobilizes his personal memories, in collaboration with his autobiographical community, to challenge the national drama of "threat, vengeance, and salvation"[78] that many other Americans used to justify the wars in Iraq and Afghanistan in the name of righteous retaliation and national defense. Such a national emotional drama highlighted a "confrontation between evil and good," and framed the nation "as a victim" while promoting intense sentiments that encouraged many "to enlist in the military in order to eradicate the enemy or support efforts to round up all Arabs on American soil."[79] By reinterpreting his past, Ronn (in cooperation with Christie and many other IVAW members) uses his autobiographical recollections to invert the moral core of these popular arguments and shape the collective mnemonic record of the ongoing war in Iraq. He works to determine how the war should be understood and remembered (particularly by other Americans) even before the war officially has receded into the past. In the process, Ronn also challenges the cognitive and mnemonic authority of other veterans who use their personal recollections to bolster and legitimate movements in support of the war.[80]

Similarly, Anuradha also publicly promotes the mnemonic norms of this autobiographical community. Writing in both a personal and collective voice, Anuradha establishes a mutually affirming relationship between her life experiences (her autobiographical reflections) and the personal stories of her fellow autobiographical community members. She describes her awakening to truth as part of a common awakening to a shared worldview:

I joined the Marines in 1999 and I left in 2004 when I realized that my conscience and my values could no longer allow me to serve in uniform. I'm now a part of IVAW—Iraq Veterans Against the War. Perhaps some of you have heard of IVAW. A group of young soldiers who'd been sent to Iraq a few years ago to defend freedom and democracy came home from the war completely changed. They'd experienced the trauma of combat and had witnessed atrocities committed against Iraqis that they were quite sure hadn't been shared with the American public. [. . .] So they swore they'd work to expose the darker side of the war on Iraq to Americans [. . .]. Those who have been sent overseas for a bunch of lies [. . .] need to spread the message to young people that heroism is defined in many other ways: by service to your fellow human being, by sacrifice to your community, by kindness to your neighbor, by the telling of *truth. It is our duty to protect our children, and to wake our country up.*[81]

As Anuradha describes awakening to the "truth" about her past perceptions, experiences, behaviors, and relationships, she works to shape the collective mnemonic record of the war by asserting how others should understand this nationally and internationally relevant event. She conveys a sentiment of betrayal while emploting and contrasting the feeling tone of war with the feeling tone of peaceful interpersonal connection, cooperation, and truth. Such a sentiment of betrayal serves to reinforce her authority to redefine the rationale for war to be a "bunch of lies." Her story shows how "emotion is concomitant with an articulated judgment concerning a given state of affairs" and occurs "within a social matrix of goals and aspirations."[82] Anuradha's words reveal a tension between her autobiographical memories of her service and the way the war is perceived by other Americans. Her "duty [. . .] to wake our country up" implies that (most of) the country is currently asleep, just as she herself used to be. Combining her autobiographical memories with the moral imperative inherent in her awakening account, Anuradha tells the nation how this war ought to be perceived and remembered.

Many IVAW members use nationally relevant historical analogies[83] and shared historical reference points to fuse their personal stories with the national collective memory as they use their autobiographical memories to weigh in on a political and moral dispute over the character of the ongoing wars in the Middle East. For example, Victor writes,

Regarding the meaning of the word "patriotism"—Iraqis fighting for freedom from oppression get called things like "terrorists," "insurgents," "evil-doers," and even ironic things like "Islamo-fascists" by shallow-thinking Americans. Did King George of England call George Washington, Thomas Jefferson, and Ben Franklin similar names? Should we stop celebrating these guys on the 4th of July every year and denounce them as "terrorists," or something else even more hypocritical? What would you do if your country was invaded by another in the name of spreading communism, toppling your despotic leader, and removing your illegal WMD's [weapons of mass distruction]? Would you call yourself a patriot, or a terrorist?[84]

Victor voluntarily reenlisted in the army after September 11, 2001, to fight terrorism. As he describes his own awakening, he uses a temporal frame alignment strategy[85] to equate Iraqi resistance to the US military with the foundational American collective memory of Patriot resistance to the British during the Revolutionary War. In the process, he equates the current policies of the US military with eighteenth-century British tyranny. As Victor reaches into the US collective memory with this historical analogy, he uses a familiar mnemonic framework to elaborate his newly acquired perspective on his personal experiences in Iraq. He uses this historical analogy to invert the binary moral code at the core of popular justifications for war, to reverse the alignment of those contending discourses of liberty and repression[86] that he once used to justify his own pro-war actions. Victor works to shape the collective mnemonic record of the Iraq war by suggesting that Americans should remember this war as the moral and political antithesis to the values of honor, freedom, and patriotism that they collectively associate with their historic war of independence. By aligning his personal account with an established "meaning-constitutive tradition," he thereby influences "the thinkability of particular acts and projects."[87] Further, while the moral polarization intrinsic to the story formula requires storytellers to make sharp sociomental distinctions, it also "might be effective in encouraging audience emotional engagement for precisely these reasons."[88]

Similarly, when IVAW members gave personal testimonies at an event they named "Winter Soldier: Iraq and Afghanistan," they drew a historical analogy to the "Winter Soldier Investigation" organized by Vietnam Veterans Against the War in 1971. Further, they drew a secondary analogical contrast to the notion of a *"summer soldier"* or *"sunshine* patriot," terms coined by Thomas Paine in 1776 in reference to those who only stood by their country during good times. Paine's concepts initially inspired members of Vietnam Veterans Against the War to coin the term *winter soldier* to depict their antiwar activism as a patriotic duty. By organizing to end the war, they claimed, they were standing by their country during troubled ("winter") times. By using the term *winter soldier* to frame their personal testimonies about war, IVAW members acknowledged the legitimacy and influence of their Vietnam-era predecessors and fused their personal accounts and future-oriented projects with American collective traditions and memories of opposing tyranny (in both 1776 and 1971). Framing their personal testimonies with such national references, these storytellers work to shape the collective meaning and memory of the Iraq war. They salt their autobiographical narratives and frame their autobiographical memories with collective mnemonic references as they work to encourage others to awaken and see the "truth" as they have.

In a similar fashion, the six former communists who told their stories in Richard Crossman's *The God That Failed* used their autobiographical accounts to shape the cultural perception and mnemonic record of Soviet Bolshevism and mid-twentieth-century Cold War politics.[89] As with IVAW members, when these awakeners published their accounts, they were working to define a widely relevant and ongoing political situation. However, their testimonies were certainly also relevant for posterity's sake. From a contemporary perspective, the phenomenon in question (Soviet communism) has already receded into the past, and these autobiographical reflections have become part of the mnemonic record of the Cold War. Indeed, their personal awakening stories can be read as "history."

Just as Crossman's *The God That Failed* used autobiographical accounts and personal memories to redefine Cold War–era politics at a time when much of America was divided on the question of socialism, Peter Collier and David Horowitz's *Second Thoughts: Former Radicals Look Back at the Sixties* uses several autobiographical reflections to redefine the 1960s as a period of cultural decline and delusion as opposed to a period of progress and enlightenment. Notably, the title of the book implies the mnemonic revision, as "second thoughts" necessarily supersede previously embraced but now-undermined "first thoughts" when *"former radicals"* (an autobiographical community) *"look back"* at the past. In a striking example, Horowitz uses a historical analogy to recast a central, iconic faction of the sixties Left as terrorists, criminals, and "ruthless exploiters." After claiming to have discovered a murder perpetrated by members of the Black Panther Party, Horowitz writes,

> Because of what I knew, I myself now lived in fear of the Panther terror. In my fear it became impossible for me not to connect these events with the nightmares of the radical past. Just as Stalin had used the idealism and loyalty of my parents' generation to commit his crimes in the '30s, so the Panthers had used my generation's idealism in the '60s. My political odyssey had come full circle. [. . .] My dedication to the progressive cause had made me self-righteous and arrogant and blind. Now a cruel and irreversible crime had humbled me and restored my sight. [. . .] The Stalinists and the Panthers may have operated on stages vastly different in scale, but ultimately their achievements were the same: Stalin and the Panthers were ruthless exploiters of the radical dream; just like our forbears, my comrades and I were credulous idealists who had served a criminal lie.[90]

Evoking a historical analogy to the widely held collective memory of Stalinism (which was unpopular on both sides of the political spectrum in the United States during the late 1980s when Horowitz published his account), Horowitz uses his personal memories to shape the mnemonic record of the 1960s. Using highly charged moral and emotional cues (including references to nightmares, cruelty, arrogance, ruthlessness, exploitation, and criminal victimization), he equates the Black Panther Party with the Soviet regime of the 1930s and 1940s. He also equates his self-ascribed "self-righteous and arrogant and blind" faith in 1960s New Left progressivism with his parents' "credulous" commitment to the Soviet promise of a generation earlier. Symbolically equating the death of his left-wing beliefs with the death of his Marxist parents, Horowitz opens his longer autobiography, *Radical Son*, with a description of himself standing and reflecting at their graves. In both works, he revises his personal history (and theirs) in order to advance his conservative political agenda. He uses his personal reflections to undermine one way of viewing the national past in favor another and to set the mnemonic record of a significant political and cultural era of US history.

Whereas IVAW members and ex-Leftists of various perspectives and generations use their autobiographical memories to shape the collective memory of nationally and internationally relevant political issues and events, religious converts use their revised autobiographical memories to shape the collective memory of humanity with regard to the question of ontological and spiritual reality. In this vein, converts to Mormonism use their personal stories as autobiographical testimony to "the restoration of truth"[91] that they claim occurred when God delivered the Book of Mormon and established the Mormon Church through their prophet, Joseph Smith. As Richard, for example, accounts for his awakening to the "truth" of Mormonism, he models his own autobiographical story on the iconic collective memory of Joseph Smith's awakening. In the process, he makes a public statement affirming the truth of past events, offering a mnemonic account for others to adopt and share. He writes, "The missionaries knocked on my door [. . .]. We had the first discussion at the ward building the next day, and when the flip chart showed a young, 14 yr old boy [Joseph Smith], looking up at two bright heavenly beings, *I knew upon sight it was an event that actually occurred.* The elders asked me if I believed it could be true. I told them I could totally believe it happened, because in my own searchings *I also became disillusioned in the religions of the day.*"[92] On the one hand, Richard testifies to a foundational collective memory of the Mormon community—he is certain of the divine visitation that led to Joseph Smith's awakening as he "knew upon sight it was an event that actually occurred." On the other hand, Richard models his life story in a particular way. Like Joseph Smith, who according to Mormon doctrine became disillusioned with all other religions before literally seeing the light while kneeling in a grove, Richard "also became disillusioned in the religions of the day." Whereas two radiant beings—God and Jesus—appeared before Smith to restore the "truth," two Mormon missionaries revealed this "truth" to Richard. As Richard models his personal awakening on the foundational narrative of Joseph Smith's conversion, he uses the mnemonic norms and recounting conventions of his newfound autobiographical community to shape the collective memory of humanity by attesting to the truth of a significant past event (Smith's conversion) and performing the relevance of that event in the present (by virtue of his own conversion). He uses his personal story to shape how others ought to understand and articulate the collective spiritual history of humanity. In the process, Richard, like other members of his autobiographical community, simultaneously works to undermine all other "religions of the day" as well as nonreligious worldviews.

Similarly, as Deborah reinterprets her personal past, she also works to advance the mnemonic norms and recounting conventions of the Mormon community. In the story of her awakening, Deborah incorporates the Mormon doctrine of preexistence into her personal past. She writes, "As [the missionaries] began to explain that we lived with our Heavenly Father before birth, I began to remember my conversations with God as a young child. I vividly remembered living with my

Heavenly Father and His Son, Jesus Christ. I remembered walking with my other brother, Lucifer and begging him to listen to Father and not to be so stubborn. I remembered crying when some of my friends were cast out of Heaven."[93] As Deborah describes her awakening, she fills a mnemonic void, taking on new memories of past experiences, feelings, and relationships. Her immersion in this new group puts her "in touch with a past stretching back some distance."[94] In this case, she personalizes and testifies to the shared Mormon belief that human beings coexist as "intelligent" brothers and sisters and common children of God in heaven before conception,[95] at which point they transition into a living earthly body (a collective, historically oriented belief that, although taking various forms within Mormonism,[96] is not shared by any other Christian religion). She was in heaven before birth because every one of "God's children" existed in heaven before birth. Just as she remembers, we all should remember. Deborah, like Richard, uses her autobiographical memories to say something about how all of humanity ought to view the past. Like other Mormon converts, she uses her autobiographical reflections to weigh in on a cultural contest over the nature of collective ontological reality.

To directly undermine the memory work of Mormon converts, converts turned apostates use a *re*awakening narrative to revise and undermine their former awakening experiences. Reawakeners use the same story formula to reject an autobiographical community that they once used to embrace it. They cast what they once thought to be the discovered light of truth to be the darkness of falsehood. Whether focused on political, religious, sexual, scientific, or psychological subject matter, all reawakeners reinterpret their past perceptions, beliefs, relationships, and behaviors (again) as they weigh in on a cultural contest over truth and meaning. For example, an ex-Mormon going by the name "Exmo #2" writes,

I was a convert and highly active in women's leadership callings for nearly 10 years. I had a burning bosom, warm inspirations, converted friends, read the scriptures daily, attended the temple regularly [. . .]. Basically, a card carrying, stamped on the forehead, Golden Convert. I loved mormonism. I don't regret most of what I learned about people and myself through my experience. I had some good friends, but now that I'm completely and officially out and have my opinions about it, they don't have any more time for me. They don't brook opposing opinions very well, even when they want to. It's passing a bit too close to the anti christ and apostate evil world to brush shoulders with someone as far "in" as I was who has gone so far away as to say "Joseph was no prophet, Joseph was just a guy who, like my ex husband, couldn't keep his pecker in his pants and justified it with the temple ceremony and marriage, which just so happens to be so damned sacred it has to be kept a secret. How convenient.[97]

As Exmo #2 tells her story, she uses a reawakening-narrative formula to redefine her prior conversion and undermine central tenets of the Mormon doctrinal view of the past she previously embraced and "loved." Whereas she once discovered Mormonism to be "true," she now rejects that discovery and redefines the mnemonic foundations of Mormonism (including its prophets and historic customs) as "false." As she connects with an online community of ex-Mormons, Exmo #2 uses a reawakening formula to establish a new future-oriented project as an apostate to the Mormon Church.

Likewise, Arthur Koestler, once an active member of the German Communist Party, uses a similar formula to reject his prior awakening to communism. Using a logic of mnemonic transformation (notably, the same formal logic used by Marxists to reject their "false" bourgeois consciousness), Koestler writes, "I became converted because I was ripe for it and lived in a disintegrating society thirsting for faith. [. . .] But we all moved happily though a haze of dialectical mirages which masked the world of reality. [. . .] Those who *were caught by the great illusion of our time*, and have lived through its moral and intellectual debauch, either give themselves up to a new addiction of the opposite type [fascism], or are condemned to pay with a lifelong hangover. [. . .] Hence the deep, instinctive resistance of the political dope addict to the cure."[98] As such reawakeners use their autobiographical memories to weigh in on some widely relevant and contentious issue, they reject their prior awakenings and (once again) redefine experiences, relationships, and behaviors that are important to their lives. They invert the moral coding of the story as they redefine their previous awakenings, yet the generic story formula remains the same as the reawakener switches from model A to model B depicted here in figure 4.

Regarding figure 4, the storyteller's movement from position 1 to position 2 in model A (in the section demarcated by the heavy dashed vertical lines) is replicated by the movement from position 2 to position 3 in model B (also demarcated by heavy dashed vertical lines). In telling a story about moving from model A to model B, reawakeners reinterpret the memories and perceptions they previously regarded as "true" to be "false" and vice versa. Structurally speaking, the period of the awakener's life denoted by position 1 often moves from the realm of "darkness" (below the x axis in model A) to the realm of "light" (above the x axis in model B). The period of the awakener's life denoted as posi-

MODEL A: An Awakening Narrative

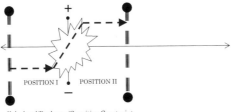

MODEL B: A Reawakening Narrative

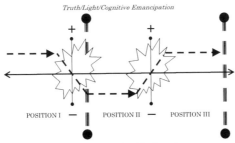

4 Awakenings and reawakenings

tion 2 moves from "light" to "darkness" as the storyteller reinterprets and undermines one awakening in favor of another.

Reawakening narratives further demonstrate the remarkable flexibility of the awakening-narrative formula, which can be adapted to suit multiple changes of mind in a person's life. Cierra, a practicing Pagan, takes her reawakening one step further, as is evident by the title of her story, "From Christian to Pagan to Christian and Back to Pagan Again."[99] Reawakeners express the same cultural contention across a single narrative plot that is otherwise expressed by two dueling awakeners. Their individual stories thereby expose an ongoing battle between competing mnemonic authorities in the broader autobiographical field. Such stories often include recantations, retractions, or reconversions[100] and involve vocabularies of disillusionment or disenchantment that the storyteller uses to reject a previously discovered worldview along with the community with which they were previously joined.[101] In the process, they use their autobiographical memories to undermine the legitimacy and authority of other awakeners who claim to have discovered a "truth" that the reawakener now rejects and redefines as a "false" discovery. In such cases, as Jeffrey K. Olick and Joyce Robbins argue with regard to national history, "contestation is clearly at the center of both memory and identity."[102]

While different in many ways, all of these awakeners use their autobiographical memories to shape collective memories. As they account for their awakening experiences, they work to define the shared experiences of a broad and heterogeneous social group, whether a nation or all of humanity. They use their autobiographical accounts to vie for mnemonic authority and establish the mnemonic record of morally and politically significant events and issues.

Shaping the Cultural Milieu for Personal Memory

Awakeners also use their autobiographical accounts to shape the cultural milieu for individual recollections with regard to morally charged personal issues. As they discover difficult and previously unknown yet already-there "truths" in their personal pasts, they articulate these "truths" to explain present problems, establishing a developmental cause-and-effect chain between the newly discovered past and the newly interpreted present. In the process, awakeners promote mnemonic norms and recounting conventions that others can use to portray similar issues in their own lives.

For example, as "repaired" heterosexuals tell their awakening stories they promote a recounting model that others can use to look into their own personal pasts in order to discover and identify the causes of their homosexual attractions and behaviors. These awakeners are guided by various practitioners of reparative therapy who serve as mnemonic authority figures. Exemplifying and encouraging this framework for personal memory, sexual reparative therapist Joseph Nicolosi (founding member and former president of the National Association for Research and Therapy of Homosexuality) writes of his patient Albert, "It is quite common to *find* anxious mothers *in the backgrounds* of homosexual men. These intrusive, hovering mothers intend the best for their sons, but are unable to recognize and respond to their authentic needs."[103] He tells him, "The essence of therapy is *to slowly recall the hurt*. Then to slowly reclaim the true [masculine, heterosexual] self that the hurt has made you detached from. [. . .] [T]herapy *brings out buried feelings*, and this is as it should be."[104] In his biographical sketches of several patients, Nicolosi clearly describes the relationships, scenarios, and associated emotions he claims homosexuals *should* find in their pasts in order to understand

and overcome pain and delusion. He reinforces a social model, along with conventional feeling rules and emplotted emotional themes, for individuals to remember with regard to the issue of homosexuality.

While advancing such a cultural framework for mnemonic revision, Nicolosi encourages homosexually inclined individuals to discover the personal origin of their deviation from a positively valued course of development. In the process, he contrasts two biographical trajectories—one healthy, the other pathological. He spurs his patients to reject the latter and reroute their lives along the former. He argues, "At a critical period in your development—the *gender identity phase*—you had to individuate yourself from your mother and develop a masculine identification through your father. It was your father who personified the demands of the outside world. [. . .] But you never received the necessary support from him, or any other masculine figure."[105] By discovering "intrusive, hovering mothers" and unsupportive, distant fathers in their pasts,[106] "repaired" heterosexuals learn to code their personal experiences with homosexuality as feminine, deviant, and regressive while defining their newly embraced heterosexuality as masculine, normal, and progressive.

Using these conventional polarized sex and gender distinctions, Alan writes, "I came to see that my homosexual problems were largely a problem of undeveloped manhood. Every man has to go through certain developmental stages; there is no real shortcut to growth. I saw that somehow on my road to manhood, *I had taken an emotional detour.* Fearing that I would never be 'man enough' myself, I bailed out of my personal growth into manhood and started obsessing on the manhood of others."[107] When Alan reinterprets his past in this way, he contrasts the trajectory his life once took (one that he associates with significant problems) with his newly illuminated future-oriented course of action. By defining homosexuality as a temporally situated deviation from the proper course of development ("I bailed out of my personal growth"), he justifies defining it as a moral deviation from positive sex- and gender-based behaviors and relationships. Using a similar sex-gender moral coding strategy, Jerry contrasts what he calls "the gay world" with what he calls the "the male world."[108] Likewise, Frank describes his newfound autobiographical community as "the world of men to which I belong and had not been a part of before."[109] Rob contrasts the "gay scene" with a "community of men,"[110] and Richard opposes the "sad, 'gay' world" to the "world of men."[111] When these awakeners look to their pasts to discover the causes of homosexual attraction in what they deem to be disturbed childhood sex and gender relationships, they also use their personal memories to contrast "gay" with "male" and establish autobiographical models that others can use to assert hetero-sexual behavior and masculine gender performance as the "normal" and "healthy" course of male development.

Proponents of sexual reparative therapy use the contrast between these two contending trajectories to outline and justify a remedial and restorative future project, one that is, they claim, necessary to overcome delusion and discover the "truth." Thus, Charlie reports, "Today, my therapy unravels the lies that inflicted this male insecurity upon me. My therapy has been a sophisticated process of discovering the truth, trying it on, and living it out confidently for the first time in my life."[112] Chuck testifies, "After many positive and self-affirming years of reori-entation therapy, I have come to the whole-hearted truth about myself: that my seeking romantic and sexual relationships with other men was, for me, a repetitive compulsion to get my family of origin and emotion-ally absent father to love me."[113] Without community-based recounting conventions and a shared project of heteronormativity, each of these awakener's personal stories would be anomalous and socially insignifi-cant; there could be no normal "road to manhood," no "developmental stages" that "every man has to go through," and thus no "emotional detour" that binds them together. Inversely, without their individual stories, the collective perspective of the sexual reparative commu-nity would be hollow and lacking in the "embodied memory"[114] and mnemonic authority conveyed by personal testimony and case-based example. As these awakeners account for their personal discoveries, they use their autobiographical memories to advance a situated version of truth and assert how other homosexually inclined individuals should remember their own sexual feelings, behaviors, and relationships. In the process, they weigh in on a cultural dispute over the nature of human sexual orientation, countering the notion, prevalent in gay-positive autobiographical communities, that "coming out" as homosexual is an expression of "truth."[115]

The sexual reparative community's framework for autobiographical memory is contested and undermined by members of ex-ex-gay[116] or "sexual reparative survivor" communities who reawaken to (re)discover their "true" homosexuality. Brian writes,

Around the time I began attending Columbia College I became a member of a cult-like fundamentalist group that espoused the belief that I could be "healed" of my homosexuality and only then could I be saved. This is the faith based version of the so-called "reparative therapy" movement. For three years I had lived as a gay man, but desperate for eternal salvation, acceptance and unconditional love I threw myself into their programs. A central part of their teaching was the "ex-gay" lie that I was "healed" of my sexual orientation through faith—and blind faith can believe or justify anything. [. . .] The cult-like group I joined taught that if you quit the homosexual behavior and accept Jesus that you are no longer gay, you are "HEALED!" [. . .] Part of the inhumanity of the ex-gay myth is the way it draws more people into the unreality of the idea that people are "created" universally heterosexual. By this time, the stakes were very high for me to maintain my sham heterosexuality. [. . .] This restarted the long slide into depression which had haunted me since I was fourteen years old.[117]

Brian reinterprets his prior awakening experience to be a "myth," a "lie," and an "unreality," one that was the source of his previous years of unhappiness. Using quotation marks to undermine the worldview and basic tenets of sexual reparative therapy, he deems his former autobiographical community "a cult-like fundamentalist group." In a similar strategy of mnemonic revision, Paul defines "ex-gay" movements as "snake oil" whose "salespeople are [. . .] pseudo-scientists" who promote "a self-illusion of being 'cured'" and "mind tricks and the delusion of progress."[118] Likewise, Tracey writes, "I now know that 'reparative therapy'—which purports to be able to change one's sexual orientation from homosexual to heterosexual—is a lie."[119] Brian, Paul, and Tracey reinterpret their prior awakenings in favor of an antithetical worldview. They use their revised memories to deem reparative therapy a pathological delusion and associate homosexuality with health, happiness, progress, and truth. As they take a stand in the cultural battle over the moral character of sexuality and sexual orientation, they reinforce a general model that others can use to recall similar experiences and relationships in their own lives. These stories show that what is regarded to be the correct way to account for one's past and what is viewed as the incorrect way to recall depends on the autobiographical and mnemonic community of the storyteller at the time the story is told.

Using autobiographical stories and biographical case studies in a similar fashion, feminist scholars, recovered memory therapists, and many self-identified survivors actively create a developmental framework that reinforces the authenticity of recovered memories with regard to the trauma of child sexual abuse. They advance the notion that many adults (with particular emphasis on women) are suffering from a variety of behavioral and psychological symptoms (including depression, anxiety, promiscuity, unexplained nightmares, and more) that indicate the likelihood of long-forgotten and yet-to-be-discovered abuse experiences in their personal pasts. Ellen Bass and Laura Davis, cultural entrepreneurs and mnemonic authority figures in this autobiographical community, articulate this idea in their well-known book *The Courage to Heal*. They write, "Children often cope with abuse by forgetting it ever happened. As a result, you may have no conscious memory of being abused. [. . .] You may think you don't have memories, but often as you begin to talk about what you do remember, there emerges a constellation of feelings, reactions, and recollections that add up to substantial information."[120] These and other advocates provide guidelines for individuals to reinterpret their own past experiences and relationships.[121] They encourage individuals to explore their pasts and discover sexual abuse as the hidden cause of their current problems.

When self-identified survivors share their stories in various venues, they use their autobiographical memories to reinforce this cultural framework for personal recollection. For example, Linda personifies the psychological phenomenon of dissociation that recovered memory therapists argue to be at the core of abuse-related amnesia when she recalls, "I learned young how to cope with 'Daddy's game.' Many a night I spent having a tea party in my mind while we played his game. [. . .] And the fact that I repressed the memories of my abuse for years only adds to my family's disbelief."[122] Similarly, Ann remembers, "As I read the courage to heal among other books it tells me to tell my story to feel better so well here it goes. I can remember being so young my dad walking to my room after mom left for work and my younger brother was sleeping. He would say this is a special game for daddy's and their girls and not to tell anyone. I can't remember all details yet as I repressed a lot of them."[123] Both Linda and Ann replace one version of the past (a "game") with another (sexual abuse) in order to locate the origin of their current troubles in overwhelmingly painful and abusive past events. Michele also transforms the past through the lens of her present suffering when she writes,

I am 19 years old and in my freshman year in college. I have just remembered the sexual abuse I endured as a child. [. . .] About two months ago, I began having horrible nightmares and flashbacks . . . my father had sexually abused me. [. . .] I remember him bathing me in the bathtub on other occasions, but it wasn't the normal bathing a parent does for their child. [. . .] Then he would lead me into his bedroom and tell me to lie down on the bed and spread my legs so he could "check if I was clean enough." I did, and he would then take a rough washcloth and rub my genitals with it.[124]

As Michele revises her perception of the past, she uses quotation marks to explicitly reinterpret particular childhood events—those associated with bathing in this case—and redefine her relationship with her father (quite like Desi, who reinterprets her childhood bathing experiences as she redefines her relationship with her grandmother[125]). Like Linda and Ann, Michele assigns blame for her troubles and establishes a future-oriented remedial project that involves sharing an enlightened under-standing of her own victimization. When such awakeners tell their stories, they draw a stark moral contrast between the evil acts of the sex-ual perpetrator, on the one hand, and the innocence and virtue of the storytelling victim-now-survivor, on the other hand.[126] In the process, they use their autobiographical memories to reinforce the social frame-work for individual memory advanced by recovered memory authorities such as Bass and Davis. Like the other awakeners cited above, they use their personal memories to shape the mnemonic norms and recounting conventions of the cultural environment with regard to a salient moral issue.

To undermine the claims of the recovered memory community, re-tractors tell formally similar stories about reawakening to reject their once-recovered memories of child sexual abuse. Beth writes, "At the end of 2 1/2 years of therapy, I had come to fully believe that I had been impregnated by my father twice. I 'remembered' that he had performed a coat hanger abortion on me [. . .]. I also 'recalled' that he had inserted a curling iron, scissors and a meat fork inside of me, and other 'horrors.' I came to believe this without a doubt and could 'remember' it hap-pening detail by detail."[127] Just as Michele (and Melissa, whom I cited previously) uses quotation marks to transform the past and describe recovering memories of sexual abuse, Beth uses them to undo a prior mnemonic transformation and *retract* a recovered memory of sexual abuse.[128] Retractors revise the past to discover that their once-believed-in abuse experiences never actually happened. They use the awakening-narrative formula to rename "recovered memories" "false memories" and establish a future-oriented project as victims of "false memory syn-drome." In the process, they mobilize their newly defined autobiograph-ical memories to assert how others should account for similar issues in their own lives.

Like the recovered memory movement, the false memory community relies on an ideology of victimization. However, the false memory com-munity identifies recovered memory therapists as perpetrators (asso-ciated with evil and falsehood) and reconstructs the retractor-family alliance (which, they claim, was disrupted by a therapeutic authority) as morally pure victim.[129] They invert the moral coding inherent in the survivor's story, yet the generic story formula remains the same. In this vein, Maria undermines her former therapist's mnemonic authority as she defines her therapy—a once-embraced space of "truth" and reality—as a space of "falsehoods" and mental confinement from which it "feels like there is no escape."[130] Describing her time in therapy, Trish remembers, "When I look back now I define the last four years like I was in a cult; the only member of the cult was me and the cult leader was my therapist."[131] Diana describes her therapy as a "cult," "a nightmare world," "a world of unreality and madness" where she "lived in total fear" with a "delusional belief system."[132]

Through their accounts of their personal discoveries of "truth," these reawakeners throw their autobiographical weight behind the False Memory Syndrome Foundation as this organization denies the legitimacy of recovered memories and defends the sanctity of the family. Like religious converts turned apostates and ex-gay individuals who become ex-ex-gay, such reawakeners symbolically redefine what was once brought to "light" to have really been a delusional "darkness"—a *false awakening*. Using such a narrative strategy, retractors reinterpret their pasts and use their autobiographical memories to assert how others should interpret such issues, experiences, and relationships in their own lives. Whereas false memory proponents accuse the recovered memory camp of "making monsters" and conducting "witch hunts,"[133] recovered memory proponents accuse the false memory camp of harboring perpetrators and undermining victims. Both "survivors" and "retractors" reinterpret their past perceptions and relationships as they "awaken" to oppositionally situated "truths" in a cultural contest over the veracity of claims concerning child sexual abuse.

Conclusion

All awakeners reinterpret their past experiences and relationships in order to explain a major transformation of mind and justify their present beliefs. They use their newly revised memories in an effort to shape social memories pertaining to widely relevant and controversial moral and political issues. Whether primarily working to shape the collective mnemonic record of some event or phenomenon or working to define the cultural milieu for individual recollection pertaining to a salient moral-personal issue, these awakeners deploy their autobiographical accounts and personal memories within a larger multifarious cultural arena. They work to promote certain interpretations and meanings while undermining the legitimacy of others. As their stories show, the work of mnemonic revision in general involves repositioning oneself in the world—an active shift in sociomental allegiance. While the communities we belong to shape our personal memories and model the way we tell stories about our lives, individuals are also active agents who use their autobiographical stories to ally with a community and vie for cognitive and mnemonic authority. By emphasizing such autobiographical work, we can elucidate underexplored social dynamics (especially interpersonal and intergroup contentions) involved with meaning, memory, and commemoration. Exploring the strategic use of autobiographical memory allows us to better recognize the role individuals play as active participants in social contests to make shared cultural realities.

As awakeners tell their personal stories, they adopt the mnemonic conventions and recounting norms of a new autobiographical community while relegating another community to the realm of "falsehood" by leaving it in the past. They express a duality of negative and positive sentiments as they simultaneously separate and join, reject and embrace, mourn and celebrate. Just as new generations typically set themselves in opposition to their elders,[134] so do awakeners set themselves apart from their previous communities. The temporal organization of the awakening story—the organization of progress, development, and direction in the autobiographical account—is key to the establishment of moral contrast and to the definition of falsehood and truth. Despite the particular subject matter at hand or any awakener's particular standpoint, falsehood is always something one has left behind and truth is always a progressive venture. Thus, awakening stories show us that the social construction of truth and memory is often intertwined. They are complementary narrative accomplishments, taking form in different autobiographical communities where we share our stories with some in order to undermine the claims of others.

FOUR

Vocabularies of Liminality

At times you may experience flashbacks [. . .]. These experiences can be disruptive and terrifying. You may respond with shock, horror, or disbelief. You may
feel panicky and suicidal, or relieved to finally know the truth about your life.
LAURA DAVIS, *THE COURAGE TO HEAL WORKBOOK*[1]

Our life is a long and arduous quest after Truth.
MAHATMA GANDHI[2]

Just as we cannot teach a child that a caterpillar and butterfly are the "same" being without describing a cocoon,
awakeners cannot adequately explain their major transformations of mind without reference to some sort of *sociomental* cocoon. In other words, individuals who claim such
a radical change of mind must account for a liminal awakening experience, a transformative episode that separates
their past commitment to "falsehood" from their current
grasp of some "truth" yet also allows for their passage from
one phase to the other. As Victor Turner shows, liminal
spaces and periods of time are, by definition, separate and
set aside from the regular occurrences of everyday life.[3]
Such zones of seclusion facilitate an individual's separation from, and reintroduction to, the shared lifeworld of
society in order to mark a ritual transition or transformation in that individual's life. The ritual practice of seclusion
marks a distinct ending to an individual's prior phase of
life; social disappearance symbolizes the death of the old.
A ritual reintroduction to society marks the beginning of
another phase; emergence from seclusion symbolizes the
birth of the new. Further, Turner argues, individuals who

are undergoing such a transition typically take on a "liminal persona," which involves being reduced to their bare essences where they "have nothing" and exist in a vulnerable "stage of reflection," "divested of their previous habits of thought, feeling, and action."[4] Expanding on a class of what Émile Durkheim earlier referred to as rituals of the "negative cult,"[5] Turner argues, "If our basic model of society is that of a 'structure of positions,' we must regard the period of margin or 'liminality' as an interstructural situation."[6]

As awakening stories show, such spaces and periods of transformation take narrative form as well.[7] They manifest as interstitial scenes according to the logic of the autobiographical plot. Awakeners use *vocabularies of liminality* in order to depict their cognitive and epistemic metamorphoses and justify their adoption of worldviews that radically contradict their previous ways of seeing and knowing. While vocabularies of liminality take on particular characteristics and themes relative to the autobiographical community with which an awakener affiliates, they also share important generic structural properties. Such vocabularies serve three interrelated purposes.

First, they allow awakeners to distinguish between different and discrete *autobiographical periods* and treat their past and present as separate, mutually exclusive chunks of autobiographical time. Vocabularies of liminality provide a narrative "splitting"[8] mechanism that awakeners use to justify ending an older period of life and starting a new autobiographical phase. As awakeners convey their sociomental transitions, they apply a logic of periodization to their life stories that is similar to the way national communities distinguish between historical periods before and after political revolutions and religious communities associate a new spiritual era with an earthly manifestation of the divine.[9]

Second, just as awakeners use vocabularies of liminality to "split" their past and present life periods, they also use such vocabularies to "lump" together a variety of otherwise different events, experiences, perceptions, beliefs, behaviors, and relationships *within* each period.[10] Whereas "splitting entails widening the perceived gaps between entities so as to reinforce their mental separateness," Eviatar Zerubavel explains, "lumping involves playing down mental distances within entities . . . deliberately ignoring differences within mental clusters."[11] Thus, as awakeners use vocabularies of liminality to split past and present eras of autobiographical time, they also engage in a "mental coloring"[12] to blend all the details of each respective autobiographical period so that each is portrayed as one homogenous phase of the awakener's life. The combined acts of autobiographical splitting and mental coloring make the distinctly diametric moral charging of the story possible. Awakeners disregard intra-era variation in order to contrast the bad "falsehood" with the good "truth."

Third, whereas Turner highlights the process by which individuals occupy a liminal space to signify their passage between two status positions in the social structure, awakeners use vocabularies of liminality to depict the condition of being "betwixt and between"[13] two positions in a *sociomental* sense. They use these vocabularies to convey *passage* through the cultural boundary separating two mutually exclusive cognitive standpoints or belief systems. Unlike the way individuals commonly maintain multiple group affiliations at one time,[14] one cannot simultaneously embrace two sociomental communities that adhere to antagonistic worldviews. Given the cultural tension that defines their relationship, the boundaries between such groups cannot be casually traversed.[15] One must do autobiographical work to explain a shift in allegiance from one to the other. Thus, awakeners use their vocabularies of liminality to dramatize the moral complexities involved with crossing the cultural boundaries that separate contentious autobiographical communities in the autobiographical field. No matter what the topic at hand, they portray a mental, emotional,[16] and/or physical crisis and convey a sense of betrayal, existential uncertainty, and moral anxiety that stems from losing one's sociomental home. They contrast this state with an expression of profound discovery, salvation, and cognitive rebirth associated with finding a new community of "truth." Consequently, as they tell their stories, awakeners reinforce the "great divide"[17] that separates one moral world from another.

Each of these purposes is exemplified by the structural position of the tunnel in Plato's allegory of the cave. An underanalyzed feature of this well-known allegory, Plato's tunnel provides a buffer zone through which no sunlight passes from the upper world to the lower world of the cave, where fire provides the mere illumination necessary to perceive shadows. Without the tunnel, the world of the cave and the world of light would bleed into one another. The cave would resemble a room with windows as opposed to the contained sociomental prison necessary to Plato's moral. Consequently, falsehood/illusion and truth/reality would blend together to create a world of cognitive ambiguity. In order to first be pained and disoriented and ultimately to discover knowledge of the good, Plato's escaped prisoner must travel through the tunnel, which provides a figurative passage to cognitive emancipation while also separating his state of emancipation from his past state of bondage. Further, this passageway separates the community of light and freedom from the community of darkness and captivity. Plato reinforces this gulf between the cave and the upper world with his comment that one who has seen the light of the sun and attained knowledge of the good would rather occupy the lowest position of the upper world than the highest position of the lower world.[18]

At the diegetic level of autobiographical performance, awakeners commonly locate their awakening experiences in culturally relevant in-between spaces to relay the transformative impact of their awakenings and enhance the diametric moral contrast between contending world-views in their stories. Such storied liminal zones provide a dramaturgi-cal element of *setting* and typically involve props and characters that awakeners use to convey their sociomental transformations. These are culturally defined spaces of receptivity where major changes of mind take place. For example, the Christian apostle Paul was struck by light-ning on a road separating Tarsus and Damascus. In this story, the road, a literal geographic passageway between two points, symbolically comple-ments Paul's awakening—his cognitive passage from one mental loca-tion to another.

Take as another case Malcolm X, who describes his awakening to Islam and black nationalism by writing, "Where else but in a prison could I have attacked my ignorance by being able to study intensely sometimes as much as fifteen hours a day?"[19] Likewise, referring to his time in prison, Arthur Koestler writes, "I had made the acquaintance of the different kind of reality, which had altered my outlook and val-ues, and altered them so profoundly and unconsciously."[20] By their own accounts, both Malcolm X and Arthur Koestler experienced profound changes of worldview in prison, a space that is structurally separated from the rest of society and symbolically (and temporally) located in between criminality (or persecution) and reform.[21] In a narrative sense, this space serves as a sequestered buffer that enhances the contrast between their former and current mindsets. Their existence in prison not only sets them apart from the common spaces of social life but also marks both storytellers as exceptional in relation to others who have not been incarcerated.

Such symbolic sociomental liminal zones are also evident in the nar-rated experiences of self-identified survivors of child sexual abuse, who commonly describe recovering memories in a therapy session, while watching a film, during a birthday or another anniversary, or while dreaming. In another case, Joseph Smith received the "true" vision of Mormonism at night, once in the woods and later in the form of a visit by the angel Moroni as he slept. Nighttime is culturally recognized as a temporary hiatus to the conscious, official world of daytime activity. Freud's patients (along with many others) awaken to "truth" in psychotherapy sessions—formal meetings that are geographically, temporally, and relationally set aside from quotidian life. Siddhārtha Gautama achieved enlightenment while traveling, away from home. The prophet Muhammad awoke while retreated to a cave in the mountains. Moses awoke in the desert. The Roman emperor Julian awoke while studying, eventually at university in Athens. From the perspective of the student, the university (like the prison) is structurally and temporally separate from the rest of life. It is a place one enters with the expectation of change. John Newton described embracing God during a violent storm at sea that almost sunk his vessel. The storm, the sea, and the state of transporting all serve to reinforce Newton's in-between status in the account.

To the same end, like the legend of the Roman emperor Constantine, many veterans account for a change of consciousness during their deployment to war. Military deployment and war in particular are separated worlds distinguished from "home." These worlds, not to mention often being located in a foreign land, have separate moral codes[22] and meaning systems. The fact that many Vietnam and Iraq veterans had such profound changes of mind while deployed is not simply a function of seeing war but is equally a function of being separated from (and at times a function of returning to) "normal life."

Likewise, many religious converts describe awakening in prison, in an Alcoholics Anonymous meeting, or during special visits from missionaries. The act of sending missionaries door-to-door is not only an effective way of reaching large numbers of people in a relatively organized fashion but also places the bearer of "truth" in the structural position of the stranger, as described by Georg Simmel, a transitory manifestation of foreign perspective that enters one's personal life space and temporarily transforms it. Such a peculiar combination of "nearness and remoteness," attachment and wandering, grants the missionary a position of exception and fresh perspective.[23] Like Plato's ex-prisoner who returns to share the "truth" with his former bondsmen, missionaries cross the threshold into "darkness" in order to bring the "light." Such in-between spaces—including special visits, storms, sleep and dreams, roads, caves, secluded meetings, journeys, deserts, mountains, anniversaries, and the night—allow storytellers to describe their transformative experiences by grounding them in between the common spaces of everyday life.

Dividing past and present while distinguishing "falsehood" from "truth," awakeners use vocabularies of liminality to center their life stories on sociomental transformation. The structural centrality of the

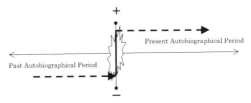

MODEL A: A Sociomental Express Elevator

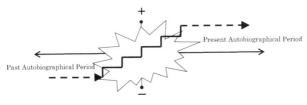

MODEL B: A Sociomental Staircase

5   Sociomental express elevators and sociomental staircases

liminal awakening experience also indicates its autobiographical weight. Even when the period prior to the awakening experience and the period following the awakening experience take up a much greater amount of the narrator's lifetime in a chronometric sense, the awakening episode (whether lasting a mere moment or several years) typically assumes a more highly marked and sacred place in the awakener's autobiographical account. In a narrative sense, the liminal transformative experience takes center stage in the storyteller's life.

Along with the formal and dramaturgical properties I have outlined, vocabularies of liminality occur in two ideal-typical configurations. Awakeners use both versions to portray a dramatic transformative experience and to mark the distinction between "false" and "true" states of mind in their lives. However, these ideal-typical versions of liminality differ in terms of the narrated duration of the awakening episode, and functioning as "vocabularies of motive,"[24] they differ in terms of the awakener's attribution of agency, intention, and will in the account.[25] Consequently, they exemplify two distinct variants of what Kenneth Burke calls the "scene-act ratio."[26] In other words, they can be distinguished by the way awakeners account for actions and use time frames, settings, characters, and props to describe their liminal life-altering changes of mind.[27] Further, these versions of liminality can also be distinguished by the way awakeners express the emotions of the liminal persona. The ideal-typical characteristics of these two vocabularies of liminality are aptly captured in the metaphoric contrast between the *sociomental express elevator* and the *sociomental staircase*. (see fig. 5). Keeping the culturally sanctioned vertical organization of cognitive authority in mind,[28] I develop these metaphors in order to highlight the ways that awakeners depict an experience of cognitive and epistemic transformation in their lives as they navigate complex and contentious autobiographical fields.

Sociomental Express Elevators

The metaphor of the express elevator (fig. 5, model A) signifies a direct, expedited ascent to a higher level of consciousness. When we take an express elevator to the top floor of a hotel or an office building, we are rapidly carried up to a new higher level; the door opens and we are there. When awakeners use such a vocabulary of liminality, they describe being acted upon by some overwhelming force. They portray themselves without agency—as powerless beings who are thrust into a shocking change of mind. Their awakening experiences are usually abrupt and intrusive and occur despite the awakener's will or intention. Like Martin, the born-again Christian who recounted "a series of cold surges" radiating throughout his body as "[v]ivid scenes" from his past "began to flash before [his] eyes,"[29] this version of the awakening story often involves a stunning discovery or sudden, disruptive realization of "truth."

Fiona, for example, describes recovering a memory of sexual abuse. She writes, "Then I had a panic attack out of the blue. One morning I woke up and I remembered being a little girl, lying in my bed, door shut, crying my eyes out, my night light all blurry through my tears. And I knew. [. . .] I called [a] sex abuse hotline [. . .] and the operator referred me to my therapist."[30] As she recounts having "a panic attack out of the blue" and immediately knowing she was sexually abused as a child, Fiona describes a rather sudden and overwhelming discovery of "truth." In her story, the "panic attack"—a particular version of sociomental express elevator—serves as a narrative mechanism that allows her to account for a major sociomental transition in her life. Like Martin, Fiona "flirts with a breaking down of the ability to narrate, an overcoming by the sheer power of the experience itself."[31] Both recount their awakening experiences in a highly dramatic way—as a narrated depiction of a shock that accompanies the reality switch.

Likewise, Shadow describes a similar elevator-like awakening experience when she writes, " [. . .] [T]he memories & nightmares began after i was raped last year & i can't push them away any longer."[32] By attributing her discovery of "truth" to an external "trigger" event (a more recent sexual assault), Shadow forfeits any claim to having had the conscious intention to discover that "truth." In the same vein, Robin, who writes as someone suffering from multiple personality disorder, describes an awakening that was imposed by an external event, in her case the death of her father whom she accuses of sexually abusing her. Taking her forfeiture of agency even further, Robin locates the intention behind her awareness of "truth" in her alternate personalities. When she writes, "A few years ago my father died and I believe that is why my alters [alternate personalities] felt it was time to tell me their stories,"[33] Robin effectively removes the will to discover from the first-person "I" in her story. While such external trigger events take many forms, they all serve as "nuclear episodes" in the autobiographical account, "particular events, in particular times and places, which have assumed especially prominent positions in our understanding of who we were and, indeed, who we are."[34] When awakeners tell elevator-like stories, they often make such trigger events the causes of their radical changes of mind.

To portray the involuntary essence of such elevator-like discoveries, awakeners often attribute agency to "truth" itself, which, according to their accounts, acts through various media. Sagha writes, "I was slapped by the cold wave of memories."[35] Similarly, Patrick writes, "The biggest flash back that always haunt me was when i was on the couch taking in the sun rays from the big window [. . .] [u]ntil my grandfather came up stairs. [. . .] Where at 1st thought he was just resting his hand until i saw he was playing with me. I didn't know what to do so i did the same back. *This flash back keeps coming back to me like some type of bad dream. At 1st i thought it was a dream.*"[36] Patrick's discovery of "truth," like the act of dreaming, is not within his control. Notably, Patrick couples his forfeiture of agency in the awakening experience with his portrayal of his innocence and victimization in childhood. Both experiences, the abuse and the discovery, *happen to* him, despite his will. In the same vein, psychiatrist Lenore Terr describes the case of Eileen Franklin-Lipsker, who had an elevator-like recovered memory of her father (George Franklin) murdering her best friend (Susan Nason) in front of her twenty years earlier.[37] Terr, who worked with Eileen, describes a particular moment in which Eileen noticed her daughter, illuminated by the afternoon light beaming through a window in their home, looking up at her. Terr writes, "And *at exactly that moment* Eileen Lipsker remembered something. She remembered it as a picture. [. . .] Eileen Franklin Lipsker's buried *memory, once it started rising to the surface, could not be stopped.* [. . .] On a quiet winter afternoon in 1989, a suburban housewife's mind almost shorted out with overload. Her heart pounded mercilessly against her chest."[38] Like Martin, the born-again Christian, Eileen's memories are accompanied by an uncontrollable mental and somatic "overload." Memory itself is given the power to act in the story, as recalled by Terr, and indeed it does act on Eileen as "once it started" it "could not be stopped." Whether or not Eileen wanted to know the "truth" about Susan is beside the point. The memory wanted to be known, so it acted. Notably, such a vocabulary of motive releases Eileen from direct responsibility for the will or desire to accuse her father of murder. The memory, by this account, left her with little doubt and few options.

Despite manifesting two oppositional standpoints in an autobiographical field, self-identified survivors who recover memories of sexual abuse and retractors of sexual abuse memories often use similar express elevator vocabularies of liminality to account for their awakening experiences. Debbie writes,

I caught part of a show about FMSF on television just at the point I realized that none of the "memories" in therapy were true. At the time, I was in shock and walking about saying to myself over and over again, "Oh my God, it didn't happen. What do I do now?" [. . .] I called [the FMSF], scared, and very afraid as I'd heard the FMS people were perps [perpetrators of sexual abuse] and didn't know if I could trust them or not. [. . .] They gave me support, love and they helped me out of the shock I was in so I could start to think for myself again. I was then able to realize even more what was reality and what had not been reality.[39]

While "flashbacks" are typically associated with the aftereffects of trauma, many individuals tell stories that make use of the flashback model. Aided by an external event (the television show) in her discovery of "truth," Debbie experiences an awakening that takes the form of a shock-like realization that leaves her in a panicked state of disarray. More, the intensely fearful character of her situation exemplifies the way awakeners who use an express elevator vocabulary of liminality typically portray themselves as overcome by an *emotional flood.* They portray the emotions of the liminal persona as extreme, disruptive, involuntary, and overwhelming.[40] In a narrative sense, Debbie uses her fear to explain the experience of traversing the boundary between autobiographical communities. She contrasts her fear with a feeling of comfort to justify granting cognitive authority to the False Memory Syndrome Foundation.

In a story that is strikingly similar to Debbie's account, as well as Fiona's story about recovering memories of sexual abuse, Gerilena writes,

I woke up one morning in tears. It was Father's Day. A loud voice inside me said, "You were not abused by your father. It's a LIE. It's all a lie!" I believe now that it was the Lord speaking to me in His loud voice. About a day or two after my realization, I was told about False Memory Syndrome (FMS) by my sister. I called the FMS Foundation and I started to cry when I read the information they sent that explained everything that had happened to me. I began to look at it all with new eyes. I became aware, relieved, and crushed inside knowing full well I had been deceived [. . .].[41]

Flooded with overwhelming emotion, Gerilena forfeits cognitive authority in her account, first to a voice, then to her sister, then to the False Memory Syndrome Foundation, and later to "the Lord." Like restitution narratives of illness in which "the active player is the remedy: either the drug itself . . . or the physician,"[42] her story externalizes agency. Using an express elevator vocabulary, Gerilena gives "truth" itself the power to act as is evident by the title of her account, "The Truth Set Me Free."

Like Gerilena, many awakeners who recount such overwhelming awakening experiences also describe immediately needing the guidance of a grounding cognitive authority figure to alleviate the sociomental anxiety stemming from their express elevator–like discoveries. They use such cognitive authorities to counter a sense of being "crushed," to use Gerilena's words, with a reassuring sense of being "aware, relieved" and thus to convey a sociomental passage marked by polarized feeling states. Such cognitive authority figures serve as symbolic representatives of an alternate sociomental reference group.[43] Just as the figure of the sovereign stood for the authority of the newly enlightened state in Thomas Hobbes's express elevator account of the rise of modern society,[44] these figures represent the authority behind the awakener's new autobiographical community.

As with Lenore Terr's portrayal of Eileen Franklin Lipsker's discovery, awakeners who use an express elevator vocabulary also commonly complement their portrayal of emotional flooding with a loss of physical, bodily control. Dustin, a Mormon convert, writes,

We sat down in the theater to watch the Joseph Smith video [. . .]. Then it happened, as Joseph was kneeling in the grove [. . .]. I had felt it! For the first time my heart burned, chills ran up my spine and tears rolled down my face. The spirit hit me so strong that I didn't care if I was the only blubbering fool in a theater of about 100 people. I knew that the church was true and that I had to be baptized. [. . .] I called the missionary. [. . .] From that point forward my life has been blessed so immeasurably that I can't imagine where I would be today without it.[45]

Dustin's involuntary bodily sensations (his "burns" and "chills") and flood of emotion (the "tears" rolling down his face and his "blubbering," which are euphoric expressions of joy in his case) provide complementary physical and affective manifestations of his lack of agency, a somatic expression of the uncontrollable character of his mental discovery. His tears also serve to convey a transformative cleansing of the mind, heart, and soul, a narrative cleansing function that is especially evident when Charlene Cothran, "redeemed" lesbian and former editor of *Venus* (a magazine she previously published for African American lesbians), writes, "A river of tears flowed as Jesus washed me and forgave me and redeemed me for His work."[46] Dustin and Charlene are under the power of an overwhelming force, a spirit that possesses them and forces them to know what is "true."

Using a similar overwhelming bodily possession to account for an involuntary discovery and transformation, Rod, a born-again Christian, writes,

I was smoking four packs of camel cigarettes a day, and had no intention of slowing down, I pulled a cigarette out of the pack and as I tried to put it in my mouth, my hand threw it to the ground. I was so surprised, because I didn't feel anything in hand, I didn't want to throw it down, and I really wanted a cigarette. So I pulled another one out of the pack and as I tried to put it in my mouth, my hand threw it down. [. . .] So I pulled out the pack and flipped one up and held the pack real tight and started putting it to my mouth, really concentrating to get that cigarette into my mouth and beat whatever this was that was in control of my hand. Suddenly my hand threw the whole pack to the ground. [. . .] Then, while my mind was trying to figure out what was going on, I heard my mouth saying, "O.K. Lord, if you don't want me to smoke. I will never touch another one." Then I thought I had gone crazy. Then I started thinking . . . who is Lord? Who could make my hand throw down cigarettes? Who could speak through my mouth? Who is Lord? These thoughts were bombarding my mind when suddenly, I met the personality of Jesus Christ.[47]

When Rod is visited by the spirit force, he loses complete control of his body. He forfeits all agency in the account to explain his awakening experience. Using a more subtle tone, Anna (who claims to have led an "anti-cult" group against Mormonism for years) forfeits her agency to the same spirit character. She writes, that after reading the book of Mormon for the first time, "the spirit was able to reach me and help me turn my life around."[48] Richard reports that an "unseen person sat next to me and whispered in my ears that what you just read is true."[49]

Just as Debbie used a television program to account for her shocking realization of her "false" memories of abuse, an individual who goes by the name "Mountaingirl" uses a television program to account for her sudden and unsolicited mental discovery of the "lies" of Mormonism. Like a holy spirit to a convert, the program provides an external authoritative link to the "correct" definition of her situation. She writes, "I saw an educational program on secret societies including free masonry. [. . .] As this TV show was on I was in the other room listening and I was hearing the [Mormon] temple rites being recited, verbatim. I quickly ran to the TV and sure enough that was what I was hearing. These were supposedly the rites that Masons practiced! I was reeling with disbelief at first and then a quiet acceptance overcame me that it really was all a lie."[50] Mountaingirl conveys an initial moment of shock as she "quickly ran to the TV" and was then "reeling with disbelief" (this shock is also conveyed by her use of an exclamation point in the passage). By using the television program to account for her realization of "truth" (a program that she was not even watching but only listening to from another room where she was presumably focused on something else), Mountaingirl portrays her awakening as accidental and unmotivated. She did not seek the "truth"; rather the "truth" (as with a spirit possession) found and imposed itself on her.[51] Likewise, C. L. Hanson describes an elevator-like awakening after realizing that her high school best friend (a Lutheran) held beliefs that contradicted the tenets of Mormonism. She describes this as her *"moment* of epiphany" and exclaims, "It *hit me* [. . .]. And that was it. That moment was the end of my belief in Mormonism."[52] C. L. Hanson's elevator-like awakening experience is both powerful and relatively instantaneous—a combination of attributes that is reflected in the common etymological root of the words *momentous* and *momentary*. Echoing sentiments expressed by both Debbie and C. L. Hanson, former Christian and creationist Kim describes having an elevator-like experience while watching a Stephen Hawking lecture. Flooded with euphoric and overwhelming emotion, Kim writes,

[. . .] [M]y atheist friend asked me if I saw how it was at least possible without a god. I said yes. That was all it took. *My [religious] belief vanished in that moment.* [. . .] That moment was perhaps the most, for lack of a better word, *transcendent* moment of my life. [. . .] I saw the universe as I had never seen it, and will never see it again. *Everything made crystal-clear sense.* [. . .] I saw in that instant why the universe was billions upon billions of light years wide with billions upon billions of galaxies like ours. [. . .] In that moment, the greatest "Ah Ha!" moment of my life, *I GOT IT!* It was like a supernova of the mind (now my mind is pulling in information like a black hole!) I also knew in that moment that I would never accept another supernatural claim without real evidence ever again.[53]

Such elevator-like discoveries are also evident in the accounts of awakeners who focus on a salient political issue. Using Oliver Stone's 1986 film *Platoon*, Vietnam veteran Arnold Steiber describes an overwhelming *sensory-based* flooding experience to portray an awakening that led him from a mental void to conscious antiwar activism. Arnold writes,

When I left Vietnam in early 1971, I pretty much closed that chapter of my life. [. . .] About seven months ago I was home alone at night. I turned on the TV. The movie "Platoon" was playing. [. . .] Wow. Stuff was there. Especially the kids. The violence was real. *I could smell Vietnam. I could hear it. I could feel it.* [. . .] The next day I went on the Internet and looked up Vietnam Veterans Against the War [. . .]. Wow. This was good. Maybe that's why I was in Vietnam—to help others realize that violence is not the answer. [. . .] I woke up, and it feels right.[54]

The film leads Arnold to embrace a new peace-oriented belief system, engage in political action, and discover a new sense of his life's purpose. Like a holy spirit to a religious convert, the film speaks to him and spurs him into, as the title of his essay reveals, "Waking Up to Peace." Likewise, Iraq Veterans Against the War (IVAW) member Adam, once a pro-war marine, attributes the initial loss of his "shield"—the metaphor he uses to describe the Marine Corps mindset and emotional composure—to his participation in the IVAW political protest "Operation First Casualty." In the wake of his experience at this momentous political event, Adam writes, "That was when I got to become human again."[55]

Beyond the shocking impact of films and public protest actions, political awakeners also describe how personal events and issues serve as catalysts for major world-altering transformations of mind. Peter Collier, for example, describes an elevator-like moment of "truth": "It was about this time that my daughter Caitlin was born and my father was diagnosed as having terminal cancer. Being sandwiched *so suddenly* in between life and death *jolted me* and *made me feel* that I had been living through a kind of rhetorical gauze for the past decade."[56] This jolting moment in Collier's life led him to abandon his 1960s left-wing radicalism.

David, who accounts for his reawakening to discover his "true" homosexuality, describes a similar life-changing moment of discovery after nearly attempting suicide several times. He writes, "That was the moment that my life truly started to change. I was admitted to a treatment center for my alcoholism and depression and I never returned to the 'ex-gay' ministries, churches, or reparative therapists that had been my way of life for almost ten years. [. . .] I started trying to accept myself the way I was."[57] After working in various ways to embrace heterosexuality for nearly a decade, David's "moment" of breakdown, his cessation of work, caused him to realize he was "truly" homosexual.

Despite many differences among them, each of these awakeners forfeits agency and describes being acted upon by an overpowering force in order to convey the experience of crossing the cultural and sociomental divide between contentious autobiographical communities. It happens rather quickly to all of them regardless of their will and intention and leaves them temporarily shocked, stunned, or overwhelmed with a new life-changing awareness of "truth." Such awakeners portray their express elevator–like moments as panic attacks, flashbacks, jolts, blackouts, confused or dazed states, temporary blindness, bodily possessions, convulsions, intrusive thoughts, unsolicited messages, nightmares or dreams, body memories, hallucinations, and more.[58] To portray such momentous events, awakeners use various dramaturgical devices. These include symbolic props and supporting characters, such as other people, organizations, lightning bolts, storms, messengers, spirits, voices, alternate personalities, films, television programs, and various other nonbiological actors.[59] Awakeners attribute agency to these props and characters. They give them the ability to convey information and compel new discoveries. By using these various literary devices to explain involuntary, near-instantaneous, and radical transformations of worldview, they impose a staccato-like structure on their autobiographical accounts.[60] More, in Kenneth Burke's words, the scene or setting expresses "in fixed properties the same quality that the action expresses in terms of development."[61] Using such sociomental express elevators, awakeners often depict their "liminal personae"[62] in concentrated form by describing a profound loss of emotional, bodily, and/or sensory control in order to convey the intensity and overwhelming, uncontrollable character of their discoveries. In the process, they justify their embrace of a new worldview by appealing to an authoritative force that exists outside their conscious design and beyond their control. Consequently, such accounts typically appeal to faith. Whether psychological, political, sexual, scientific, or religious in focus, they ask us to believe in some "power" that often works in mysterious ways.

Sociomental Staircases

In contrast to the elevator, the metaphor of the staircase (fig. 5, model B) implies a step-by-step ascent—a gradual transformation of consciousness that unfolds over a relatively greater amount of time and involves the deliberate activity of the awakener. A staircase will allow us to cover the same vertical distance that an elevator will; it just requires us to ascend in discernible increments, by our own effort. You have to walk up a staircase, one step at a time. When awakeners use such a vocabulary of liminality, they typically describe embarking on a self-motivated quest for truth and knowledge. They exercise agency in their stories and bring about their own discoveries. Like Fritz (the Episcopal minister turned atheist-humanist who started to doubt his faith and to look for answers while studying at Princeton, well before leaving his ministry)[63] or Ben (whose sexual reorientation unfolded over twenty-seven months of conscious commitment to therapy),[64] awakeners employing a staircase vocabulary of liminality take charge in their stories, which often highlight the intentional application of the mind to the question of truth and typically appeal to reason.[65] As is the case with Jean-Jacques Rousseau's philosophical account of the protracted, multiphase rise of modern society,[66] several notable yet relatively minor events are nested in the broader transformative episode. Each of these nested events contributes to the cumulative transformation of the storyteller's consciousness.

Bill, a former Mormon, describes his awakening as a long, intentional search for truth. He writes, "After about a five year process of deep study and introspection, about six months after my visit with the bishop in his office, my conscience finally led me to write my resignation letter. [. . .] The drip drip on my conscience began on my mission. The path to my awakening started when I was a missionary in Rio de Janeiro, Brazil."[67] Bill then reflects on his long search for truth and describes finding several illuminating clues before achieving his full realization. Notably, the "path" to his awakening involves a conscious mental pursuit characterized by study and introspection. Like Charles, who depicts his rejection of young-earth creationism and acceptance of evolutionary theory as "a life long journey of learning,"[68] Bill exercises agency to seek answers as he works to find "truth." By articulating a "drip drip" on his conscience, Bill uses the metaphor of a leaky faucet to describe how his emerging doubts spurred him into a quest. Notably, such a "dripping" phenomenon can be contrasted with the "flood" of realization that occurs in express elevator stories. With regard to affect, such awakeners convey a protracted *emotional reasoning*. Their liminal feelings are paced and inseparably coupled with a conscious intellectual pursuit. Moonshine writes, "Suffice it to say, for me, the beginning of the end came while studying church history from the historian's view. Thirty books and buckets of tears later, I came to realize that 'a church that will not tell the truth simply <u>CANNOT BE TRUE</u>.'"[69] Like Bill's metaphoric leaky faucet, Moonshine's tears indicate the protracted pace of her awakening. In order to have "buckets of tears," time is needed. Further, Moonshine's reading (an intellectual pursuit) spurs her accumulation of tears and demonstrates the intention behind her discovery. Similarly, another ex-Mormon who goes by the screen name "dbradhud" writes, "The more I read from the church history, the worse I felt. The more I studied, thought and prayed, the more problems I found with the church and what it claimed to be. I started compiling a list of problems. It became harder and harder for me to go out and teach. [. . .] Finally, I realized that I couldn't do it anymore—tell people that I knew the church was true when I had such serious doubts."[70] By actively and intentionally reading church history, studying, and reflecting, dbradhud, like Bill and Moonshine, takes charge over his awakening. Even when the "truth" is represented as a painful discovery, these awakeners look for it, cultivate it, and "face" it. Their difficult feelings occur on pace with and as a consequence of their investigations.

As they portray their liminal journeys, Bill, Moonshine, and dbradhud account for their gathering of the "truth" piece by piece. Such pieces of the "truth" become steps in a more general process of *sociomental accumulation* that forms a staircase-like plotline culminating in the fulfillment of an awakening. Such awakeners often describe a restless longing for an elevator-like experience that never comes. Their frustration spurs them to quest for answers. RuneWolf, a Pagan who was raised Methodist, writes,

For some time I had been restless and discontented with the Church. [. . .] I was looking for the "burning bush," what later decades would come to call "peak experiences." [. . .] What I wanted from Church was to feel the breath of God blow through my soul, and I just wasn't getting it. So I went out to find it on my own. My quest, as it were, started out pretty well. I began to read extensively on other religions and spiritual paths throughout history and the contemporary world, assimilating what I liked and leaving the rest.[71]

After exploring several paths and later joining Alcoholics Anonymous, RuneWolf writes, "I found my way to the arms of the Goddess. Like so many of us, after years of wandering, I came home at last."[72] Likewise, Rob, a "repaired" heterosexual who titles his account "A Hard-Work Miracle," recalls wanting a "flash of light" but never receiving it. Rob describes reading several books as he searched for the truth and meaning that such flashes of light usually impart. He writes, "I started reading anything I could get my hands on from a reparative-therapy perspective— Nicolosi, Medinger, Eldridge. Their books helped me better understand my desire for men and masculinity. I learned it was a natural drive for gender connection that had been misdirected into sexual desire [. . .]."[73] Rob later continued this search by attending weekend retreats called "Journey Into Manhood" and "New Warriors," their names expressing the protracted and agentic character of his quest. Rob uses each book, therapy session, and retreat in his story to describe how he accumulated his awareness of "truth" over time, in a step-by-step fashion that matches the pace set by the "drip drip" that characterizes Bill's apostasy.

Stressing such a process-oriented approach, sexual reparative therapist Joseph Nicolosi prepares his patient Father John for a similarly protracted and challenging journey that he will have to "fight for." He writes, "Essential to healing homosexuality is changing this perception you have of yourself as the passive, helpless victim. Real change requires more than just putting the lid on a sexual behavior. We're looking for a larger transformation. [. . .] But this is something you will have to fight for. Forever—I'm not talking about a week. Some days will be big battles; some, small battles. But every day has to be a battle of some sort [. . .]."[74] Adopting this perspective on the step-by-step process of transformation (as epitomized by daily "battles" in Nicolosi's view), many "repaired" heterosexuals associate the discovery of "truth" in their lives with the prolonged process of psychological healing. Such an agentic engagement with therapeutic work counters the lack of agency built into the psychoanalytic view that, without treatment, individuals are "victims of unconscious forces."[75] Using a staircase vocabulary, Scott writes, "The *road* to healing was a difficult one filled with ups and downs. Along the way, *I faced* feelings of rejection from my peers and father. *I worked* to overcome feelings of inadequacy and incompetence as a man. As *I worked* with my counselor to fill my emotional needs, extinguish harmful behaviors, and heal emotional wounds, I noticed my homosexual compulsions becoming less intense. With time, they began to subside. Then, subtly, I noticed heterosexual feelings starting to emerge. These new feelings grew slowly as *I continued progressing* through the recovery process."[76] As with "quest stories" about illness that "meet suffering head on,"[77] Scott emphasizes the protracted character of his drive to comprehend and change his homosexual attractions. As he works to achieve "healing," he ultimately discovers the core "truth" about his sexuality—the causes and consequences of his "homosexual compulsions" and the hidden nature of his "heterosexual feelings." His "healing" process is, among other things, a staircase-like discovery of "truth" that leads to a new sexual worldview and lifestyle. Such a stress on process is evident in Dan's comment that "[t]here is joy in the journey itself"[78] and is captured by the Japanese poet Matsuo Bashō's sentiment that "every day is a journey, and the journey itself is home."[79]

In the same vein, many self-identified survivors who recover memories of child sexual abuse also stress a staircase-like commitment to psychotherapy and link the protracted process of discovery to the process of working to heal. Stephanie writes, "I have started to live my life day by day and [some] days I want to recall more of what he did to me [and some] I don't if I feel I can't deal."[80] Ella writes, "I don't remember lots of things. I started to face the memories about 3 years ago. I just wasn't ready before then. [. . .] And I have been working with a therapist and I have been very open to my feelings, talking to my child inside, but it's very hard anyway."[81] As she works with a therapist to understand the "truth" about her life, Ella slowly acquires an understanding of her present feelings. For both Stephanie and Ella, the difficult work of psychological discovery and healing also explains their prior lack of awareness and justifies a protracted venture. Such a staircase-like logic is evident when Lilita writes, "I have been facing my memories and feelings for three years. I knew there was a lot, a lot to face, so it makes sense why I postponed it."[82] Despite taking an oppositional stand, several who retract memories of childhood sexual abuse use a similar staircase-like vocabulary to describe their healing reawakenings. Beth, for example, describes her discovery as "The Process" and meticulously details the steps involved with her "Journey Home and Back to Truth."[83]

While some awakeners use a staircase-like vocabulary of liminality to describe gathering the truth piece by piece (a process of sociomental accumulation), others use such a vocabulary of liminality to describe trying and rejecting various answers until they discover the real "truth"—a process of *sociomental elimination*. For example, as Mormon convert Douglass describes his self-motivated and protracted journey to discover spiritual "truth," his account is riddled with false leads, dead ends, and turning points.[84] Douglass writes,

I studied philosophy and theology in the Roman Catholic college-seminary and spent three years in the Society of Jesus, a Roman Catholic religious order, preparing for priesthood. And that is where *the first turn in the road* appeared. [. . .] My desire to marry and my *growing disillusionment* with the Catholic Church put me on *a long path of searching.* I realized that I never really had a personal relationship with Heavenly Father or Jesus Christ and *I searched long and hard* where I might find that relationship. [. . .] That began *a long period of spiritual wandering.* I worshipped with Lutherans, Episcopalians, Baptists, and Pentecostals. I visited Hindu Ashrams and practiced Zen Buddhism. I eventually found a place in the Russian Orthodox Church, but while its liturgy was most beautiful, I found no spiritual sustenance for the remainder of the week. [. . .] I knew I had to find out what this "Mormonism" was all about. Thus began *a ten year investigation.* [. . .] [Today] I testify that the Book of Mormon is true and Joseph Smith is a prophet and the Church of Jesus Christ of Latter-day Saints is the True Church and is led by prophets in our day.[85]

Douglass exercises agency and consciously searches for "truth" in his story. Despite several setbacks along the way, his intention and will never faltered; it was clear from the outset. While these disappointing setbacks are typical of the way many Mormon converts model their accounts on the iconic story of Joseph Smith, such sociomental dead ends, false leads, and cognitive turning points serve a more general function as stages in the process of reaching an end goal. In retrospective narrative form, they become steps in a staircase-like plotline culminating in the fulfillment of an awakening to "truth."

Exemplifying this narrative model in an account titled "Searching All the Wrong Doctrines," Stephen, a born-again Christian, writes,

[. . .] [I]n my teens and gradually I decided that church was okay for some but it wasn't essential. [. . .] I drifted from church to church, religion to religion. Each time, I KNEW I'd found the truth, only to drift away when I changed my mind about what I believed. I went from Buddhism, to Hinduism, to Judaism and back again. At one point I even became involved in an online Wiccan group. [. . .] I drifted from denomination to denomination in search of God's church. Nothing seemed right and yet everything sounded right! How could this be? [. . .] The last few years have seen me visiting (and each time joining, never to return) countless churches: Pentecostal, Apostolic, Roman Catholic, Nazarene, Primitive Baptist and lastly Russian orthodox.[86]

After claiming to have been repeatedly "betrayed" while following his "heart" for years and searching "to find the truth," Stephen found his answers and his "home," he tells us, at an Easter Sunday service at the church to which he now belongs. From this, his new autobiographical community and narrative standpoint, he writes, "Gone are the doubts. Gone is the tendency to have a complete doctrinal reversal the next morning."[87] From his current standpoint, Stephen reconceives each of his prior religious affiliations as disappointing but eye-opening steps in his overall staircase-like "search" for ultimate "truth." Likewise, Jerry, a "repaired" heterosexual who sets out on a self-labeled "quest" to find the truth about his sexuality, describes seeking answers from two psychotherapists, various "circles" in the gay community, and a pro-gay Catholic group before discovering the "truth" that his homosexuality was a symptom of unhealed psychological wounds.[88] Julia Sweeney, former *Saturday Night Live* cast member and apostate to the Catholic Church, describes exploring the practice of meditation, reading "the Tao Te Ching, the Bhagavad-Gita, the Tibetan Book of the Dead, Rumi, The Essential Kabbalah, and The Way of the Pilgrim," as well as attempting to be a Bhuddist and looking for God in nature as she was searching for spiritual truth. Sweeney, who ultimately rejects religion and "let[s] go of god" to become an atheist, articulates each of these projects as experimental though faulty stages in her self-described "spiritual quest."[89] All of these awakeners describe an extended period of searching marked by several disappointing sociomental false leads or dead ends before finding what they now regard as the "truth."

Whether describing a process of accumulation or elimination, awakeners who use a staircase-like vocabulary of liminality typically portray their sociomental journeys as a period of cognitive anxiety and distress. Like the state of aporia, or "profound uncertainty," that results when Plato's prisoner sees sunlight for the first time,[90] awakeners often describe struggling with the epistemological and existential difficulties of being in between autobiographical communities. Such quest-like undertakings, as Alasdair MacIntyre argues, are "not at all that of a search for something already adequately characterized."[91] In an express elevator awakening, "truth" makes itself painfully known to the awakener. However, in these staircase narratives, each awakener conveys a more extended awareness of his or her own doubt and uncomfortable moral uncertainty. According to their own accounts, they suffer a period marked by "definitional ambiguities"[92] that spurs the quest for answers. "Truth" only comes later, after a certain state of sociomental torment and disorientation. Cheryl writes,

As I began to deal with my own internalized homophobia, I fully rejected the notion of "ex-gay." What followed was *the beginning of a long, hard struggle* with spirituality and genuine self-acceptance. *I began to wrestle with what it means* to be a lesbian. I wondered if my sexual orientation and the church were compatible. Reality quickly raised its head and within a couple of weeks, members of the church I attended began to harass me. Phone calls at work, unending questions and Bible beating became a regular part of my life. Finally, the leader of Regeneration [A Baltimore-based ex-gay group] requested that if my partner and I would not change our ways, we needed to leave the church we were attending. We did.[93]

Like the "repaired" heterosexuals quoted above, Cheryl uses a staircase vocabulary to describe her active, "long, hard struggle" of personal discovery. As she "began to wrestle" with meaning, she suffered various consequences of her sociomental and cultural transition. Similarly, Kathryn writes, "I also want to highlight how coming out is not necessarily a linear process, consisting of a single, dramatic coming out, followed by automatic, profound transformation. Rather, coming out can be, and was for me, an ongoing, gradual process akin to unveiling—*one painful layer at a time*."[94] Kathryn's gradual unveiling, though depicted as epistemologically progressive, is also quite painful and distressing. Removing "layers," like drips and steps, signifies a change that proceeds by "short, slow" increments characteristic of the "legato" phrasing we use to narrate a "gradual process" of historical development.[95] Such a difficult state of transition is also evident when Jerry, who now identifies as a survivor of sexual reparative therapy, writes, "It was the pain and suffering that caused me to search for truth both spiritually and psychologically."[96] Likewise, a sociomental and emotional struggle is clear in Karen Armstrong's account of rejecting her vows and life as a Catholic nun, living with undiagnosed epilepsy, and eventually finding her place as a scholar of comparative theology, a journey she refers to as a "spiral staircase" and "climb out of darkness."[97] The epistemological uncertainty that spurs the staircase-like quest is also evident in Kristi's reflection on her "long process of questioning and searching for answers." An Evangelical Christian turned scientific atheist, Kristi writes, "Thought is the beginning of doubt, and doubt is a gateway to reason."[98]

Staircase-like vocabularies of liminality are also evident in the stories of political awakeners. Describing his rejection of his once-embraced pro-Sandinista, pro-Castro worldview, Xavier Arguello, writes, "[. . .] [D]isenchantment also has something to do with a slow, personal process of maturation. To open one's eyes takes time."[99] Former 1960s radical David Ifshin describes his evolving views on the Vietnam War as "A Political Journey."[100] IVAW member Christie's awakening unfolded as she asked questions over time and "[s]lowly [. . .] began to comprehend what it meant to belong to the service [the US army]."[101] In a similar vein, Adrienne Kinne, former Arabic linguist for US military intelligence and IVAW member, lays out a staircase-like agenda for active duty military personal during an interview with the political newsletter *CounterPunch*. An awakener herself, Adrienne assumes the role of cognitive authority figure while giving other veterans a vocabulary of motive with which they can articulate their own transformations of mind. She comments,

> I would encourage all soldiers to question everything they have taken for granted as being the truth as told to them by their unit, their president, and their country/media and to start thinking for themselves. I would suggest that they shouldn't let some abstract feeling of loyalty to the military override their own morals and consciences. I would encourage them to watch [. . .] documentaries, and to start reading books [. . .]. I would also encourage soldiers to start talking to one another, really talking, about their experiences. [. . .] It's very hard for soldiers to break free of the hold the military has over us [. . .]. But in order to make the transition from soldier/veteran to resister/ activist, we all have to be open to the concept that everything we thought we knew about reality could be wrong or only half-truths.[102]

Adrienne's agenda stresses rejecting mindless "abstract" loyalty and engaging in the active and conscious yet difficult mental pursuit characteristic of all staircase-like vocabularies of liminality. She asks other soldiers to rise to the occasion and seek out "truth" for themselves.

Despite the many differences among them, all of these awakeners describe an intentional discovery of "truth." They raise questions, actively search for answers, and discover the "truth" over time. They embrace their own cognitive agency as they convey the experience of crossing the cultural divide between contentious autobiographical communities. Awakeners who use express elevator vocabularies ask us to know on faith that they were acted upon; however, those who use staircase vocabularies ask us to know by an emotionally informed process of reasoning how and why they acted as well as what they discovered. They prolong their liminal persona and the scene of their awakening to fit their protracted mission. Whether describing stages of accumulation or a frustrating process of elimination, such awakeners portray a step-like, gradual process of discovery. By giving process to discovery, they give meaning to their disillusionment and the experience of cognitive ambiguity. In an elevator-like story, truth finds the awakener, but in these staircase-like models, the awakener seeks and finds truth.

6 Michelangelo's *The Conversion of Saul* (1542–1545). Michelangelo Buonarroti, via
Wikimedia Commons, retrieved June 2009, http://commons.wikimedia.org/wiki
/File:Michelangelo_-_Bekehrung_des_heiligen_Paulus.jpeg.

Consequently, they portray their current autobiographical community
as the culminating point of their quest, the "truth" or "home" that they
discovered at the end of their arduous "path."

These two ideal-typical vocabularies of liminality, sociomental express
elevators and sociomental staircases, are epitomized by the Christian
account of Saint Paul's conversion and the Buddhist story of Siddhārtha
Gautama's enlightenment, respectively. Further, the ideal-typical characteristics of each vocabulary are evident in popular depictions of these
stories that portray sociomental liminality in visual form. By analyzing
such visual depictions of liminality, we can further see how the scene of
liminality fits the organization of the act of awakening and the attribution of intention (similar to what Burke calls "purpose") and agency in
each case.[103]

In Michelangelo's depiction of Saint Paul's conversion (see fig. 6), Paul
is literally overwhelmed by a powerful force (not unlike Iraq veterans

who describe having a powerful realization after a firefight and sexual abuse survivors who report having "flashbacks"). Paul's original intention (to persecute Christians in Damascus) is thwarted and his horse is fleeing in the opposite direction. The agency in this image is clearly located in the figure of God, which hovers over Paul and his band of compatriots in a symbolic depiction of moral and cognitive authority. The narrative mechanism of a lightning bolt serves to bridge the upper and lower sections of the scene, connecting God to Paul and conveying the shock associated with rapid awakening experiences. In this account, the "scales" fell from Paul's eyes a mere three days later and he could "see" the "truth."

Consider a depiction of Siddhārtha Gautama's journey painted on the wall of a Buddhist temple in Laos (see fig. 7). Siddhārtha willfully disregards his father's will and leaves the protection of his castle (which appears in the far background of the scene, symbolically positioned in Siddhārtha's past). In this image, the young prince exercises his own

7   Painting from a Laotian temple depicting Siddhārtha Gautama's initial expedition out of his father's castle. "Picture of a painting in a Laotian Temple," via Wikimedia Commons, user Sacca, retrieved June 2009, http://commons.wikimedia.org/wiki/File:Four_Heavenly _Messengers.jpg.

8   Painting from a Laotian temple depicting Siddhārtha Gautama leaving his ascetic comrades. "Picture of a wallpainting in a monastery in Laos," via Wikimedia Commons, user Sacca, retrieved July 2009, http://commons.wikimedia.org/wiki/File:Buddha_walking_away_from _ascetics_who_torment_their_bodies.jpg.

agency as he initiates what will become a six-year journey that will culminate in his enlightenment. Notably, Siddhārtha is the highest figure in the scene (as opposed to Michelangelo's depiction of Saint Paul's conversion where God is the highest figure and Paul is the lowest). Siddhārtha is clearly in charge of his horse and chariot. Taking these initial "steps," he encounters four messengers—an elderly man (who is depicted on the road, behind Siddhārtha's chariot), a sick man, a corpse, and an ascetic— who provide "clues" to the "truth." This painting visually synchronizes several occurrences (portraying successive messengers in one scene) that are not synchronous in the narrative in order to portray the process of movement along a road. Unlike the elevator-style conversion of Saint Paul, only specific snippets of Siddhārtha's staircase-style awakening can be captured in any one painting (symbolized by the visual implication that Siddhārtha's chariot will eventually move down the road, out of the frame that surrounds the scene). In another depiction, set later in the course of Siddhārtha's journey, the young prince abandons his fellow ascetics after outgrowing and rejecting their teachings (see fig. 8). In the wake of this sociomental false lead, Siddhārtha intentionally moves onto the next step in his quest. We see his back as he leaves his interim community in the past.

Combining Elevators and Staircases

Arguing that sudden, radical discoveries are actually marked moments obscuring a more unconcious, sequential process of realization, Arthur Koestler writes, "The moment of truth, the sudden emergence of a new insight, is an act of intuition. Such intuitions give the appearance of miraculous flashes, or short-circuits of reasoning. In fact they may be likened to an immersed chain, of which only the beginning and the end are visible above the surface of consciousness. The diver vanishes at one end of the chain and comes up at the other end, guided by invisible links."[104] While writing about the creative process, Koestler stresses the notion that sociomental express elevators actually involve unconcious associative links (the links of Koestler's chain, however buried and un-conventional, are equivalent to steps in a staircase). However, Koestler himself is a reawakener who previously accounted for his prior awaken-ing to communism by describing a more radical elevator-like "mental rapture." He wrote, "[. . .] [S]omething had clicked in my brain which shook me like a mental explosion. To say that one had 'seen the light' is a poor description of the mental rapture which only the convert knows (regardless of what faith he has been converted to). The new light seems to pour from all directions across the skull; the whole universe falls into pattern like the stray pieces of a jigsaw puzzle assembled by magic at one stroke."[105] Koestler's later critical interpretation of "miraculous flashes" harmonizes with his repudiation of his past Marxist worldview. He sees his once-believed elevator-like awakening to communism, in retrospect, as a false awakening on a more protracted staircase-like path (a link in his journey to "truth"). Despite emphasizing the "fact" of staircase-like associative links over the "appearance" of elevator-like "miraculous flashes," he uses both vocabularies to tell his story.

Alternatively, Thomas S. Kuhn is widely known for dispelling the notion that a cumulative development of knowledge leads to scientific breakthrough. Instead, Kuhn argues, science moves forward by radical paradigm shifts—sudden changes in ways of seeing the world that are comparable to perceptual gestalt switches.[106] However, Kuhn argues, these paradigm shifts typically occur when cumulative scientific work produces "novelties" or anomalies that violate "the paradigm-induced expectations that govern normal science."[107] Despite the fact that Kuhn emphasizes paradigm-shifting moments and Koestler stresses a linked sequential process, the claims of both men ultimately show how these mechanisms can be coupled in our accounts of progressive enlightenment.

The metaphor of the express elevator and the metaphor of the staircase illustrate two ideal-typical vocabularies of liminality. As ideal types, they are useful for emphasizing and accentuating the distinctive aspects (i.e., what is *typical*) of different narrative strategies that are, in many cases, more complex and less refined. As Max Weber writes, ideal types are "formed by the one-sided *accentuation* of one or more points of view and by the synthesis of a great many diffuse, discrete, more or less present and occasionally absent *concrete individual* phenomena, which are arranged according to those one-sidedly emphasized viewpoints into a unified *analytical* construct."[108] Thus, ideal types are analytic tools that we construct to separate, highlight, and detail various social phenomena. "An ideal type . . . serves the investigator as a measuring rod to ascertain similarities as well as deviations in concrete cases."[109] In the case of awakening narratives, though some are very elevator-like and some very staircase-like, many awakeners combine elements of both ideal-typical vocabularies to articulate their liminal transformative experiences. They couple staircase-like themes of protracted doubt, intention, and self-motivated searching with elevator-like themes of momentous realization, surrender, and external validation to justify their discoveries and synchronize their portrayals of individual will with the determinant cognitive authority of a new community.

When used in combination, express elevator and staircase vocabularies often serve to reinforce one another. In such cases, awakeners typically describe a sudden, elevator-like "snapping" experience[110] or "tipping point"[111] that signifies a qualitative change at the beginning, middle, or end of a protracted quantitative gathering of information in a staircase-like search for answers. The "shock" is nested in the "quest." Film directors Andy and Lana Wachowski used such a combination of the elevator and the staircase to portray the fictional character Neo's awakening in their 1999 film *The Matrix*. Before his awakening, Neo is haunted by doubts about the authenticity of the world. He is searching for something but he is not sure what that something is. At one point, the character Morpheus, who plays the role of a cognitive authority figure, offers Neo a choice between two pills, one red and one blue. If Neo chooses the red pill, he will know the truth but can never return to his life of ignorance. If he chooses the blue pill, he will return to his delusional world without the haunting hint of its false character. After choosing the red pill, Neo is uncontrollably thrust into a shocking awakening and quickly learns exactly how the world he has always known is an illusion.[112] This jolting realization, however, does not end Neo's quest but rather catapults it to a new level. Neo continues to search for answers and discover pieces of the truth throughout the trilogy. Thus, the Wachowskis nest an elevator-like experience within a staircase-like quest for enlightenment that only ends in the third and final film when Neo realizes his destiny. The directors blend qualitative and quantitative transformations of mind to depict Neo's awakening. They also combine themes of agency (Neo chooses to know) and destiny to cast Neo as a powerful figure ("The One") who is both free and at the whim of forces much larger than himself.[113]

Likewise, Ronn (whom we discussed earlier and who went to Iraq with a self-described "kill them all" mentality) also uses a combination of elevator and staircase vocabularies to account for a major mind-changing event that provoked his more protracted search for truth about the war. Ronn describes experiencing elevator-like intrusive thoughts after killing an Iraqi civilian when an incendiary device engulfed part of his convoy on a road between Baquba and Muqdadiyah in Iraq. These thoughts take over his mindset and eventually lead him to the conclusion that war is senseless and wrong. Ronn writes,

And the more I thought about it, the more I realized I shouldn't [think about it], but I couldn't help it. Who was he? He was probably just someone who woke up that morning in his bed and assumed that he would end his day in the same place. [. . .] And who was the screaming woman? Was it his wife? His sister? His mother? Was he old enough to have a daughter that age? [. . .] And it made me think about life in general and how senseless something like war is. [. . .] War is simply people killing each other. What a silly concept![114]

In some ways, Ronn's road to Muqdadiyah experience resembles the story of the Christian apostle Paul. His intrusive thoughts (an official criterion of the posttraumatic stress disorder diagnosis[115]) overwhelm him. However, they also spur him to ask a number of questions about the nature of the war and his position in it. Ronn then proceeds to seek answers. His elevator-like experience leads to a staircase-like process, the culmination of which led to, in his words, "The Death of a Pro-War Conservative." With such a title, Ronn uses the metaphor of death—which can be culturally conceived as an *event* and as a *process*—to describe his sociomental transformation. With regard to a very different issue, Alan describes an elevator-like experience that spurs his quest to know the "truth" about the natural history of the earth and our human origins. After attending a creationist seminar with his pastor, Alan recounts, "I came away from that meeting with my faith in evolution shaken enough to make me have to embark on what turned out to be a three or four year intensive study of all the available material on creation/evolution. At the end of that time, I was convinced that the creation point of view, from a scientific standpoint, was the only credible position that a thinking person with a scientific background could accept."[116] Likewise, Julie also describes how an unsolicited elevator-like experience thrust her into a staircase-like drive for answers. She writes, "My 'awakening' came abruptly and harshly through a traumatic experience. [. . .] I found myself questioning everything. Why didn't I feel comforted? Where was the Holy Ghost? I teach the primary children it will comfort them! I speak at their baptisms about this wonderful new gift! But where was it when I needed it the most?"[117]

Whereas Ronn, Alan, and Julie describe intrusive elevator-like experiences to explain and justify initiating a search for answers, Jerry depicts an intrusive religious sociomental express elevator in the midst of his sexual staircase. As he searched for answers about his sexuality, he "fell into a deep depression" after coming across several false leads and dead ends. Jerry writes, "I remember standing in the shower one time, heavy with depression. I felt myself starting to collapse. I thought I was about to have a psychotic breakdown. But all of a sudden I felt these large, supernatural spiritual hands behind my back lifting me back up on my feet. I felt a surge of strength that whispered, 'Keep going.' I recognized immediately that it was the Lord intervening, giving me his strength to lean on when I couldn't do it by myself any longer."[118] In Jerry's case, an elevator-like experience comes as an intervention. The voice and hands of a spirit character act on their own to reinforce Jerry's agency and spur him to keep searching. While not causing a complete awareness of "truth," this intervention plays a pivotal role in his quest.[119]

In the same vein, Richard uses a flashback and recovered memory express elevator to describe a significant discovery in the midst of several years of work in sexual reparative therapy. Richard writes,

While pounding away at what I thought was some abuse caused by my mother, I had a flashback. All of a sudden, I saw male genitals coming toward my mouth. I screamed. I felt shocked. I felt horrified. I cried and the tears flowed for the next few years, as I worked through memories of sexual abuse that occurred when I was between the ages of five and six years old. [. . .] I learned that my neurology was programmed to respond to men in sexual ways. For me, intimacy with a man equaled sex. I learned that to be close to a man, I must give him my body.[120]

Richard's unintentional and overwhelming discovery provided the evidence he needed to reinterpret his homosexuality as the pathological consequence of sexual abuse perpetrated by a male friend of the family. He uses an express elevator mechanism to mark a sociomental turning point in his more protracted staircase-like journey. According to his account, while he was working to discover "truth," he was looking in the wrong direction. The "truth" then forced itself upon him, took command of his affect in unexpected ways, and provided a guiding discovery that shaped the remainder of his sexual work.

While sociomental express elevators can serve to provoke a quest for answers or serve as a midjourney turning point, they can also function to deliver "truth" after a long arduous period of searching, doubting, or questioning. After an increasingly desperate search for answers about the moral purpose of life and the nature of sin, the Christian saint Augustine has an elevator experience. He writes,

I was asking myself these questions [about life and the nature of my sins], weeping all the while with the most bitter sorrow in my heart, when all at once I heard the sing-song voice of a child in a nearby house. [. . .] [A]gain and again it repeated the refrain 'Take it and read, take it and read'. [. . .] I stemmed my flood of tears and stood up, telling myself that this could only be a divine command to open my book of Scripture and read the first passage on which my eyes should fall. [. . .] I seized it and opened it, and in silence read the first passage on which my eyes fell [Romans 13:13–14]. [. . .] I had no wish to read more and no need to do so. For *in an instant, as I came to the end of the sentence, it was as though the light of confidence flooded into my heart and all the darkness of doubt was dispelled.*[121]

Such a culmination is also evident when Louis Fischer describes his and his comrades' ultimate rejection of Soviet communism as an "ideological melting point."[122] Melting, like boiling, implies a qualitative change that occurs at a specific point in time, but one set at the culmination of a longer, developing, and intensifying process of transformation.

In all of these cases, awakeners combine the ideal-typical components of the sociomental express elevator with the ideal-typical characteristics of the sociomental staircase. Nesting elevator-like events in their staircase-like quests for truth, they blend a forfeiture of control with expressions of agency, strategic surrender with the exercise of will, and faith with reason to reinforce the legitimacy of a newly embraced cognitive authority. Combining such seemingly contradictory components into their autobiographical accounts, awakeners convey the qualitative and quantitative dimensions of their liminal awakening experiences to justify a major change of mind.

Conclusion

The metaphoric contrast between sociomental express elevators and sociomental staircases heightens our attention to the ways that individuals account for the organization and manifestation of social forces—including agency, intention, will, authority, and time—when explaining radical changes of mind and justifying their claims to have discovered truth. Awakeners use these vocabularies to depict and emplot their liminal personas as they portray life-changing awakening experiences that separate two distinct periods in their life stories. In the process, they construct and display a sharp epistemic and sociomental discontinuity in their lives. Awakeners use such vocabularies of liminality to ground their awakening experiences in between two mutually exclusive moral universes and validate their transition to a particular place in the moral order. Whether surrendering to a force of "truth" greater than oneself or deliberately choosing to navigate the righteous path to "truth," individuals use these symbolic narrative mechanisms to account for the difficult experience of traversing the sociomental gulf dividing contentious autobiographical communities in the autobiographical field.

FIVE

The Temporally Divided Self

I still marvel at how swiftly my previous life's thinking pattern slid away from me, like snow off a roof. It is as though someone else I knew of had lived by hustling and crime. I would be startled to catch myself thinking in a remote way of my earlier self as another person. MALCOLM X[1]

In the epigraph above, Malcolm X reflects on his time studying at Norfolk Prison in Massachusetts. As he describes his rejection of one "thinking pattern" in favor of another, he also makes a sharp distinction between his previous and current lifestyles, his "earlier self" and his present storytelling self. As he begins to think of his past self as "someone else [he] knew," he goes on to strategically undermine and reject that Harlem "hustler" known as "Detroit Red"[2] in an effort to establish his identity as "Malcolm X," a black nationalist Muslim minister and activist. By symbolically separating himself into two temporally divided entities, as well as figuratively engaging, debasing, and defeating his past self, Malcolm X undermines the legitimacy of one way of living and being in the world and bolsters the legitimacy of another. He depicts a cultural and political tension as a conflict between two dueling personas, a conflict that plays out in autobiographical form.[3]

Such a performed temporal division of self is also exemplified by the Christian account of the apostle Paul.[4] In a narrative sense, Paul critically characterizes his preawakening self in order to establish his moral authority while taking a stand in cultural disputes between traditional Jewish authorities and the Christian sect,[5] on the one hand, and between Roman political authorities and the Christian community, on the other. For example, when defending himself in front of a violent mob of Jews, who seized and beat him in Jerusalem and were intent on killing him because of his Christian ministry, Paul says, "I am a Jew, born in Tarsus of Cilicia, but brought up in this city. Under Gamaliel I was thoroughly trained in the law of our fathers and was just as zealous for God as any of you are today. I persecuted the followers of this Way [Christianity] to their death, arresting both men and women and throwing them into prison [. . .]. I even obtained letters from them to their brothers in Damascus, and went there to bring these people as prisoners to Jerusalem to be punished."[6] In his defense to the Roman king Agrippa shortly thereafter, Paul, who evokes his Roman citizenship to establish his right to a hearing, states,

[. . .] [A]ccording to the strictest sect of our religion, I lived as a Pharisee. [. . .] I too was convinced that I ought to do all that was possible to oppose the name of Jesus of Nazareth. And that is just what I did in Jerusalem. On the authority of the chief priests I put many of the saints in prison, and when they were put to death, I cast my vote against them. Many a time I went from one synagogue to another to have them punished, and I tried to force them to blaspheme. In my obsession against them, I even went to foreign cities to persecute them.[7]

After each vivid account of his past persona, Paul immediately debases his former self by recounting the story of his conversion. As he portrays his temporally situated duality of identity, Paul establishes a cultural and political license to undermine the lifestyle of those who persecute Christians while contrasting that lifestyle with his current persona as a Christian missionary. Notably, Paul's past identity is only portrayed from the perspective of his present concerns and objectives. The "darkness" and "sin" of his preconversion life is all that we are told about Paul's previous existence.[8]

As they tell stories about their lives, awakeners articulate who they *are* by undermining and invalidating who they *were*. Establishing a direct link between worldview and identity, they base their newly established selves on the active portrayal and negation of their former selves.[9] In the process, awakeners commonly discuss the past self as if they were describing a completely different person. Such a "second self is a temporal production, lodged in the past but told in the present."[10] Thus, the awakener's past self has a symbolic, functional position in his or her present life. This past self takes storied form as awakeners engage in a performative type of self-interaction,[11] a particular style of cultural identity work, in order to make controversial claims and weigh in on contentious moral and political issues. They actively perform what George Herbert Mead refers to as an "internalized conversation"[12] for various audiences in order to articulate their position in a broader cultural dispute.

Building on Charles Horton Cooley's notion that our "looking-glass self" emerges from the way we imagine other individuals see us—from an "imputed sentiment" or "the imagined effect" of our reflection in another person's mind[13]—Mead argues that the self consists of different components which he refers to as the "I" and the "me." Mead's "me" stands for the dimension of self that is defined by others in the world— the self that exists as "the organized set of attitudes of others which one himself assumes." Alternatively, the "I" is the more autonomous, freely acting part of the self that manifests as "the response of the organism to the attitudes of the others."[14] We experience these two dimensions of the self, according to Mead, as an inner conversation or dialogue that allows us to engage the world around us.[15] Without the capacity for an "I" we would not have any sense of ourselves as independently acting individuals. Without the capacity for a "me" we would not have any sense of our fit within a community. Both aspects of self are necessary, and an individual "*is* a self in semiotically constituted *relations* to others in the world" and simultaneously "to his or her own being."[16] Further, any individual only "becomes a self in so far as he can take the attitude of another and act toward himself as others act."[17] In short, this internal conversation is necessary for one to experience who one is *and* to situate oneself in relation to other individuals and communities.

Mead recognizes a temporal dimension of this inner dialogue when he writes, "The 'I' in memory is there as the spokesman of the self of the second, or minute, or day ago. As given, it is a 'me,' but it is a 'me' which was the 'I' at the earlier time. If you ask, then, where directly in your own experience the 'I' comes in, the answer is that it comes in as a historical figure."[18] Thus, according to Mead, we act as an "I" but only end up knowing or reflecting on this acting "I" in retrospect, after it has ceased to be an "I" (an acting agent) and becomes a "me" (a socially determined self defined in hindsight). When we reflect on ourselves, our acting, reflecting "I" portrays and engages various older "I's" (previously acting selves) that have expired. We define and experience our old selves from our present position and impose our social "attitudes" on our past selves just as we impose them on other people. More, as Lonnie Athens argues, such self-interacting (what he refers to as "soliloquizing") makes "self portraitures" possible.[19] These portraitures are internal depictions of ourselves that we put together by assuming the perspective of our interlocutors and communities of reference. Thus, the communities with which we are involved (both past and present) are crucial to our self-definitions, and our expressed identities expose something of our relation to these communities. We are both temporally and relationally situated at the same time, and these temporal and relational dimensions of existence complement each other.

By combining Mead's emphasis on self-interaction and time with a view of the self as emplotted in narrative form, situated in a cultural milieu,[20] and actively portrayed and performed in relation to various audiences, we can begin to get a more thorough picture of the cultural foundations and significance of identity. From this perspective, our present storytelling "I" actively portrays and mobilizes various "me's," which take form as narrative constructs as we engage in ongoing dialogue with others in the world and situate ourselves in relation to them. By considering how awakeners construct and mobilize their self-portraitures, how their autobiographical stories serve as externalized performances of the reflexive foundations of identity, we can gain insight into the connection between identity and the more salient moral and cultural relations of the broader autobiographical field, the fragmented space of multifarious identity conflicts and contradictory lifestyles in which our self-stories are received.[21] Awakeners are partisan players who wield their identities (past and present) in a contentious cultural arena. While the self is a reflexive project,[22] it is also an autobiographical act[23] as well as a locus of cultural conflict and a means of displaying cultural and cognitive authority.

Just as formulaic "dramatis personae" give shape to the folktale,[24] awakeners cast past and present selves as dueling characters—ignorant antagonist and enlightened protagonist—that interact in the awakening account and give dramatic life to the story.[25] In line with Alasdair MacIntyre's more general point that characters are "the moral representatives of their culture . . . the masks worn by moral philosophies,"[26] awakeners construct and portray contradictory *self-character schemes* that serve as proxies for their past and present autobiographical communities. Notably, the term "character merges both *persona*, the character in the story, and quality, having a good [or bad] character,"[27] and indeed awakeners' self-character schemes are polarized morally coded assessments[28] that are often "laden with affect."[29] They are situated and personified depictions of the worldviews, belief systems, and values of contending autobiographical communities in the broader autobiographical field. Thus, they are "created from the symbolic axes of the discursive space in which" the storyteller is situated.[30] As opposed to the way that some individuals work to articulate a biographically continuous "true self,"[31] or the way that identity "integrators" simultaneously embrace different facets of identity as harmonious parts of their one whole self,[32] awakeners arrange their past and present self-character schemes into a moral power struggle between polluted and pure styles of being in order to take a stand in a cultural contest. As awakeners construct and portray dueling self-character schemes, they color them with various expressions of intelligence, perception, lifestyle, habit, taste, demeanor, affect, attitude, and/or embodied style of being. Awakeners then use these depictions to typify and classify the adherents to different worldviews while they dramatize a historically evolving moral and cultural tension.

While the plot of the awakening story is marked by a polarized discontinuity of self-character schemes, awakeners stabilize their narrative identities by resolving the tension between the dueling characters in their stories, by "expressing and then coming to terms with conflicts between contradictory aims."[33] They defeat or overcome the past self, and the resolution of the tension between characters is necessary for awakeners to integrate an otherwise awkward identity transformation into a coherent "moral career."[34] Further, the defeat of the past self allows awakeners to act as cultural representatives of their current autobiographical communities. When awakeners portray their temporally divided selves, their self-character schemes become *character models* in the public arena, "schemas and narratives of selfhood"[35] or "possible selves"[36] that others can use as identity tool kits with which to craft, express, and situate their own identity transformations. In other words, other individuals can "define their parts" by looking to these character models, which place "a certain kind of moral constraint on the personality of those who inhabit them in a way in which many other social roles do not."[37] Their storied temporally divided selves then serve "as boundary-maintaining devices in the sense that they demonstrate to whatever audience is concerned where the line is drawn between behavior that belongs in the special universe of the group and behavior that does not."[38] Like Pierre Bourdieu's concept of habitus, the active mobilization of self-character schemes provides a framework for others to experience "a sense of place and out-of-place" in the field.[39] However, the particular moral charge any given awakener associates with a given character model will depend on his or her sociomental orientation to the contention at hand. "What is considered authentic" from one community standpoint "is thought to be damaging to the self" from another.[40] What is "ego-alien"[41] to the convert is ego-appropriate to the apostate. Awakeners weigh in on prominent cultural tensions by bringing dueling characters to life in the public sphere, casting them as moral idol and counteridol, cultural ideal and counterideal, good lifestyle and bad lifestyle.

Portraying the Temporally Divided Self

All awakeners debase their past self in some way. Just as individuals reproduce the social distance between themselves and those they categorize as "other,"[42] awakeners inflate the moral and cultural distance between their past and present selves in order to undermine and reject their former way of being in the world. While the awakener's past self typically manifests as an explicit narrative sketch, similar to what Anthony Paul Kerby refers to as a "subject of speech," the awakener's present self often manifests more implicitly, and by contrast, as a "spoken subject," an acting narrator implied by the narrative itself who is there to be interpreted by the audiences receiving the autobiographical account.[43] As such, past self and present self take form as self-character schemes set in binary opposition to one another with regard to some morally charged issue.

Carol, a self-identified survivor of child sexual abuse, writes, "I was so young and dumb I thought it was really a game that big people play and I played like that with my sisters and cousins thinking that I was grown up because some one had taught me what adults did."[44] As Carol recalls the sexual abuse in her childhood, two versions of self are present—one who is "so young and dumb" that she "thought it was really a game," and one who tells the story, realizing that she was deceived and taken advantage of. In just a few words, Carol makes a distinction between different and mutually exclusive ways of being that are rooted in her perception and understanding of significant interactions. The social act of writing her story involves establishing a sharp distinction between her past and present personas. Carol as autobiographer takes a distanced, critical standpoint as she undermines and rejects the perspective of Carol as autobiographee—a past version of self who was abused and then unknowingly re-created that abuse with sisters and cousins in her story. She performs a sociomental tension between herself as "animator" (the one who transmits the story, bringing it to life) and her past self as "principal of the embedded, reported action."[45] She uses her autobiographical story to transcend the unknowing past self, account for that character's actions, evoke sympathy, and establish her present identity as a survivor as she makes a controversial accusation in a cultural milieu where memories of child sexual abuse are highly suspect.[46] Elizabeth, who retracts her once-believed memories of child sexual abuse, uses a similar strategy when she portrays her past self as a brainwashed "faithful disciple" of her former therapist and thus "the pitiful casualty of a horrendous crime."[47] Likewise, Murphy, a born-again Christian, writes, "I *didn't know* I was a radically-depraved and God-hating person."[48]

In a similar vein, "Exmo #2" portrays her dueling self-character schemes to explicitly criticize her former autobiographical community when she writes,

Do I think most of the mormons I've known are EITHER dishonest, ignorant, OR stupid? Yes. And *so was I when I was there. I was dishonest* in trying to believe that "we" were in the One and Only True Church [. . .]. *I was ignorant* because I only listened to the adrenalin rushes that burned my bosom instead of also looking at facts. [. . .] *I was stupid* when I let my ex husband have Priesthood Power in our house. [. . .] *I was stupid* when I believed that Ezra Taft Benson was a prophet [. . .].[49]

Like Carol, as well as David Horowitz who describes his past self as "self-righteous and arrogant and blind,"[50] Exmo #2 takes a distanced, critical perspective as she describes and undermines the person she used to be. She crafts a literary picture of her past self and depicts that character as "dishonest," "ignorant," and "stupid" in order to discredit her former mindset along with others who currently embrace the beliefs associated with that worldview. As Erving Goffman notes, such a "self-deprecator . . . is not the self that is deprecated. He secretes a new self in the process of attesting to the appraisal he is coming to have of himself."[51] Further, Exmo #2 uses her dual self-character schemes to convey a present feeling of shame over her past lifestyle as she engages in a cultural debate over the nature of ontological "truth." In a similar vein, an ex-Mormon who goes by the name "Tinkling Brass" writes, "I am embarrassed to admit that I could have ever been so completely taken in by a con-man [Joseph Smith] that lived nearly 200 years ago."[52] Hamar writes, "I have said many times how embarrassed I have been that I truly believed in the whole package for 30 years before I and DW had our awakening."[53] Likewise, Charles, a creationist turned evolutionist, writes, "It makes me sick to think that I felt like that [. . .]. It wasn't until I realized that I had made a complete fool of myself that I returned to face my original problem."[54] Kim, who describes her past self as "a Fox News watching, young earth Creationist Southern Baptist," later asks,

"How could I have ever been that person?"[55] While these feeling states of shame and embarrassment manifest in the present, their object of reference is the past self. Depicting a more angry and aggressive feeling state to the same end, Richard Crossman describes the plight of former communists who now hold a more "enlightened" liberal self-concept when he writes, "The Yogi looks in the mirror, sees the Commissar, and breaks the glass in rage."[56]

As awakeners convey various feelings such as embarrassment, shame, pity, anger, or disgust to characterize and debase their past selves, they cast their newly embraced selves, in contrast, as more authentic. Authenticity, a highly valued moral and cultural ideal,[57] is either accompanied by a state of happiness and pride or, as is the case when the awakener is still suffering, carries the promise (or hope) to achieve such a positive affective state. As emotion codes, authenticity and pride are emergent through and grounded in dialogic contrast with the deluded past self.[58] Thus, these feeling states serve to inflate the cognitive and emotional distance between the awakener's past and present personas and, by proxy, the awakener's past and present autobiographical communities. Expressing a clear sense of authenticity in just a few words, Julie writes, "I discovered me."[59] Brian, a reawakener and self-identified survivor of sexual reparative therapy, titles his account "A Journey toward Living an Authentic and Integrated Life" and explicitly (re)embraces his "authentic" gay self.[60] Christine writes, "I [. . .] re-came out to myself in 2003."[61] Expressing the tension between past and present selves as an emotional transformation, "Warmfuzzylogic," a former Mormon, writes, "[. . .] [T]he remainder of my life will be lived at a level of happiness that I didn't know existed in my youth."[62] Rick, who came out as gay after being "ex-gay," writes, "If someone had told me a few years ago that I would one day be an out, proud gay man, I would not have believed it."[63]

In addition to affect, many awakeners express the cultural antagonism between their past and present selves, and by proxy their past and present communities, as a question of embodied lifestyle. They debase their past lifestyles by undermining particular tastes, behaviors, and modes of appearance and embodiment that they associate with their former way of being in the world as they weigh in on matters of cultural dispute. To this end, Brooke uses photos to contrast her preawakening, punk-rock, Pagan self with her enlightened, happy, born-again Christian self (see fig. 9). Notice the striking difference between her preawakening and postawakening appearance and manner.[64] As Brooke

9   Brooke, a born-again Christian, contrasts two pictures in her awakening story. The photo on the left, labeled "before deliverance," portrays her past self, and the photo on the right, labeled "after deliverance," portrays her present self. Photos courtesy of Brooke Donnelly, retrieved October 2013, www.myJesusmyLord.com.

conveys a figurative interaction between past and present versions of herself, commenting "Jesus set me free from idolatry, homosexuality, witchcraft, drugs, alcohol,"[65] she displays her self-character schemes in different costumes with contrasting modes of embodiment and displays of affect. As Arthur W. Frank notes with regard to illness narratives, "Such autobiographical work is recursive and self-reflexive: the narrative performance makes a claim that the narrative itself validates."[66] Like other awakeners, Brooke uses her past self as both ignorant antagonist and literary *foil*, a character in her autobiographical drama that makes her present self appear morally superior by contrast.

In a similar vein, Malcolm X describes his former "conk," a popular African American hairstyle of his time that required a painful process of straightening one's hair with a lye-based substance called "congolene." He writes,

How ridiculous I was! Stupid enough to stand there simply lost in admiration of my hair now looking "white" [. . .]. This was my first really big step toward self-degradation: when I endured all of that pain, literally burning my flesh to have it look like a white man's hair. I had joined that multitude of Negro men and women in America who are brainwashed into believing that the black people are "inferior"—and white people "superior"—that they will even violate and mutilate their God-created bodies to try to look "pretty" by white standards. [. . .] It makes you wonder if the Negro has completely lost his sense of identity, lost touch with himself. [. . .] To my own shame, when I say all of this I'm talking first of all about myself.[67]

Hair in Malcolm X's account, and the body more generally, becomes a marker of his dueling self-character schemes and a locus of the moral and cultural battle he engages. As his story demonstrates, the triumph of the positively coded self-character scheme comes to life with the degredation of his prior "self-degradation." In this sense, Malcolm X's awakening involves a discovery of what W. E. B. Du Bois terms "double-consciousness" and a redefinition of the past self as one who lived according to the ideals of an oppressive force.[68]

Likewise, Rod, a born-again Christian, uses an old grainy photograph of himself on a motorcycle with dark sunglasses and an angry affect titled "Before Being Born Again" to portray his past drug-, sex-, and alcohol-abusing self, commenting, "My life was such a confusing mess when I was 30 years old, and I thought I was living in a world that every man wanted."[69] The photograph is a portrait of his past self that complements his written description of his now-rejected "space of lifestyle,"[70] one that consisted of "work, alcohol, drugs, sex, cycles, and hate" in which he "had sex with different women every night" and "did all the drugs [he] wanted and stayed drunk."[71] He uses this image to engage and undermine this past version of himself from the standpoint of his newfound autobiographical community. By undermining their past lifestyles, such awakeners embrace new embodied practices, tastes, attitudes, and mannerisms that are linked to their newly embraced values and epistemological worldviews.[72] Striking a moral contrast between past and present self-character schemes, they posit those characters as representatives of contentious communities to weigh in on issues of significant moral and political concern.

As awakeners symbolically debase and overcome their past selves, they establish a unique epistemic, cognitive, and moral footing—a socially founded right to be self-assured about their present system of beliefs because they have lived the life of "darkness" and can therefore testify to the false nature of the rejected lifestyle and its associated worldview. This socially established cognitive authority explains why many religions hold converts and returned apostates, or "prodigal sons,"[73] in an even a higher regard than those who always believed. As character models, the convert and the prodigal son, like the awakener and reawakener more generally, provide living testimony to long-time believers that only shame and sadness await outside the fold. The awakener's past self serves as an admonition to others. Such a socially established cognitive authority also explains why the modern antiwar movement holds antiwar veterans in such high regard, often positioning them at the front of marches and rallies. The antiwar veteran symbolizes the willful rejection of the self at war. Sean, a member of Iraq Veterans Against the War (IVAW), comments, "[. . .] [L]ike so many Americans, I lapped up the spoon fed garbage the government fed me and went off to war. It took me over 2 years after I got back home to realize what a fool I had been."[74] Daniel, another IVAW member, writes, "I enlisted in September 2005 as an Army Reserve MP [military police officer]. I served three years, from Ft. Leonard Wood, MO - to Bocas Del Torro, Panama. What I saw in those three years changed a gung-ho MP, ready to kill for God and Country, into a Conscientious Objector willing to die for the truth."[75] Both Sean and Daniel portray their temporally divided selves to weigh in on a morally and politically salient debate over the character of the wars in Iraq and Afghanistan. As they critically engage and undermine their past selves, they work to discredit the self-concepts of others who currently subscribe to their former pro-war ideology.

To this end, Victor, like many other IVAW members, displays photographs of himself at war (see fig. 10). While such images serve to authenticate his veteran status, they do not stand on their own. As Victor displays his armed and combat-ready self, he frames this past self with a caption describing his political awakening. Notice how he switches voices—from a third-person voice (describing the photos as if he were talking about someone else) to a rebuking second-person voice in order to facilitate the figurative interaction between past and present personas in his account. The caption reads, "Former active duty Army Intel Analyst who joined an Army Reserve PSYOPS [psychological operations] unit shortly after 9/11, after a five year break in service, just in case his country needed to call on seasoned ex-warriors for the war with Afghanistan—a war he thought was justified. Having served in Iraq in 2003, where he was awarded the Bronze Star Medal, he has since given up any beliefs he held about the Global War on Terrorism being waged

10 Victor, an antiwar veteran, displays pictures of himself at war to establish a temporally divided self. Photos courtesy of Victor Blazier.

honorably by the current Administration. [switch in voice] You don't defeat terrorism by becoming a terrorist."[76] Victor's photos of himself at war only take on meaning because his autobiographical caption, set in the context of an antiwar website, serves as a storied performance of his "reorientation," in the terms of Robin Wagner-Pacifici's "political semiotic."[77] As Victor displays his old identity, he describes that character with a distanced third-person voice. He switches to a critical second-person voice to engage (with the personal pronoun "you") and redefine that past persona. As he describes his past self as a "terrorist," Victor portrays this self-character scheme as a proxy for others who currently justify the war as an effective venture of *counter*terrorism. Engaging in such voice work, he performs the "positioning of a new identity after the undoing of the old."[78]

When portraying their temporally divided selves, some awakeners perform an *apologetic metanoia*—a transformation of self that stems from publicly repenting and seeking forgiveness for the actions of the past self-character. In a letter to her parents, after retracting her previous accusations of incest, Jessie writes, "I cannot seem to let go of my so heavy guilt for everything. [. . .] I beg your forgiveness. [. . .] Never again will I allow myself to lose control of me. [. . .] Please [. . .] believe I am now me. And most of all, please believe that monster was NOT me. That monster is dead."[79] In this desperate plea to her parents, Jessie completely dissociates her pleading, letter-writing self from her past self—the out-of-control "monster" who once believed she was sexually abused but is now "dead." Emphasizing the same terminology used by Richard Ofshe and Ethan Watters, whose book *Making Monsters*[80] advances a scathing indictment of recovered memory therapy, she uses her personal account to lend credence to the notion that those who make accusations of child sexual abuse based on recovered memories are not only wrong but are diabolical characters. Like self-identified survivors who recover memories of abuse, Jessie uses her temporally divided self to take a position in an ongoing cultural controversy over the veracity of claims concerning child sexual abuse. However, whereas self-identified survivors evoke a sympathy linked to their past innocence, Jessie establishes her guilt, expresses regret, and begs for redemption. As she posts her story to the website of the False Memory Syndrome Foundation, her past "monster self" becomes a proxy for others who make similar accusations based on recovered memories. Jon, an IVAW member, expresses a similar sentiment when he says, "I am no longer the monster that I once was."[81] In Jon's case, his past self serves as a proxy for soldiers who are actively and unapologetically waging war in the Middle East.

In an intentionally creative fashion, Aaron Hughes contrasts his past self who participated in the Iraq war with his present self—an artist "drawing for peace." While Aaron publicly admits his guilt over his past actions at war, he atones by creating artwork intended to undermine those actions. Such a public performance of repentance expresses a profound change in the character of one's thoughts and behaviors. In Aaron's case, he expresses the feeling of guilt as a way of distancing his present self and current life objectives from any moral or political justification for the actions of his past soldier self (see fig. 11). Such a duality of self-character schemes carries an implicit apology for past actions, one that lies at the emotional core of many antiwar veterans' public testimonies.

Such an apologetic metanoia is more explicitly communicated by Josh Stieber and Ethan McCord in their open letter to the Iraqi victims of an attack perpetrated in part by the US army company in which they served. Josh and Ethan write,

We humbly ask you what we can do to begin to repair the damage we caused. [. . .] We acknowledge our part in the deaths and injuries of your loved ones [. . .]. [W]e are acknowledging our responsibility for bringing the battle to your neighborhood, and to your family. [. . .] Please accept our apology, our sorrow, our care, *and our dedication to change from the inside out.* We are doing what we can to speak out against the wars

11 Aaron Hughes, a member of Iraq Veterans Against the War, creates art for peace in a
military-issued jacket as passersby look on. Photo courtesy of Aaron Hughes, Drawing for
Peace, 2006.

and military policies responsible for what happened to you and your loved ones. Our
hearts are open to hearing how we can take any steps to support you through the pain
that we have caused.[82]

A video of the attack Josh and Ethan reference was leaked by US army
private Chelsea (then Bradley) Manning and then made public by the
controversial organization WikiLeaks and dubbed the "Collateral Murder" video, prompting the two veterans to publicly apologize for their
past actions. In the video, Ethan can be seen running with an injured
child in his arms after her family's van was destroyed by gunfire from
an American Apache helicopter. Her father had just been killed trying
to rescue an injured journalist. When Ethan speaks publicly about his
experiences, he refers to this incident as a source of his posttraumatic
stress and posits his suffering apologetic self in contrast to the soldier at
war (see fig. 12).

Such an apologetic metanoia is also apparent in the public performance of a self-described ex-"homophobe" who rallied at a Gay Pride
parade in Chicago (see fig. 13). As this awakener performs his apologetic transformation, he conveys peace (with a hand symbol) and
expresses happiness (with a smile) in moral contrast to his "homophobe" past self. His apologetic posture frames his dialogue with the
gay pride community marching in the parade. Like the various other

awakeners I previously discussed, he links his past and present self-character schemes to "particular feelings that serve as guidelines"[83] for others to situate their identities in relation to these issues.

In addition to the way some awakeners assume an apologetic posture, many awakeners engage in various forms of story performance and use other expressive tactics to dramaturgically *channel* a different character in order to portray their temporally divided selves. In such cases, the awakener's past self serves as an explicitly present and pronounced "dialogical other" and, as such, "becomes as much the teller of the author's story as the author" is the one who tells about the past self-character.[84] To this end, Gayatri, a self-identified survivor

12 Iraq war veteran Ethan McCord speaks as a part of the "Operation Recovery" campaign organized by Iraq Veterans Against the War. Photo by Maria Saenz-Luna, © 2010 Iraq Veterans Against the War, image retrieved October 2010, http://www.ivaw.org/gallery /operation-recovery.

13 An ex-"homophobe" rallies at a Chicago gay pride parade. © Michelle Gantner, Maladjusted Media.

of child sexual abuse, writes, "The only problem was that her friend's father was a monster sometimes. He would want to play monster games and he had big monster hands. He would hurt the little girl with his hands. [. . .] But he said that it was a nice game."[85] Speaking about herself in the third person, Gayatri channels and performs her childhood perspective in order explain how her abuser masked sexual contact and led her childhood self to perceive it as a "monster game." Her past self enters to give voice to her past situation in the autobiographical story. She distances her past and present personas as she portrays her past self as a proxy for child victims who are too young to fully comprehend sexually abusive experiences. As a self-identified survivor posting her account to a public survivor website, Gayatri now clearly understands her experiences, not as a monster game but as sexual abuse. Both versions of self are integral to the contemporary account; however, Gayatri's past self is more explicitly present as the character performing her story.[86]

To a similar end, Christine recalls her child sexual abuse in a second-person voice, describing it as if it happened to an alternate "you" when she writes, "[Y]our mother's boyfriend [. . .] raped you when you were eleven years old."[87] By engaging in this voice work, Christine as writer assumes the role of cognitive authority figure in the present. Not only does she now understand what happened in her past, but she explicitly defines it for both her past and present selves. Likewise, Mary Ellen describes her past self as if she is talking about another person when she writes, "I have only begun to see it. [. . .] I am different. I am a 10 year old girl in bed [. . .]. I am still little Mary Ellen. [. . .] I want little Mary Ellen to heal. I want her to grow up. I want her to know that the world is safe. I want her to know that I will take care of her."[88] Such a strategic separation of self as narrator (and present caregiver) from the self who experienced the situation of concern allows the storyteller to revisit and intervene in the past in order to redirect the course of one's development and convey a sense of self-transformation.[89] From her present standpoint, Mary Ellen reaches out to her past self to offer comfort and care.

Engaging in remarkably similar voice work, Dan uses a discourse of sexual and psychological regression when he separates his present "repaired" heterosexual self from the injured "inner child" that he believes was at the root of his now past homosexuality. He "symbolically returns to childhood"[90] when he writes,

By establishing contact with this subconscious, inner child, I was able to find out each day how my inner child was feeling and what his needs were. Then I could consciously find ways to either help my inner child understand and deal with *his inappropriate feelings* or find ways to meet *his needs* in a healthy way. *In a sense I became parent to myself.* I was amazed at how resourceful my adult self could be when *it was asked* to parent my inner child. I was also amazed at *how much my inner child could tell me* about things that were repressed.[91]

By channeling his injured inner child, Dan manifests the cause of his past gay lifestyle in the character of that younger being. More, by engaging in dialogue with that character (notably, from the morally superior position of "parent," a process often referred to as "re-parenting"), Dan intervenes in his own past development and reroutes his life along what he deems to be the right and true course. By revisting and "healing" his injured child self, he debases and undermines his past gay self while authenticating his storytelling "repaired" heteroself. Later, Dan reflects, "I faced my shadow, my demon, and walked away a new man [. . .]."[92]

In another explicit performance of temporal division, Yvonne, a self-identified survivor of child sexual abuse, uses a third-person voice to split her life into two personas, each with a different name. In her story titled "Becoming Yvonne," she recounts the death of Anita and the birth of Yvonne to make a clear distinction between past and present self-characters. She writes,

Earthly years place her at nearly thirty seven and yet she is only nine and a half months old. [. . .] Nine and a half months ago Yvonne was born. [. . .] [A]s she looks out to sea she sees that the immense space ahead portrays the beginning of her life [. . .]. Like a chick that gains strength from breaking its own shell, Yvonne had to enable her birth herself. [. . .] Nine and a half months ago Anita was released. [. . .] With the birth of Yvonne, Anita can now after thirty six heavy and exhausting years hand over her physical body. She knows that Yvonne will take better care of it than she did. [. . .] Anita knows that in Yvonne all her dreams that were so horribly taken from her, the dreams that she only dared to dream of in her make believe garden that she escaped to when bad things happened, in Yvonne these dreams can become true.[93]

Employing various metaphors and imagery, Yvonne crafts a narrative of death and rebirth, the mythical archetype for which is the phoenix, to portray her temporally divided self.[94] Such an explicit fracturing of the self into dual identities, each with their own name and storied voice, is a direct form of the more common tendency for awakeners to take on a new title (such as "survivor" or "Mormon") or rename themselves (such as when Malcolm Little became Malcolm X) after an awakening experience. Such new titles and new names are identity markers that reinforce the gulf separating past and present selves in the awakener's story. In this vein, Brian, a gay man who previously subscribed to a religious sexual "reparative" therapy program, closes his reawakening story with the claim "I am not a victim, I am a survivor."[95] He takes on a new title to express his allegiance and commitment to a new autobiographical community. Ronn, an IVAW member, releases his past self when he titles his story "The Death of a Pro-War Conservative."[96] Likewise, when the Egyptian pharaoh Amenophis IV took the new name Akhenaten, "obliterating [the cosmological god] Amun from his name and, in intention, from the whole of Egypt,"[97] he not only divided his past self from his present self but also severed his ancestral lineage from his newly defined living being. Christian turned Pagan Cierra uses a similar strategy when she writes, "I am a child of the Goddess—not a child of Christ."[98]

Using other creative tactics, some awakeners engage in quite direct dramatic re-creations of their past selves for an audience. Awakeners use such "narrative strategies of re-enactment"[99] to perform the cultural conflict at hand. More, they use the performative frame to take a stand in that conflict by resolving the tension between past and present selves. Consider, for example, how IVAW members reenact scenes from the Iraq war as "street theater" in the United States.[100] Staging battle scenes not only allows veterans to expose and confess their wartime activities to a civilian audience, but also allows them to separate themselves from these activities, which are now keyed as a skit,[101] and redefine them as they undermine the political justifications for war with their present performances. By reenacting a wartime scene, and later formulating this reenactment as an autobiographical story, Paul portrays his past soldier life from a present, critical standpoint—that of an awakened antiwar activist who is "reliving the nightmare" of Iraq. However, for Paul this event was more than just a political action, it was an evocation and embodiment of his past self. Reflecting on his performance, he writes,

It was just like I remember it, the screams, the detentions, the pushing, and the chaotic reaction as we put our imaginary rifles in their faces. It was real, very real. [. . .] Personally, as soon as we began patrolling the streets, I caught myself slowly shifting into the role I had once performed on the streets of Iraq. Perhaps people saw us and thought us to be acting, but I can only say of myself, after a short period I found myself honestly checking windows of tall buildings looking for snipers. My arms had become rigid as if they were made to hold a rifle. No longer was an alley just that, they all became danger areas I needed to use increased vigilance while crossing. In short, within just a short while I was reliving a nightmare.[102]

Not only did Paul assume his past mindset, but according to his own account he also assumed the "direct embodiment" of his past self, the "inculcation of the dispositions" that once "remodeled [him] according to the specific demands of"[103] the military and war. His body, and stated awareness of his body, is integrated into the self-narrative and crucial to the plot of the story as the cognitive and affective realms of experience come together with the corporeal dimension in a doubly reenacted self-character scheme. Even the world changed around him as he performed his past self.

Further, Paul also portrays a reliving of his postwar transformation of self in the wake of this event. He writes,

Once the action had ended, *I was able to slowly re-emerge from the soldier I once had been what seems like a lifetime ago.* As time went on, I gradually checked windows for snipers less and less. It became easier to walk by an alley without checking it for "the enemy." Most importantly, I viewed people as, not a potential threat like I had during the patrol, but as what they really were, Human Beings. It was a reminder to how much we dehumanized each other while at war, and I was thankful that I was able to recognize how wrong engaging in such a process of degradation is.[104]

By recalling his dramatic reenactment, Paul explicitly portrays his past and present self-character schemes and captures the tension between their contradictory modes of embodiment. As he performs the embodiment of his past self at war and subsequent reemergence into the embodied self at home, he critically undermines the former self-character scheme by describing it as one who degraded and "dehumanized" others he now views as "Human Beings." He resolves the conflict between past and present selves to reject the self at war. Frank, a "repaired" heterosexual, expresses a similar sentiment while also portraying the embodied dimension of transformation when he writes, "I have become transformed. I have experienced physical changes in my voice, and most importantly, I have experienced emotional changes. [. . .] I have indeed become a man."[105]

Such explicit dramaturgical reenactments of the past self take a variety of forms. For example, beyond those who portray their past selves with a distanced, third-person voice, Sylvia Fraser uses a first-person childhood voice to perform her past, abused child self when she writes, "I cry when my mother puts me to bed. I didn't used to be afraid of the dark but now I know that demons and monsters hide in the cubbyholes by my bed. I'm afraid one will jump out at me, and rub dirty dirty up against me with its wet-ums sticking out."[106] Fraser, like Paul and other awakeners, gets into character in order to perform a temporally expired version of self. As she tells her story, she assumes the voice of the child to make a claim in the present. In general, when individuals talk about the past in the present tense, they do so to convey "emotional intensity and vivid perceptual experience."[107] Capturing the past self in the present tense allows storyteller and audience to share in the past experience and know the past self as it is told so they might also share something of the dramatic transformation of identity at the core of these awakening stories.

Awakeners use affect, voice work, body imagery, apology, and other perfomative mechanisms as dramaturgical strategies to enact, engage, and undermine their past selves, thereby basing their current situated expressions of identity on the rejection of their former ways of seeing and being in the world. Their dueling self-character schemes serve as portraits of different socially rooted lifestyles and their associated cognitive, emotional, and embodied norms. Further, awakeners reinforce the contrast between past and present personas in their stories by expressing a distressing sentiment of cognitive alienation (a painful sociomental distance from one's former autobiographical community) and contrasting that state with a sentiment of cognitive solidarity (a sociomental nearness to a newfound community). Thus, cognitive alienation (with associated feelings of malaise, fear, betrayal, isolation, and dissatisfaction) and cognitive solidarity (with expressions of relief, security, and belonging) become aspects of identity and the performance of self. Highlighting these themes, Jared, an IVAW member who enlisted in the army in 2003 in order to fight in Iraq, writes,

What is a family anyways? Is a family only defined by bloodlines whose only purpose is to spend birthdays and holidays with? What happens when your family won't support you anymore because you speak out against an illegal war, something they haven't begun to comprehend. Yes, I have a family. I have a mother and father to spend holidays with, just so long as i don't mention Iraq Veterans Against the War. Then that family begins to look and sound like two strangers with a distant grasp on reality. [. . .] I have met a new family recently at the Midwest [IVAW] strategy retreat. [. . .] And to this family I would like to say thank you, regardless of whether or not our fight ends the war in Iraq and brings back our brothers and sisters, the bonds I share with all of you will live in my heart forever.[108]

Jared complements his temporally divided self by expressing a formidable sociomental tension with his biological family, who, given their continued commitment to Jared's former worldview, now "look and sound like two strangers with a distant grasp on reality." Inversely, he uses a vocabulary of cognitive solidarity to account for his membership in a "new family," a political organization in this case. His "bonds" to this new family are inseparably connected to this group's shared cognitive norms and autobiographical conventions. The sociomental character of Jared's expression of solidarity is evident when one considers that he does not claim to feel the same way about all groups of veterans. If feelings of solidarity resulted strictly from shared experience, as some may suggest, then Jared would feel similar "bonds" with veterans who profess a pro-war worldview. The fact that Jared contrasts the "bonds" that "live" in his "heart" to a particular way of seeing the war shows his sentiments and expressions of solidarity to be fundamentally cultural and cognitive in essence. They stem from a shared identity rooted in a shared definition of war, not from his military service alone.

James expresses similar sentiments of sociomental alienation and solidarity to complement his temporally divided self when he comments,

For those of us who have Mormon family, they don't support us at all. Hell, most of us who HAD Mormon friends [they] dumped us, because we're suddenly too evil to be around. Suddenly, all of the people you depended on and care about tell you that you're the scum of the earth and they don't want anything to do with you, or they insist you conform. Intolerance continues . . . until it is unbearable. [The online

Recovery Forum is] not support to stop attending church, it's support to fill in for the "friends" [notably in quotes] and family who dumped us cold because they are intolerant enough to view us as evil.[109]

James uses a vocabulary of cognitive alienation and cognitive solidarity to account for the social repercussions of his divided self. He locates the blame for his ostracism on his former thought partners, the friends and family of his past self, whom he now describes as "intolerant," closed-minded, and disdainful as he casts his present self as unjustly persecuted, as did the Christian apostle Paul, due to his newfound "truth."

Conclusion

If, as Kai T. Erikson argues, "the interactions which do the most effective job" of publicly defining a community's cultural boundaries are "those which take place between deviant persons on the one side and official agents of the community on the other,"[110] awakeners show us that "agent" and "deviant" can be different versions of the same being. Despite many differences among them, all of these awakeners express a sociomental distinction between two dueling personas in their autobiographical stories. They mobilize contradictory self-character schemes— morally coded personified representations of the ideologies, worldviews, sentiments, and lifestyles associated with different autobiographical communities—giving dramatic form to a *sociomental migration* and thereby expressing the contours of the broader autobiographical field. As opposed to the conventional notion of migration, which refers to the physical movement of an individual or group from one geographic location to another, this notion of sociomental migration refers to a shift in an individual's cultural and cognitive allegiances—a change in orientation to the social source of one's worldview.[111] Thus, as awakeners evoke, portray, engage, and undermine their past selves, they simultaneously reject one set of cognitive, affective, and corporeal norms and embrace new conventions of perceiving, feeling, and embodiment. Just as anthropologists have used historical time to split and distance their own cultural group from the otherwise contemporary culture they study,[112] awakeners split their proxy personas along an autobiographical timeline and thereby distance their newly embraced community of "truth" from a rejected community of "falsehood." By emploting a moral polarization of identity, they reinforce the cultural boundary between dueling communities in a contentious cultural arena.

While awakeners are individuals defined by temporally divided group affiliations, both antagonistic groups remain vital to the individual's sense of self. Whereas George Herbert Mead suggests we assume the perspective of the "generalized other," internalizing "the attitude of the whole community" to experience a "unity of self,"[113] awakeners show that our self-concepts often reflect cultural tensions and moral conflicts—the contradictory "attitudes" of multiple communities. In this sense, the awakener's past community continues to play an active role (via its negation) in shaping the awakener's present identity. More, awakening stories show us just how identity can be a locus of cultural conflict and a means to assert moral and cognitive authority. In all of these cases, awakeners do identity work to validate the broader sentiments, perspectives, and objectives of a particular group and attest to the authenticity of that group's standpoint in relation to various alternatives. In the process, they provide character models that potential believers can use to "see the light" and claim an identity that represents that particular community's collective worldview.

SIX

Culture and Autobiographical Narrative

There are three stages in this journey that I have been on! The first, the social science stage; the second, the psychedelic stage; and the third, the yogi stage. They are summating—that is, each is contributing to the next. It's like the unfolding of a lotus flower. Now, as I look back, I realize that many of the experiences that made little sense to me at the time they occurred were prerequisites for what was to come later. [. . .] For me, this story is but a vehicle for sharing with you the true message . . . the living faith in what is possible.

RAM DASS, *REMEMBER: BE HERE NOW*[1]

Arriving in India in 1964 was like walking into a concert that had been playing for five thousand years with seven hundred million people in the band.

BHAGAVAN DAS, *IT'S HERE NOW (ARE YOU?)*[2]

Remember: Be Here Now and *It's Here Now (Are You?)* are influential Eastern-oriented New Age autobiographical accounts written by Americans Ram Dass and Bhagavan Das, who went on quests for self-discovery that took them to India, where they studied under the guru Neem Karoli Baba and assumed new names (Ram Dass was formerly Richard Alpert; Bhagavan Das, Michael Riggs).[3] These awakeners tell of experiencing something akin to the ancient Greek practice of *theoria*. Their contact with another culture both prompted and justified their claims to enlightenment, self-discovery, and cognitive authority. Their stories are representative of the dawn of our late modern era when Eastern mysticism was first becoming widely influential in the West

and in the United States in particular, and thus, they capture something of the cultural visions and tensions of that time.[4] Ram Dass and
Bhagavan Das look to worldviews rooted in the Axial Age to counter
what they deem to be the destructive influences of modern culture.[5]
Both describe their lives as journeys of enlightenment punctuated by
radical moments of epiphany. Both reinterpret their past worldviews and
lifestyles and contrast photographs of their past and transformed selves.
While looking across a cultural divide as well as to tradition steeped in
centuries of history, Ram Dass and Bhagavan Das present their lives as
moving along a trajectory between the polar forces of falsehood/illusion
and illuminating truth.

Taking a broad, comparative approach, I have mapped and detailed
the patterned characteristics of the awakening-narrative formula. I have
shown how various groups with diverse interests, spanning multiple
cultural and historical contexts, make use of the same story formula to
advance strikingly different, and often oppositional, claims about truth
and reality. Whether concerned with the experiences and consequences
of war, the nature of political economy, the character of sexuality, the
foundations of human existence, the alienation of late modernity, the
trauma of childhood, or some other matter, awakeners link their lives
and struggles to the plight of an autobiographical community. Stressing
their discovery and awareness of "truth," they express and advance their
respective newly embraced communities' conventions of perceiving, feeling, remembering, and recounting. Such autobiographical communities
take form in relation to one another in a broader autobiographical field
that contains multiple and competing versions of truth.

When they tell stories about their lives, awakeners delineate cultural
and epistemic tensions concerning the nature of truth and the definition of various moral and political issues. They define and reinforce the
contours of the autobiographical field. As Andrew Buckser argues with
regard to religious conversion, the process of awakening itself can make
otherwise backgrounded boundaries separating groups rise to the fore
of collective attention.[6] Thus, the prominent awakening stories of any
given historical era, like the stories of Ram Dass and Bhagavan Das, capture and epitomize the defining cultural contentions and conflicts of
that era. Just as the stories of these two mystics convey a critique of contemporary Western culture, the Axial Age traditions that inspire them,
as Robert N. Bellah argues, "all involved social criticism and harsh judgments on existing social and political conditions" of that distant past
era.[7] Despite the seemingly personal character of these morally charged

autobiographical stories, they are cultural tools that individuals use to make their lives relevant to the multifaceted and contentious world around them.

Individuals and communities use the awakening-story formula to define goodness and articulate moral order in contrast to some equally defined evil, illusion, and moral disarray. This structural dualism facilitates a generic type of signifying work that is quite durable, yet the story type is flexible in terms of content; "what changes is the signifieds, the social entities conceived as embodying the pure and impure symbolic representations."[8] Thus, the story formula allows for the recurring and ubiquitous morally charged activity of polarizing falsehood and truth. However, it also facilitates innovative discovery and adaptation—it allows for new versions of "falsehood" and "truth" to be devised and mobilized. Individuals and communities use this narrative formula, with its corresponding diametric cultural codes, to make sense of the world in the face of complexity—to resolve contradictions about moral obligations and to negate the feelings of anxiety that often stem from moral uncertainty.

In the process, somewhat ironically, awakeners and their communities exacerbate, reproduce, and reconstruct cultural tensions, distinctions, and patterns of discord as well as, at times, all-out conflict. Given the structural organization of the story formula, awakenings define and preserve standpoints from which communities provoke and engage in cultural battles. These stories often thwart mediation and may inherently resist the type of communicative dialogue that would lead to the synthesis of ideas and to resolution between contending parties.[9] While the sociomental diversity of our cultural landscape has certainly increased over time, there has been a concurrent impetus to sectarianism. Regardless of how one feels about any of the various conflicts and tensions I have discussed throughout this book, there are consequences to this promotion and preservation of antagonism in the world. As they tell their stories in public arenas, embracing one truth upon the rejection of others, awakeners fuel the cultural tensions and conflicts from which they seek relief in their communities of like-minded others.[10]

While I have been guided by my commitment to a particular narrative formula, this study of awakening stories has important implications for a cultural and cognitive sociology of autobiographical narrative more generally. Given the various facets of this analysis, such a cultural and cognitive approach to autobiographical stories should encompass several interrelated principles.

First, autobiographical narrative is an expression of socially situated and relational identity. When individuals tell stories about their lives, they often communicate rich sentiments and values as an aspect of their being. They define important events, issues, and situations in the world as a way of attributing meaning to their lives. In other words, when we tell stories about our lives, we reflexively manifest ourselves as the knowing and feeling storyteller. In the process, we establish our position vis-à-vis others—our cognitive orientations[11] and moral solidarities and antagonisms—within a diverse cultural arena marked by both a growing multiplicity of particularly salient moral and political concerns and a variety of contentious standpoints organized around those concerns. Autobiographical stories are like coordinates that individuals use to locate themselves within this complex cultural arena. They are narrative anchors and social identity posts that individuals use to take a stand on important issues of the day and emplot their life course within the flow of history.[12]

Second, while individuals make "use of the particularities of the historical situation, the symbolic resources at hand, and the constraints and opportunities provided by institutional structures,"[13] they also draw on historically durable and generic story formulas to make their claims. The awakening-narrative formula is one such durable, socially patterned, and flexibly applicable cultural tool. Another is the "rags to riches"[14] story formula that individuals use to portray a self-made triumph and success (like the story boasted by the fictional character Josiah Bounderby in Charles Dickens's novel *Hard Times*, which is formally quite similar to the autobiographical story of African American entrepreneur Booker T. Washington,[15] or the iconic biographical account of US president Abraham Lincoln). Yet another is the formulaic moral tale about heroic personal sacrifice for the greater good (like the Christian story of Jesus, which is formally reproduced by C. S. Lewis as the character Aslan the lion in book 1 of *The Chronicles of Narnia*, or the fate of the protagonist Neo in the third installment of Andy and Lana Wachowski's *Matrix* trilogy, *Matrix Revolutions*). Such formulaic story types, like the awakening-narrative formula, are durable cultural resources that individuals and communities adapt to their particular concerns and situations. They follow the same social pattern across divergent settings. Such autobiographical formulas are an important part of the cultural resources we use to make meaning in the world.

Third, autobiographical narrative is a form of social memory. As individuals tell stories about their lives, they do not simply recount the personal past. They also define past actions, events, experiences, and relationships in order to give meaning to various situations, contexts, and institutions. Further, they shape their mnemonic accounts with various audiences in mind. On the one hand, individuals mobilize their personal memories to define socially relevant events, both ongoing and already passed, as they work to shape the way others perceive and remember such events. On the other hand, they use their autobiographical accounts to shape the cultural milieu for personal memory with regard to particular experiences and issues. They provide social models that others can and do use to recount their life experiences. Because these story models are often based on historical referents, such as when born-again Christians emulate the conversion of the apostle Paul, they often carry the collective memories associated with the group itself. Autobiographical communities, in turn, use life stories to assert mnemonic authority in the face of competition. They deploy life stories as tools in contentious mnemonic battles. They argue that the past has a certain meaning because their individual members offer personal testimony in support of that particular meaning. Beyond Maurice Halbwachs's assertion that "the collective memory . . . encompasses the individual memories while remaining distinct from them,"[16] such an approach to the sociology of memory suggests a dynamic reciprocity between individual and collective memories—the microlevel and macrolevel of culture—with the mesolevel autobiographical community serving as a bridge between these two levels of analysis. From this perspective, a cultural and cognitive approach to autobiographical storytelling certainly has an important place in the growing field of social memory studies.

Fourth, related to the question of memory, autobiographical narrative is a form of social time.[17] All narratives have their own temporalities,[18] and autobiographical time flows by its own storied logic. Like the awakeners cited throughout this book, many individuals use their autobiographical stories to split their lives into discrete periods. They apply a logic of periodization[19] to their personal accounts to mark socially relevant distinctions between different historical eras, community affiliations, life stages, or ways of seeing and feeling. In other cases, individuals express connections between the past and present, often asserting developmental chains of cause and effect in order to find the root of current personal circumstances in past events, situations, and relationships.[20] Such individuals use a logic of historical continuity[21] to create a sense of stability and a durable identity as they share their stories with others. Further, some individuals may portray autobiographical time as a cycle to convey the sense that their personal history is repeating itself. In each case, individuals mark some eras or episodes as more significant than others, and the extent to which some episodes occupy our attention in a narrative sense often occurs independently of any chronometric measure of time. Individuals use autobiographical time—storied continuities, discontinuities, cycles, and various combinations—to advance particular claims and explanations as they work to make meaning in the world. Such an explicit focus on the formulaic, socially constituted structure of autobiographical time will allow us to further consider how individuals and communities use seemingly personal stories as a cultural tool.

Fifth, autobiographical narrative is a form of social knowledge and ought to be a subject matter of a social epistemology. Ever since the pioneering work of Ludwik Fleck, Karl Mannheim, and, later, Thomas S. Kuhn,[22] scholars have explored and elucidated the social foundations and organization of knowledge. Advancing a "sociologically oriented history of thought," Mannheim investigated "the penetration of the social process into the intellectual sphere" and argued that modes of thought "arise out of the collective purposes of a group" and "cannot be correctly understood" if "the social implications of human life are not taken into account."[23] Further, Mannheim recognized the contentious nature of knowledge when he argued that the "diverse interpretations of the world" are actually "intellectual expressions of conflicting groups struggling for power."[24] While Mannheim and other social epistemologists consider the individual to be a vessel of socially and historically situated knowledge, they have not explicitly considered conflict as a principally cultural phenomenon nor have they considered autobiographical narrative as an analytic domain.[25] If a central goal of a social epistemology is to reveal "how knowledge operates as a principle of social organization—for example, by motivating people to act in certain ways with regard to each other and their environments,"[26] then autobiographical stories are important expressive and strategic manifestations of social knowledge. They both reflect and seek to advance certain cultural conceptions of truth and reality in the world. As awakening stories show, individuals use stories about their lives to make knowledge claims and define the parameters of truth and falsehood. Further, they use autobiographical stories to make epistemic distinctions between dueling communities and establish their epistemic standpoints and sociomental locations in the world. In short, one way people deal with their "problems of knowing"[27] is by telling stories about their lives and sharing those stories with others.

Sixth, autobiographical narrative is a form of social drama. The accounts we construct about our lives are worlds of meaning with morals and plotlines. They contain characters, props, settings and scenes, acts and events, agents and attributions of agency, purposes and intentions. In a cultural and cognitive analysis of autobiographical accounts, we should seek to reveal how such dramatic scenes, acts, motives, and interactions take storied form and how storytelling often manifests as a performative ritual activity.[28] Such a perspective expands Kenneth Burke's pentad of dramatism[29] to focus directly on the cultural significance of autobiographical storytelling by including many of the elements identified by Erving Goffman as central to the performance of self, such as the construction of personal and scenic fronts.[30] Further, we should ask what these storied dramas say about the optical norms and storytelling conventions of the storyteller and the storytelling community. The stories we tell about our lives contain performative and dramaturgical dimensions that facilitate the ascription of meaning and motive. As awakening narratives show, individuals use their autobiographical accounts to construct and portray their own agency and forfeit agency to other beings, real or imagined. They use stories about life experiences to attribute cognitive authority to themselves as well as to locate such authority in a god, a therapist, a political organization, the merits of experience, or truth itself, for example. They use narrative props and settings to convey transformative, liminal experiences. They can divide themselves into two or more characters, portraying a temporally divided form of self-interaction that mirrors the cultural and cognitive divisions between communities. Further, individuals use autobiographical dramas to portray social bonds of solidarity and express the sentiments of social alienation.

Finally, autobiographical narratives are speech acts[31] that are directed at multiple audiences. The process of telling a story about one's life—whether sharing the story in person, at a press conference, online, or in a published collection—is a social action designed to win others over to a common understanding of some issue or situation. Like the awakeners whose stories are displayed throughout this book, individuals often use their life stories as testimony and wield their experiences as evidence. They work to establish cognitive authority and win the hearts and minds of others as they advance certain claims that pertain to important issues. At another level, communities use autobiographical stories to convince a wider audience that certain morally and politically salient events and experiences ought to be defined and understood in a particular way. In the process, they also work to "proclaim or at least imply *a moral vision of society as a whole*"[32] and draw others into the fold. As Jeffrey C. Alexander demonstrates when showing how carrier groups work to define particular experiences as traumatic, autobiographical communities seek to control "the means of symbolic production"[33] and expand the adherents to their collective worldview.

A cultural and cognitive sociology of autobiographical narrative should take these seven interrelated principles into account. Using such an approach, we can illuminate the ways that social movement organizations, political parties, religious groups, therapeutic support communities, sexual identity groups, corporations, and other institutions use autobiographical stories to do cultural work and perform meaning. We can also explore how autobiographical narratives take form through different modes of expression including diaries, Internet profiles, published memoirs, poetry, music, and formal confessions. Further, we can explore the ways individuals craft and use their life stories to locate themselves in a multifaceted cultural arena—to establish their authority to define the tensions and solidarities that characterize families, religions, nations, and other communities. A cultural and cognitive sociology can illuminate the role of autobiographical stories as a vehicle for making claims regarding social problems, defining psychological concerns, expressing the tenets of faith, and proclaiming sexuality. By explicitly focusing on autobiographical narrative as an analytic domain, we can reveal important ways that individuals and communities work to make meaning in the world by telling stories about life experiences.

Notes

1. J. Newton (2003, pp. 68–71). See also S. Turner (2002, pp. 39–47). There were no slaves on board during this particular voyage.
2. J. Newton (2003, pp. 73, 80). In excerpts from primary source material, I use bracketed ellipses to indicate omissions.
3. See J. Newton ([1788] 2010, p. 4), where the older Newton writes, "What I did, I did ignorantly." See also S. Turner (2002, pp. 49–65).
4. J. Newton (2003, p. 65).
5. I enclose the words *truth* and *falsehood* in quotation marks to remind the reader that I am analyzing claims people make, not the actual veracity of their accounts. When I explicitly refer to the storyteller's perception, account, claim, or description of truth and falsehood, I do not use quotes. I treat truth as a narrative accomplishment in order to expose the typically unseen cultural dimensions of the stories we tell, dimensions that are often buried or masked when we treat the truth as objective or absolute.
6. There is a vast array of literature focused on the topic of religious conversion, which is typically treated as the preeminent kind of self-transformation. While my work is informed by studies of religion, I do not privilege religious conversion as a particularly profound or unique type of transformative experience. Rather, I see it as one version of awakening among many. For a broad collection of cultural ethnographies focused on the issue of religious conversion, see Buckser and Glazier (2003). Comprehensive reviews and theoretical assessments of this field include Rambo (1982);

Snow and Machalek (1984); Thumma (1991); Smilde and May (2010). See also James ([1902] 1987); Gillespie (1979); Rambo (1993); Cadge and Davidman (2006).

7. See also Berger and Luckmann (1966, pp. 161–62) on the distinction between "partial transformations of subjective reality" and more profound "ruptures." See Kuhn ([1962] 1996) on the notion of a paradigm shift. See Loseke (1992, p. 100) for an application of Berger and Luckmann's concept of "plausibility structure."

8. Berger (1963, p. 54). Building on this discussion, Berger and Luckmann (1966, pp. 156–63) suggest that the process of "alternation," or cases of "near-total transformation . . . in which the individual 'switches worlds,'" is exemplified by religious conversion but has expanded to be "imitated by secular agencies." They established a theoretical foundation for the sociological study of subjective transformations that informed the study of religious conversion in subsequent decades.

9. Snow and Machalek (1983, pp. 269–73). See also pp. 265–66 on "the universe of discourse."

10. The rationalist approach is closely related to the "naturalist reduction" thesis refuted by Charles Taylor (1989, pp. 19, 25), which is the philosophical position that there is one universal basis from which to judge the moral character of action and that the issue of the meanings people attribute to their lives is largely an irrelevant "pseudo-question."

11. Cf. Kerby (1991, pp. 13, 82–97). Kerby argues "for a pragmatic rather than a representational theory of truth" (p. 13).

12. Denzin (1989b, pp. 70–73). See also Denzin (1989a, pp. 128–31).

13. McAdams (1993, p. 12). For a foundational psychocultural notion of self as embedded in "one's cultural-historical existence," see Bruner (1986, p. 67). For a sociological approach to a psychoanalytic case study, see Prager (1998).

14. Stromberg (1993, p. 56). See also Fichter (1987). Fichter, whose position is more purely individualist, opens his study of religious conversion with the caveat, "The autobiographical statements of the eighteen Unificationists in this book are personal and specific, and they cannot be generalized as the typical Unification mode of conversion and recruitment" (p. 1).

15. Stromberg (1993, p. 29).

16. E. Zerubavel (1997).

17. On cultural codes, see Wuthnow (1987, pp. 66–96); Alexander and Smith (1993, 2003); P. Smith (2005). On emotion codes, see Loseke (2009).

18. E. Zerubavel (1997, p. 33). See also Fleck ([1935] 1979, pp. 38–51) on "thought collectives." On knowledge as it pertains to one's social location, see Mannheim (1936).

19. Lieblich, Tuval-Mashiach, and Zilber (1998, p. 110). Lieblich and colleagues advance an illuminating structural psychology of life stories. Arguing "that the *structure* of the story may reflect the deeper personality of the teller . . .

while the *contents* manifest the particular culture within which the story unfolds," these authors show how a formal narrative analysis can illuminate the concerns of psychology. What Lieblich and colleagues call "self-actualization narratives" might indeed reveal something about the "underlying personality" of the storyteller. Further, certain individuals may be attracted to such story types and to the process of adopting what Somers (1994, p. 610) calls "totalizing fictions" or narrative identities where "a *single* category of experience" dominates the storyteller's identity. However, awakening stories also share important characteristics that clue us into the cultural foundations and social logic behind these accounts. By viewing such stories through the lens of culture, I stress these broadly shared characteristics at the expense of the particulars of personality or personality type.

20. For a foundational discussion of cognitive sociology, see E. Zerubavel (1997); DiMaggio (1997). Foundational sociological approaches to knowledge and epistemology include Durkheim ([1912] 1995); Fleck ([1935] 1979); Mannheim (1936); Kuhn ([1962] 1996); B. Schwartz (1981); Fuller ([1998] 2002).

21. See, for example, Wagner-Pacifici and Schwartz's (1991, pp. 389–92) discussion of Vietnam veteran Jan Scruggs, who embodied the multivocal character of the Vietnam Memorial. See also Brekhus (2003, p. 29). Awakeners can be contrasted to what Brekhus calls "identity integrators." As part of his "grammar of identity" in his study of gay suburbanites, Brekhus defines "identity integrators" as those individuals who treat their gay identity as "just one of a number of facets by which they organize their life and identify themselves."

22. E. Zerubavel (1997, p. 8; emphasis in original).

23. I conceive of cognitive authority to be both a constructive force and a narrative resource. On the one hand, cognitive authority is a cultural force, and cognitive authority figures teach individuals to derive particular meanings from their experiences and interpret their lives in patterned ways. On the other hand, cognitive authority often takes on meaning in the narratives we produce. Cognitive authority figures are central characters in the stories we tell about our lives, especially when explaining our personal discoveries of "truth" and accounting for our rejection of previously held beliefs. On cognitive authority, see Fuller (1991, p. 302); Martin (2002); DeGloma (2007). On the cognitive dimensions of power, see Lukes (1974, p. 24); E. Zerubavel (2006, pp. 33–45).

24. On the "definition of the situation," see Thomas (1923). Thomas advanced the notion that the definitions individuals assign to various situations have real consequences in the world. The way we define situations influences the way we understand ourselves, others, and what goes on around us. See also Goffman (1959); Emerson (1970).

25. I am building on the notion of autobiographical work as introduced by Arthur W. Frank (2000). See also J. E. Davis (2005b, p. 530).
26. See J. E. Davis (2002, p. 22).
27. Giddens (1991, p. 76).
28. Zussman (1996, p. 143). See also J. E. Davis (2005a); Somers (1994).
29. Giddens (1991, p. 75).
30. Kerby (1991, p. 4; emphasis in original). See also Bruner (1990).
31. Kerby (1991, p. 109).
32. Frank (1995, p. 158). See also Frank (2000, p. 136) on "the performative re-creation of a self."
33. Vinitzky-Seroussi (1998, p. 59).
34. The more general dialogical approach to the study of narrative was pioneered by the Russian literary theorist Mikhail Bakhtin. See Bakhtin (1981, 1986).
35. Frank (1995, p. 163).
36. Frank (2000, pp. 135, 136). On the sociological analysis of dialogue and discourse, see also Perinbanayagam (1991); Wagner-Pacifici (1994); Steinberg (1999).
37. With regard to religious conversion, Stromberg (1993, pp. 3, 5) argues that "the conversion narrative itself is a central element of the conversion. . . . In practice, of course, what is required is not so much a conversion—by its nature a transformation of the soul that occurs outside of the public view—as a conversion narrative." See also pp. 14–15 on the view that a conversion narrative "is an observable event" and "performance." See also Ezzy (1998, p. 244). Ezzy writes, "It is therefore a mistake to assume that lived experience is in some way separate from its narration." See also Parkin (1996, p. xxxii).
38. This distinction originates with Plato ([ca. 380 BCE] 1941, pp. 80–85). Cf. Gennette (1980, pp. 227–31). See also Aristotle (2006, chap. 3).
39. Burke ([1945] 1969).
40. Mills (1940). Burke ([1945] 1969, p. 440) also uses the term *vocabularies of motive*. See also M. B. Scott and Lyman (1968); Bruner (1990); G. Becker (1997, pp. 25–36); Orbuch (1997).
41. P. Smith (2005, p. 18).
42. Goffman (1959).
43. See Austin (1962); Searle ([1969] 1999); Habermas (1987); Alexander (2004b, pp. 11–12); P. Smith (2005, pp. 33–34, 42–47); Wuthnow (2011).
44. P. Smith (2005, p. 33). See also Plummer (1995, pp. 20–24, 174–76) and Ezzy (1998, p. 244), who argues that the "story, or text, then encounters lived experience again in the world of the listener or reader who reconfigures the story as it influences his or her choices about how to act in the world."
45. C. Taylor (1989, pp. 28, 30).
46. Moonshine's story (2008).

47. On the metaphor of the journey, see Kövecses (2002, pp. 3, 4, 49, 65). See also Plummer (1995, pp. 54–56, 83–86); G. Becker (1997, pp. 6–8).

48. I am indebted to the various scholars who have pioneered the analysis of story form or plot or have developed story typologies. Their analytic approach to narrative inspires the perspective I employ in this book. See, for example, Frye (1957); Propp (1968); White ([1974] 1978, 1987); Graham (1997); Cerulo (1998); E. Zerubavel (2003); Booker (2004). For discussions of narrative plot or structure as related to the social construction of the self, see, for example, Hankiss (1981); Bruner (1987); Frank (1993, 1995); Plummer (1995); Gergen and Gergen (1997); Irvine (1999); Howard (2006); LaRossa and Sinha (2006); DeGloma (2007, 2009).

49. E. Zerubavel (2003, p. 13).

50. J. E. Davis (2005a, p. 192).

51. Ricoeur (1984, p. 3). See also Ezzy (1998, p. 245).

52. McAdams (1993, p. 30).

53. Cf. Halbwachs's ([1950] 1980, pp. 99–101) discussion of "mathematical time" and "lived time." Rather than use these concepts, I prefer the concepts of chronometric time (as measured by a timekeeping instrument), developmental time (as measured by a biologist or psychologist), and autobiographical time because they more precisely capture the different temporal frameworks that are typically deemed relevant to our experience of the life course. Further, my concept of autobiographical time calls attention to the distinctly social and storied character of an individual's life compared to the more subjective character of what Halbwachs discussed as "lived time."

54. Somers (1994, p. 617).

55. P. Smith (2005, p 14). On binary polarization, see also Durkheim ([1912] 1995, [1914] 1960); Lévi-Strauss (1963); Douglas ([1966] 2005); Alexander and Smith (1993).

56. On the social logic of classification, see E. Zerubavel (1991); Nippert-Eng (1996). See also Lamont and Molnár (2002).

57. Frank (1995, p. 3). See also H. Johnston (2009, pp. 14–15). Johnston argues that "narrative tropes allow listeners to cognitively approach the story."

58. On the notion of a structure of feeling, see Saito (2006). On "feeling rules," see Hochschild (1979, 1983). See also Gould (2009).

59. Loseke (2009, p. 497). Notably, awakening stories contain an affective conflict between the different feeling states that Northrop Frye (1957, pp. 33–43) associated with tragic (suffering) (pp. 206–23) and comedic/romantic (idyllic/triumphant) (pp. 186–206) story modes. See also P. Smith (2005, p. 26).

60. See DeGloma (2007).

61. Marshall (1994, p. 176).

62. See Plummer (1995); J. E. Davis (2005a); DeGloma (2007); Whittier (2009).

63. Israel (2007).

64. Commenting on such a binary opposition, Max Weber ([1915] 1946, p. 358) writes, "Dualism maintains that always the powers of light and truth, purity and goodness coexist and conflict with the powers of darkness and falsehood, impurity and evil."

65. Notably, the cultural notion that truth emerges from the negation of false-hood is inherent in the grammatical organization of such stories. One can "discover" or "see" the truth, but "false" is not even a noun. It does not have the object character of "truth," which can be found, discovered, seen, heard, spoken, preached, and shared. To say, for example, "I once knew the truth but now I've discovered falsehood" or "I've seen the false!" is cultur-ally absurd. Rather, falsehood is experienced as a void of truth. It appears only as the cultural inverse of truth, and when communicated in autobio-graphical form, it is always relegated to one's past.

66. Horowitz (1997, pp. 279, 280; emphasis in original).

67. Throughout this book, I provide "maps" or graphs to illustrate the charac-teristics of the awakening-narrative formula. The strength of such visual displays lies in the fact that they illustrate the basic foundational plot structure shared by a collection of otherwise diverse narratives. However, the weakness of such displays is that they inevitably simplify otherwise rich and complex stories. I ask the reader to view these structural story maps with these strengths and weaknesses in mind. While they show the foundational pattern inherent in multiple accounts, my textual interpre-tation of these stories reveals rich complexities that the models cannot display. Finally, as I will discuss in greater detail, the vertical and horizontal structure of this story map is itself a product of cultural norms.

68. Irvine (1999, p. 51).

69. E. Zerubavel (2007).

70. For a rich and thorough discussion of vertical classification as it relates to knowledge, morality, and power, see B. Schwartz (1981). On vertical metaphors, see Lakoff and Johnson (1980, pp. 22–24). On semiotics and the notion that meaning is a function of the general pattern of structural relationships inherent in a language, see Saussure ([1915] 1992).

71. B. Schwartz (1981, p. 5). See also pp. 36, 74. Notably, this linking of "up" with power and authority is complemented by the cultural norm of linking rightward movement with progress and leftward movement with decline or regression. On the cultural distinction between right and left, see Hertz ([1909] 1973).

72. Durkheim ([1893] 1984). The English words *consciousness* and *conscience* both derive from the Latin *conscientia*.

73. As B. Schwartz (1981, p. 151) argues, "Our understanding of social structure cannot be divorced from the vocabulary by which it is described." Arguing that our conceptual framework is structured metaphorically, Lakoff and Johnson (1980, p. 22) write, "The most fundamental values in culture will

be coherent with the metaphorical structure of the most fundamental concepts in the culture." We use metaphors to organize the world into different socially shared mental categories, making distinctions that shape our personal and collective identities and our understandings of the world. On the use of metaphor to structure meaning, see also Kövecses (2002, 2005); G. Becker (1997, pp. 59–79).

74. Frank (1993, p. 48). See also Loseke (2001, p. 107) on how individuals use formula stories "to make sense of their lives and experiences."

75. Genesis 1:3–4 (New International Version; emphasis added).

76. See E. Zerubavel (1997, pp. 32–34) on "optical norms."

77. Even the lost/found contrast may ultimately be informed by a vertical distinction when we consider B. Schwartz's (1981, p. 104) argument that the parent-child relationship is the primary foundation for our cultural conceptions of morality and authority. In this case, children learn that when they are picked *up* by the parent (i.e., *found*) that social connection occurs simultaneously with a raise in one's geographic position. When they are put *down*, they are left isolated by the parent (i.e., *lost*). A similar vertical distinction is evident in most religious conceptions of heaven and hell.

78. In a more general sense, Alasdair MacIntyre (1981, p. 216) argues that we can only truly understand any society "through the stock of stories which constitute its initial dramatic resources." As Philip Smith (2005, p. 3) makes clear, there is "a limited pool of narrative structures within a civil discourse [that] form the cultural bedrock upon which" our more locally situated actions are "made legitimate and thinkable." Only by exploring the formal features of awakening narratives can we truly understand the phenomenon, and social logic, of personal discovery.

79. Simmel (1950a, p. 15).

80. Simmel (1950b, 1950c, 1957, 1965).

81. Coser (1971, p. 182).

82. Snow and Machalek (1983) first proposed the notion that the "convert" is a social type. Reasoning inductively from Snow's ethnographic work in the Nichiren Shoshu Buddhist movement, they suggested that converts to religious groups share some important, general characteristics with converts to other ideologically based groups, such as communist organizations and psychoanalytic communities. Moving beyond this study, I compare a wide range of cases from a diverse array of social and historical contexts. I emphasize the generic characteristics of awakeners by exploring the common properties of their stories and the patterned ways such stories are situated in relation to multiple audiences.

83. Kerby (1991, p. 101).

84. On the polyphonic character of autobiographical stories, see Frank (2000, p. 139).

85. Bakhtin (1986, p. 91; emphasis in original).

86. Ibid, p. 89. See also Wagner-Pacifici (1994, pp. 5–7).

87. C. Taylor (1989, p. 39).
88. See E. Zerubavel (1997, pp. 12, 32, 110) on cognitive deviants.
89. Wuthnow (1987, p. 171).
90. Website of Iraq Veterans Against the War, retrieved April 2009, http://ivaw
    .org/wintersoldier (emphasis added).
91. The term *winter soldier* was coined by members of Vietnam Veterans
    Against the War with reference to Thomas Paine's words in the inaugural
    (December 1776) issue of the *American Crisis*. Paine, whose comments are
    reprinted on the IVAW website, stated, "These are the times that try men's
    souls. The summer soldier and sunshine patriot will, in this crisis, shrink
    from the service of his country; but he that stands it now, deserves the love
    and thanks of man and woman." By referencing the Thomas Paine passage,
    both Vietnam Veterans Against the War and Iraq Veterans Against the War
    claim that the war is itself a "crisis" and that their duty to their country
    involves opposing that war.
92. Lifton ([1973] 2005, pp. 75–95).
93. On the social significance of testimony, see Clanchy (1993); Boellstorff
    (2009, pp. 351–63). On the distinction between "lived history" and "writ-
    ten history," see Halbwachs ([1950] 1980, p. 69). See also Pillemer (1998,
    p. 179). On the social significance of the witness, see Frank (1995, pp. 24,
    137, 165); Tal (1996, pp. 23–59); Wagner-Pacifici (2005, pp. 29–58). On
    the phenomenon of establishing autobiographical presence, see Simpson
    (1994). On the importance of such an autobiographical presence to the
    intellectual authority of the ethnographer, see Geertz (1998, pp. 1–24).
94. Lifton ([1973] 2005, pp. 217–63). The American actor John Wayne was a
    well-known conservative icon and anticommunist spokesman during the
    McCarthy era. He was also a symbol of American machismo and bravado.
    The American rock band Country Joe and the Fish was known for its anti-
    war stance and its communist sympathies. Its well-known song "I-Feel-
    Like-I'm-Fixin'-To-Die Rag," famously performed at Woodstock in 1969,
    had satirically anti–Vietnam War lyrics. By evoking this analogy, Lifton
    captured the transformation of worldview and cultural orientation he per-
    sonally witnessed in many returning Vietnam veterans.
95. See Wagner-Pacifici (2005, p. 41) on this contradiction as it manifests
    between, in her words, "the 'third-party' understanding of a witness and
    the 'bearer of experience' meaning of witness."
96. J. E. Davis (2005a, p. 28).
97. Sewell (1999, pp. 39–40). See also Gubrium and Holstein (1994, p. 691);
    Epstein (2008, p. 167); H. Johnston (2009, pp. 4–5). The distinction
    between these two dimensions of culture is also evident in Peter Berger
    and Thomas Luckmann's (1966, p. 129–47) discussion of primary and
    secondary socialization.
98. Coining the term *autobiographical occasions*, Robert Zussman (1996, p. 143)
    has stated that "a distinctly sociological approach to autobiography" must

attend to "the social structures that dictate the occasions for and character of those narratives." Zussman (2000, p. 5) later defined autobiographical occasions as "the moments at which narrative and social structure meet." See also Vinitzky-Seroussi (1998, 2000); Irvine (1999, p. 51); Frank (2000).

99. Loseke (2001, p. 121). See also Gubrium (2005, p. 526).

100. Loseke (1992); Irvine (1999). On the contextual organization of reality, see Emerson (1970); M. S. Davis (1983); DeGloma and Friedman (2005).

101. See, for example, Gubrium (1992); A. Young (1995); Stein (2009b).

102. Vinitzky-Seroussi (1998).

103. See Denzin (1987); Plummer (1995, pp. 103–6); Holstein and Gubrium (2000, pp. 176–86); Howard (2000).

104. E.g., Stromberg (1993); Coleman (2003).

105. Gubrium and Holstein (2009, pp. 123–97).

106. Loseke (1992, pp. 96, 155); Irvine (1999, p. 46).

107. J. E. Davis (2005a, p. 16; 2005b, p. 531). See also Gubrium and Holstein (1994, p. 697; 2000, p. 99); Ezzy (1998, p. 246); Irvine (1999); Frank (2000).

108. Shibutani (1955, p. 563). See also E. Zerubavel (1997, p. 33), who uses the term *optical community* to refer to a social group for which membership "entails learning to 'see' the world through its particular mental lenses" and thus taking on shared cognitive norms. On thought collectives, see Fleck ([1935] 1979, pp. 38–51). On "interpretive communities," see Fish (1980). Wagner-Pacifici and Schwartz (1991, p. 383) treat organizations in a way that is roughly analogous to my approach to autobiographical communities when they write, "Our assumption is that specific worldviews inhere in the specialized discourses of social organizations, which include political, mass media, and military organizations. These worldviews involve ideas of what it is to be a human being in society and how human beings ought to be represented. Discourse analysis moves back and forth between organizations and the contours of their worldviews by attending to the specific words and acts of organizational members." Regarding reference groups more generally, see Merton ([1949] 1964, pp. 231–33, 247–48). On "frameworks" individuals use to orient themselves in the world, see C. Taylor (1989, p. 19).

109. As Jerome Bruner (1987, p. 21) notes, our "life stories must mesh, so to speak, within a community of life stories." See also Plummer (1995). For a similar statement with regard to social movements and their participants, see Benford (2002, p. 54). See also Hunt and Benford (1994).

110. Cf. Wuthnow (1987, p. 150). See also Weber (1968); Alexander (2004b, p. 11); DeGloma (2009).

111. On "cognitive orientation," see E. Zerubavel (1997, pp. 24–25). On establishing one's orientation in moral space, see C. Taylor (1989).

112. Loseke (2009) argues that emotion codes have affective content and impact, writing, "Widespread emotional appeal can be encouraged by the artful deployment of symbolic and emotion codes" (p. 516). Discussing

the way sexual abuse stories impact other individuals, J. E. Davis (2005a, p. 179) argues that the public telling of such stories "can elicit appropriate emotions, can help clients see their own distress and disability as the result of victimization, can reduce a sense of being unique or different, and can inspire hope in therapy and hope in a changed future." See also Gould (2009, pp. 213–65) on how "the emotion work of movements frequently *generates* feelings" (p. 213; emphasis in original).

113. As Karl Mannheim (1936, p. 99) explains, distinct truth claims stem from "different systems of thought, which are often in conflict with one another" and which are grounded in different social groups that each "move in a separate and distinct world of ideas." On the multiplicity of truths and truth cultures, see also Gubrium and Holstein (1994, p. 687); Holstein and Gubrium (2000, pp. 215–32). On the concept of "epistemic cultures," see Knorr Cetina (1999); Epstein (2008).

114. Cf. Wuthnow (1987, 1989); Alexander and Smith (2003); P. Smith (2005); Alexander (2006, 2007).

115. Synthesizing and advancing important statements made by Durkheim and Simmel, Lewis A. Coser (1956) argues that ideological conflict between groups can strengthen group solidarity.

116. Beyond Ex-Gay press conference, retrieved March 2012, http://www.youtube .com/watch?v=zc49S6JJUwg (author's emphasis). See also "Christine Bakke on Her Journey Trying to Become an Ex-Gay," retrieved March 2012, http:// www.youtube.com/watch?v=urmi4JXVD0I&feature=related.

117. "Beyond ExGay: An Online Community for Those Who Have Survived Ex-Gay Experiences," retrieved March 2012, http://www.beyondexgay.com/.

118. "Truth Wins Out," retrieved March 2012, http://www.truthwinsout.org/.

119. Nicolosi (1993, p. viii; emphasis added).

120. Steinmetz (1992, p. 496). See also See also Luker (1984); Y. Zerubavel (1995, pp. 10–12); J. E. Davis (2005a, p. 15).

121. Engerman (2001, pp. viii–ix, xxv).

122. Wuthnow (1989, pp. 13–15). See also Foucault ([1969] 1972, pp. 79–87) on the "field of discourse."

123. For a late modern conception of standpoint theory, see Collins (2000). As opposed to Collins, who elaborates a standpoint theory and "its accompanying epistemology" (p. 270) by stressing demographic variables that are "situated in a context of domination" (p. 269), I use the term *standpoint*, in the tradition of Mannheim, Shibutani, and Zerubavel, to indicate the sociomental communities to which we belong and from which we define the world. However, my emphasis on intersubjective and sociomental dynamics does not deny that power relations are inherent in these fundamentally *cultural* contests over meaning and truth.

124. E. Zerubavel (1997, p. 33).

125. On the concept of "group style," see Eliasoph and Lichterman (2003). Eliasoph and Lichterman define group style "as recurrent patterns of inter-

action that arise from a group's shared assumptions about what constitutes good or adequate participation in the group setting . . . elements of *culture* . . . [that] are patterned and relatively durable" (p. 737). I borrow this term to denote how various awakeners can use the same widespread narrative formula (roughly analogous to Eliasoph and Lichterman's treatment of "collective representations") while filling this narrative formula with group-specific, culturally grounded meanings that arise in the particular community to which they belong. In short, awakeners combine a durable, generic narrative formula with a "group style" of storytelling when they tell stories about their lives. See also Fleck ([1935] 1979, pp. 125–45) on "thought style."

126. Spillman (1995, p. 144); see also Bakhtin (1986) on the concept of speech genres.

127. MacIntyre (1981, p. 218). Cf. Frank (2000, p. 148), who comments that "autobiographical work . . . is a relation," and Vinitsky-Seroussi (1998, p. 60), who refers to "the social dynamics of autobiography."

128. Lane (1970, p. 32). See also B. Schwartz (1981, p. 94); Wuthnow (1987, p. 149); Buckser and Glazier (2003, p. xiv).

129. See Wuthnow (1987, p. 149) on "ideological fields." See also E. Zerubavel (1997, pp. 17–19) on "cognitive pluralism"; Gubrium and Holstein 2000.

130. Spillman (1995, p. 139).

131. Wagner-Pacifici (1994, p. 4).

132. E. Zerubavel (2007). See also Brekhus (2007).

133. E. Zerubavel (2007, p. 131); see also Vaughan (2002, pp. 30–33).

134. In the words of Robert Prus (1987, p. 264), I view the production and circulation of awakening stories as a "generic social process," explicitly arguing that we can observe broadly relevant cultural patterns among "materials that might otherwise seem highly diverse." See also Mullaney (2006, pp. 2–3). On "multi-area formal theory," see also Glaser and Strauss ([1967] 2008, pp. 82–89). For similar approaches, see, for example, Allan V. Horwitz's (1990) treatment of social control and Dan Ryan's (2006) work on notification norms.

135. To be clear, I find single-case and single-issue studies incredibly useful, especially insofar as they detail how local cultural forces act on individuals to shape their personal stories. However, because most studies of autobiographical narrative are limited to ethnographic analysis of a single case or setting (as are most studies of narrative identity), they do not address how and why individuals tell formally similar stories in a variety of different settings—with regard to very different subject matters—despite advancing divergent and often contentious claims and different versions of truth. Moreover, single-case studies typically fail to consider how individuals and communities tell autobiographical stories in dialogue with—and often in reactive opposition to—other individuals and communities. For an exception to the later point, see Frank (2000), who advances a broader and more

flexible notion of autobiographical stories, one that identifies a major life experience (illness) as an occasion for creating and engaging a dialogue in autobiographical form.

136. E. Zerubavel (2007, p. 140; emphasis in original).

137. Except where otherwise noted (e.g., when I add italics to call attention to a particular part of a story), I keep the original grammar of the story intact and do not correct mistakes.

138. As Robert Wuthnow (1987, p. 50) argues, a structuralist perspective allows us to emphasize "systematic patterns in cultural codes and . . . search for the underlying meaning of cultural codes through the process of identifying these patterns." See also Hayden White (1987), who argues that narrative is a "meta-code" that we use to give meaning to our experiences and transmit a shared reality. "To raise the question of the nature of narrative," White comments, "is to invite reflection on the very nature of culture" (p. 1).

139. Alexander and Smith (2003, p. 11); P. Smith (2005, pp. 38, 41, 207).

140. P. Smith (2005, p. 14).

141. Especially Geertz (1973). For illuminating discussions of Geertz's hermeneutics and its relevance to cultural sociology, see Alexander (2008); Reed (2008); P. Smith (2008).

142. This is related to the social constructionist agenda insofar as "the constitution of meaning is made the *object* of study" (J. E. Davis 2005a, p. 8) but stresses how agents must use culturally entrenched forms, binary codes, and generic tropes if their claims are to become convincing or make sense at all.

143. Literature, film, and visual art are situated in the same discursive space as the autobiographical stories I consider and thus also convey the predominant themes and concerns of the time, not to mention make use of the most salient moral polarities. Cf. Wuthnow (1989) and his treatment of Enlightenment literature. See also Kerby (1991, p. 103), who writes, "Literature provides us with a rich vocabulary for articulating, and thus interpreting, experience in ways previously unsuspected."

144. When citing these, I use the name or avatar associated with the published story. For anonymously published material, I use a pseudonym to keep the flow of the text; however, the citations for such stories reveal that the authors chose to remain anonymous. If there was no publication date associated with the account, I use the retrieval date to cite the account. With rare exception, I do not correct stories for grammatical errors. Finally, in cases where a web host deleted content between the time I retrieved the data and the time of publication, I keep the outdated URLs to show the reader that the material was once hosted on the particular site of interest.

145. P. Smith (2005, p. 51). On discourse in the public sphere, see also Tipton (1982, pp. 253–72); Wuthnow (1987, 1989); Wagner-Pacifici (1994); Alexander (2006).

146. Waskul (2003, p. 24).
147. On the online performance of self, see Walker (2000); Waskul (2003). Regarding online communities, see Cerulo (1997); Chayko (2002, 2008); P. A. Adler and P. Adler (2008). Concerning storytelling or claims making online, see Polletta and Lee (2006); Maratea (2008).
148. H. Johnston (2009, p. 21).
149. Chayko (2008).
150. H. S. Becker ([1963] 1997, pp. 147–63).
151. Examples of *public message boards* include the websites of Iraq Veterans Against the War, Susan Smiles—Surviving Childhood Sexual Abuse, Safeguarding Our Children—Uniting Mothers, Recovery from Mormonism, Postmormon, ExChristian, and Testimonies: Why I Am Pagan. Alternatively, the websites of the False Memory Syndrome Foundation, Mormon Converts, Precious-Testimonies, Faith-Travels, People Can Change, Courage, and Beyond Ex-Gay more closely resemble *controlled publications*. Autobiographical accounts posted to most sites of the latter set are typically framed with editorial comments. Many of these stories are exclusively published to the site at hand; others appear in multiple formats or locations. In many cases, those who post to these sites provide commentaries on various issues in addition to detailed autobiographical accounts. Others limit their posts to a short story or basic personal information.
152. In Habermas's (1987) terms, the Internet may sometimes facilitate strategic rather than communicative action.
153. Building on the work of Everett Hughes (1984), Jaber F. Gubrium and James A. Holstein (2000) argue that the postmodern condition is marked by a proliferation of "going concerns" that manifest as various "discursive environments." The self, they argue, has come to be defined by a growing "ability to choose between options—indeed to use some options in order to resist others, or to construct new ones" (p. 112). While I agree with Gubrium and Holstein's analysis, I, like Giddens (1991, p. 27), prefer the term *late modern* to the term *postmodern*. The latter suggests a historical rupture or division between different epochs that downplays important historical continuities in the cultural trends I discuss.
154. Weber ([1915] 1946, p. 330).

CHAPTER TWO

1. This proverb is commonly reproduced and widely attributed to the Buddha.
2. Locke ([1690] 1961, p. 127).
3. Freud ([1899] 1938, p. 308). In excerpts from these foundational awakening narratives, I use bracketed ellipses to indicate omissions.
4. In various writings, notably his "Religious Rejections of the World and Their Directions" ([1915] 1946), Max Weber argues that different "spheres

of values" (of which he distinguishes between the religious, the economic, the political, the aesthetic, the erotic, and the intellectual) increasingly operate by their own unique cultural logics, becoming more autonomous with the progress of the modern world. However, whereas Weber stresses the emergent distinctions and evolving autonomy among different realms of social life, I focus on something that they hold in common—a type of storyteller and story formula that they all share. Despite the divergent cultural logics of the variant discourses that define otherwise different realms of meaning and human activity, individuals and communities construct and deploy surprisingly similar awakening narratives as they navigate the social contours and dynamics of each sphere.

5. Wuthnow (1989). See also Michel Foucault ([1969] 1972; [1978] 1990) on "discourses of truth." See also Wagner-Pacifici (1994); Plummer (1995).

6. Jaspers ([1953] 2010). I use the terms *Axial Age* and *Axial Period* interchangeably.

7. See Weil (1975). The Axial Age is generally regarded to have been marked by upheaval and conflict. See Jaspers ([1953] 2010); Eisenstadt (1986, p. 10); Armstrong (2006a, pp. xviii–xix, 3–56). See also Bellah (2011, p. 574).

8. Building on the ideas of Jürgen Habermas, Robert N. Bellah refers to "the legitimation crisis of axial-age society." See Bellah (2011, p583).

9. See Eisenstadt (1986). See also Bellah (2011, pp. 265–82). The Axial Age signified a shift from a predominant "cosmological" worldview in which the "supernature, nature, and society" were seen to be "fused in a single cosmos" (Bellah 2011, p. 266) to new worldviews characterized by a belief in the division between the world of day-to-day life and the divine. In this era new visions were put forth to account for the questions raised by these changes. The "breakthroughs" of this era thus involved a move "from compact cosmological symbolization . . . to a differentiated symbolism of individual soul, society, and transcendent reality" (p. 271).

10. Elkana (1986, p. 64). B. I. Schwartz (1975, p. 3) describes this posture as "a kind of standing back and looking beyond—a kind of critical, reflexive questioning." See also Jaspers ([1953] 2010, pp. 61–66); Eisenstadt (1986); Bellah (2011, p. 276).

11. Bellah (2011, p. 576). Also, "the great axial utopias" stand "as a measure of just how short life in this world falls compared to what it ought to be" (p. 585).

12. Eisenstadt (1986, pp. 1, 11).

13. This new mentality is beautifully illustrated by the case of the Etruscans, who before their initial contact with the Romans only included angelic images of joy and happiness on the walls of their tombs. They conceived the afterlife to be entirely positive. With an emerging Roman threat (ca. 420 BCE), these images were combined with haunting pictures of blue devils, making the Etruscans the first known civilization to bring such positive and negative portrayals together in their tombs. Concession to the

Romans (the imposing "others" in this case) meant darkness and suffering in the afterlife. Standing against the Roman threat meant light and joy. The nature of transcendence was thus firmly linked to one's allegiances in the mundane world. See BBC (2005).

14. Thomassen (2010, p. 327).

15. On the reflexive organization of self in the "late modern age," see Giddens (1991). See also Gubrium and Holstein (2000).

16. Gergen (1991, p. 16).

17. Bellah et al. (1985, pp. 32–51, 333–34).

18. Wuthnow (1987, p. 150).

19. Kerby (1991, p. 103).

20. I must acknowledge that all periodization schemes are socially constructed. However, there is great value in understanding these pivotal moments insofar as they facilitated the broad use of the awakening-narrative formula today. On the social logic of periodization, see E. Zerubavel (1998). With regard to this notion of pivotal moments, cf. Thomassen (2010, p. 333) on "axial moments."

21. Today, Zarathustra is regarded as a prophet in the Islamic and Bahá'í faiths, and there are scattered populations of Zoroastrians living around the world, mainly in India. However, as Mary Boyce ([1979] 2001, p. 1) points out, some of the central tenets of Zoroastrianism "were adopted by Judaism, Christianity and Islam, as well as by a host of Gnostic faiths, while in the East it had some influence on the development of Northern Buddhism." References to Zarathustra's enlightenment can be found throughout various Greek and Roman philosophical treatises where he became known as Zoroaster, a name more commonly used in the Western world. There is controversy over the time of Zarathustra's life, with some scholars placing him as early as the fifteenth century BCE and others as late as the sixth century BCE. See Shahbazi (1977); Boyce ([1979] 2001, p. 2); Nigosian (1993, pp. 15–16).

22. As recorded in "The Great Hymn to the Aten," the Egyptian pharaoh Akhenaten (reign ~1352–1336 BCE) was the first to declare light, in the form of the god Aten, radiating from the sun, to be the only god and to establish the contrast between light (associated with goodness) and dark (associated with death) as a religious framework. However revolutionary, the new religious ideas of Akhenaten were short lived, and the source of the good, Aten, was said to be primarily accessible to, and manifest as, the pharaoh himself. The idea that individuals might awaken to discover the truth of a higher moral order was missing until the early prophets of the Axial Age made such claims in competition with others. See Bellah (2011, pp. 246, 276–78). See also Hornung ([1995] 1999, esp. pp. 52–57, 76–86). Such a diametric moral duality of the universe is also a fundamental tenet of the Manichaean rigid division of the cosmos into a realm of light and a realm of darkness (a "truth" that is said to have been revealed to the

prophet Mani during his awakening). See Manichaean scriptures, trans. Prods Oktor Skjærvø, retrieved July 2009, http://www.fas.harvard.edu /~iranian/Manicheism/.

23. Nigosian (1993, pp. 14–15).
24. For a complete translation, see "The Gathas ('Hymns') of Zarathushtra," retrieved June 2009, http://www.avesta.org/gathas.htm.
25. Boyce ([1979] 2001, p. 3).
26. Ibid., p. 19. See also Armstrong (2006a, pp. 9–14).
27. Nigosian (1993, p. 20); Choksy (2003, pp. 21–23); Armstrong (2006a, p. 11).
28. Boyce ([1979] 2001, p. 20).
29. *Yasna* 30.1–5, retrieved June 2009, http://www.avesta.org/yasna/yasna .htm#y28 (empahsis added). This edition was translated by L. H. Mills and originally published in 1898 in *Sacred Books of the East.*
30. Expressing this cultural contention, Zarathustra states, "[. . .] [O]n him who threatens to be my undoing, that I may fetter the men of the Lie in their violence against my friends." *Yasna* 32.16, *Ahunavaiti Gatha,* retrieved June 2009, http://www.avesta.org/yasna/yasna.htm#y28.
31. Jackson (1896); Armstrong (2006a, pp. 11–13).
32. Boyce ([1979] 2001, p. 20).
33. Cf. Bellah (2011, p. 587). See also Weil (1975, p. 29), who argues the moral division implied by this overcoming to be "the prefiguration of the concept of freedom" that emerges with modern philosophy.
34. It was Ferdinand de Saussure ([1915] 1992) who pioneered the notion that the link between a word (signifier) and the meaning it calls to mind (signified) is a product of the relation itself and "social by nature." See also E. Zerubavel (1997, p. 68); Alexander (2003).
35. Nietzsche ([1891] 1917, p. 286). Nietzsche writes, "Well! Take heart! ye higher men! Now only *travaileth the mountain of the human future.* God hath died: now do we desire- the Superman [Übermensch] to live" (emphasis added).
36. Plato ([ca. 380 BCE] 1941, p. 231).
37. Nightingale (2004). My discussion of this concept relies heavily on Nightingale's work and Bellah's (2011, pp. 577–82) application of her work.
38. Nightingale (2004, p. 4).
39. Plato ([ca. 380 BCE] 1941, p. 231).
40. Ibid, p. 229.
41. Ibid, pp. 230–31 (emphasis added). As Plato distinguished between the mutually exclusive worlds of darkness and light, he was also accounting for the death of his teacher, Socrates (p. 231n1), who, despite his lifelong pursuit of truth, was tried and condemned to death for corrupting the minds of Athenian youth.
42. On the cultural logic of vertical classification, see B. Schwartz (1981).
43. This structural affinity may, in part, be due to the fact that René Descartes, whose coordinate system makes the graph in figure 1 possible, was inspired by Plato's allegory. See Buckle (2007).

44. Nunez, the protagonist of H. G. Wells's (1904) "The Country of the Blind," experiences similarly frustrating "optical" difficulties. Combining optical and geographic metaphors to show the dilemmas involved with such a scenario, Wells locates his lost "Country of the Blind" in the deep recesses of a mountain range, separated and hidden from the rest of the world by a nearly impassable terrain. When Nunez discovers this world (by falling *down* into it), he learns that every one of its citizens lacks the biological capacity for sight. Upon his arrival, Nunez is first greeted by a local man who asks, "And you have come into the world?" "*Out* of the world," Nunez replies. Their initial exchange calls attention to their contrasting sociomental standpoints. While Nunez is first ridiculed, harassed, and feared by the citizens of the Country of the Blind, they later give him a condition that he must satisfy in order to stay and marry Medina-sarote, a woman with whom Nunez falls in love: he must give up his eyes. Ultimately, Nunez rejects this condition (rejecting the optical change that would allow him to "see" the world by this community's optical standards) and is forced to leave the country. Using the metaphoric contrast of blindness and sight to signify contrasting ways of perceiving reality, Wells portrays the often frustrating difficulties and painful consequences encountered when one traverses the structural divide between sociomental camps without a corresponding change of mindset.
45. See Gocer (2000).
46. G. J. Horwitz (1990).
47. Nightingale (2004, p. 5).
48. Ibid. Simmel's (1950c) quintessential sociological concept of the stranger captures the tensions Nightingale describes here. Simmel, too, speaking in the most general sense, attributed impartiality, objectivity, and hazard to the stranger's structural position.
49. See Plato ([ca. 380 BCE] 1941, p. 190), where he asked, "Since the philosophers are those who can apprehend the eternal and unchanging, while those who cannot do so, but are lost in the mazes of multiplicity and change, are not philosophers, which of the two ought to be in control of the state?" Elsewhere, Plato stated, "Unless either philosophers become kings in their countries or those who are now called kings and rulers come to be sufficiently inspired with a genuine desire for wisdom; unless, that is to say, political power and philosophy meet together [. . .] there can be no rest from troubles [. . .] for states, nor yet, as I believe, for all mankind; nor can this commonwealth which we have imagined ever till then see the light of day" (pp. 178–79).
50. Bellah (2011, p. 580). See also Nightingale (2004, pp. 113–16).
51. Cf. Weil (1975, p. 29), who argues, "Although the principle is proclaimed with the greatest emphasis—even in Plato's view a slave can attain true knowledge with Socrates's help—it remains only a principle. Empirically, most people lack the gifts necessary for leading the good life; they are condemned to a sub-human existence."

52. Plato ([ca. 380 BCE] 1941, p. 232).
53. Ibid., p. 229.
54. Weber ([1915] 1946, p. 330). See also Weber ([1930] 1992).
55. See Weil (1975, p. 29) on this point.
56. For the account as rendered in scholarly works on Buddhism, see P. Harvey (1990, pp. 14–22); Lopez (2001, pp. 37–42); Armstrong (2006a, pp. 326–42). For a popular spiritual rendition of the Buddha's life, see, for example, Chopra (2007). My modest rendition of the Buddha's life in this section is pieced together from these sources. While of Indian origin, the story of Siddhārtha Gautama is widely relevant in the modern Western world, as exemplified by the profound cultural impact of Herman Hesse's ([1922] 1951) allegorical novel *Siddhartha*. As Weber ([1915] 1946, p. 323) writes, "Indian religiosity . . . is the cradle of those religious ethics which have abnegated the world, theoretically, practically, and to the greatest extent."
57. See Acts 9:3–31, 26:1–18 (New International Version).
58. Armstrong (2006a, p. 327).
59. Ibid., p. 328.
60. P. Harvey (1990, p. 2).
61. Lopez (2001, pp. 41–42).
62. See Bellah (2011, p. 585).
63. Galatians 1:13 (NIV).
64. Acts 9:3–6 (NIV).
65. Acts 26:15–18 (NIV; emphasis added).
66. Acts 9:15–16 (NIV).
67. Bellah (2011, pp. 574, 575).
68. Kippenberg (1986, p. 266).
69. As James Carroll (2001, p. 132) argues, the budding Christian movement often felt the need to accentuate its differences with the Pharisees, foregrounding "the struggle with one's sibling rival" because the Jewish community was the Christian sect's direct competition.
70. Kippenberg (1986, p. 275).
71. See Armstrong (1992, pp. 45–49). See also Armstrong (2006b, pp. 33–39).
72. Augustine ([397–398] 1961, pp. 177–78).
73. See Bushman (1984, pp. 56–61; 2005, pp. 39–46); Remini (2002, pp. 38–39, 43–45)
74. Wuthnow (1989).
75. Snow and Benford (1992); Benford and Snow (2000).
76. When I discuss the Enlightenment, I refer broadly to the philosophical, scientific, and political movement that spurred the rise of the modern era. The core Enlightenment thinkers were German, French, British, and American, but its influence was much more diffuse. Early influential thinkers included Thomas Hobbes ([1651] 1962), Sir Isaac Newton (1687), and John Locke ([1690] 1961; [1690] 1980). Later Enlightenment philosophers included Jean Jacques Rousseau ([1755] 1994; [1762] 1968), Adam

Smith ([1776] 2003), and Immanuel Kant ([1781] 1993; [1785] 2008). The scientific and political theories advanced by these notable figures are, in various ways, collective awakening stories.

77. C. Taylor (2004, p. 3).

78. David Hume ([1748] 1961, p. 317), for example, writes, "[T]hought [. . .] amounts to no more than the faculty of compounding, transposing, augmenting, or diminishing the materials afforded us by the senses and experience." See also Hobbes ([1651] 1962); Locke ([1690] 1961).

79. Kant ([1781] 1993). See also B. Schwartz (1981, p. 2), who notes, "The mind, says Kant, is not a blank slate on which preorganized impressions are inscribed; it is a positive agency which molds and integrates raw impressions into finished ideas."

80. Spinoza ([1670] 2007, p. 8).

81. Wuthnow (1989, p. 324).

82. As a social and philosophical movement the Enlightenment asks, If a religious view of divine truth is wrong, how can we know that a secular view of truth is right? Or, how can we justify a secular governmental rule? Despite notable differences, most Enlightenment-era thinkers worked to show how the attainment of rational scientific truth would lead humanity into an era of civil society.

83. Hobbes ([1651] 1962, p. 100).

84. Rousseau ([1755] 1994, pp. 26–29).

85. Wuthnow (1989, p. 330).

86. See Somers (1994, p. 619), who argues the Enlightenment is a metanarrative—a master story or plot "in which we are embedded as contemporary actors in history."

87. Condorcet (1796, p. 239). See also Comte ([1830–42] 1975, pp. 279–97), who uses an Enlightenment notion of progress to introduce the field of sociology.

88. Wuthnow (1989, p. 179).

89. C. Taylor (2004, p. 176).

90. Ibid, pp. 7, 176.

91. Weber ([1915] 1946, p. 335).

92. Marx ([1845] 1978, p. 154).

93. Marx ([1845] 1963, p. 199).

94. See, for example, Marx ([1867] 2010, pp. 44–50) on commodity fetishism. On Marx's view of consciousness, see also Wuthnow (1987, p. 32).

95. See Marx ([1845] 1978, pp. 148–75).

96. Wuthnow (1989, p. 491).

97. True to Marx's dialectical approach, revolutionary upheaval is a necessary condition of true consciousness, and true consciousness is a necessary condition of revolutionary upheaval. When Marx writes that "[t]he demand to give up the illusions about [religion's] condition is the demand to give up a condition [class society] which needs illusions," he emphasizes the

inseparability of structural and mental/cultural change. For Marx, to wage revolution, one must awaken. To awaken, one must wage revolution. See Marx ([1844] 1963, p. 227).

98. Berger (1963, p. 62).

99. Engels ([1893] 1970, p. 690).

100. Lenin ([1913] 1996). Such a theory allows those advocating revolution to say that they are working in the interests of the oppressed proletarian class even when those who fall within the structural boundaries of that class do not (yet) see that they share these revolutionary interests.

101. Lukács ([1920] 1971, p. 50).

102. Gramsci (1971, p. 12). See also E. S. Herman and Chomsky ([1988] 2002).

103. McAdams (1993, p. 120). See also Wuthnow (1989, pp. 179, 316, 336–37); Zaretsky (2004). As Charles Taylor (1989, p. 28) argues, the Enlightenment eventually ushered in a "post-Romantic understanding of individual differences," which became connected to "the importance we give to expression in each person's discovery of his or her moral horizon." Freud harnessed this reconceptualization and was the first to articulate a comprehensive theory of this unique self as a process of discovery. Many others followed Freud to articulate various ways of understanding the self as a dynamic tension between one's known and unknown characteristics. See, for example, Jung (1959).

104. Zaretsky (2004, p. 11). See also Chodorow (1999); A. V. Horwitz (2002).

105. Freud ([1912] 1963, p. 49).

106. Zaretsky (2004, pp. 5–6). Zaretsky provides a detailed discussion of psychoanalysis as the "*first great theory and practice of 'personal life'*" (p. 5; emphasis in original) and argues that Freud developed psychoanalysis in the wake of "the *second* industrial revolution, amid the beginnings of mass production and mass consumption in the 1890s" (p. 16; emphasis in original).

107. See, for example, Freud ([1905] 1963, [1909] 1963, [1911] 1963, [1918] 1963).

108. Freud commonly used the term *enlightenment* (e.g., [1905] 1963, pp. 5, 6) as well as a variety of related optical metaphors to describe the process of discovering such inner "truths." For optical metaphors in Freud's analysis of Dora, see pp. 29, 45, 52, and 71, to list just a few examples. Further, the vertical implications of psychoanalytic thought are evident in the quite common practice of using the image of an iceberg to teach students of psychology the relation between the conscious mind (above the surface) and the considerably more massive unconsciouss mind (below the surface).

109. Chodorow (1999, pp. 1–2).

110. A. V. Horwitz (2002).

111. McAdams (1993, p. 33).

112. "Wolf Man" was Freud's pseudonym for the Russian aristocrat Sergei Pankejeff.

113. Freud ([1918] 1963, pp. 283–88; emphasis added).

114. Freud ([1910] 1938, p. 939).
115. Freud ([1901] 1938, p. 103).
116. J. E. Davis (2005a, p. 124).
117. Philip Rieff ([1962] 1963, p. xi) critically discusses the act of the analyst who is "engaged in an effort to change the patient's mind." See also Berger (1963, p. 64), who compares the psychoanalyst to a communist "brainwasher.'"
118. Freud ([1899] 1938).
119. Tipton (1982, p. 244). See also Plummer (1995, pp. 147–51).
120. Holstein and Gubrium (2000, p. 231).
121. H. Johnston, Laraña, and Gusfield (1994, p. 7). For other foundational statements, see Melucci (1989); Gamson (1992). See also V. Taylor and Whittier (1992).
122. Somers (1994, pp. 607–13). See also Giddens (1991, pp. 214–17), who discusses "the politics of self-identity" in the late modern era, where "life politics is a politics of lifestyle." See also Plummer (1995, p. 128).
123. See Gergen (1991); Giddens (1991); Frank (1995). See also H. Johnston, Laraña, and Gusfield (1994, p. 8), who argue that, "the organization and proliferation of new social movement groups are related to the credibility crisis of the conventional channels for participation in Western democracies."
124. Wuthnow (1987, p. 158).
125. Gergen (1991, p. 16). See also Plummer (1995, pp. 134–42).
126. Eisenstadt (1986, p. 4).
127. The sectarian character of such communities is perhaps most clearly expressed by the common sentiment that one's community-based identity affords one "a privileged state of being" (Frank 2000, p. 137), one that others (those outside the awakener's autobiographical community) are unable to fully comprehend. Such a sectarian epistemology is perhaps most clearly articulated by feminist theorists of intersectionality who argue that knowledge stems from individuals' shared social location or "standpoint" in a class/gender/race/sexuality nexus. For example, Patricia Hill Collins (2000, p. 271) writes, "The existence of a self-defined Black women's standpoint using Black feminist epistemology calls into question the content of what currently passes as truth and simultaneously challenges the process of arriving at that truth." See also, for example, Anzaldúa (1987); Crenshaw (1991).
128. Eyerman (2001); Alexander (2004b, pp. 11–12); DeGloma (2009, 2011). On "carrier groups" with regard to religious culture, see Weber (1968).
129. Both trauma carrier groups and sexual identity movements, along with the second-wave feminist movement more generally, uprooted the Freudian focus on a distinctly personal introspection (a looking *within*) and, without sacrificing Freud's commitment to interpretive personal discovery, began to identify their shared conditions, troubles, and needs (which involved

a looking *among*). Abandoning the Marxist commitment to the primacy of economic class in favor of emphasizing their common ideals, values, and lifestyles, they cooperated to achieve a shared sense of identity while making claims about their social marginalization and/or victimization. On the post-Freudian character of this late modern politics, see Zaretsky (2004, pp. 327–31). See also Plummer (1995, pp. 60, 148) and Frank (2000, p. 144), who writes, "The contemporary prophet hears divine voices coming from fellow humans, not from the clouds above." On the postsocialist character of this late modern politics, see N. Fraser (1995).

130. See, for example, Tipton (1982); Brown (2002); E. F. Johnston (2013).

131. On the notion of "rationality in recession," see Gergen (1991, pp. 77–80).

132. W. J. Scott (1990, pp. 299–300). See also A. Young (1995); Shephard (2001). For sociological insight into the modern trauma narrative, see Alexander (2004a, 2004b). See also Bar-On (1999); Eyerman (2001); J. E. Davis (2005a, 2005b); DeGloma (2007, 2009, 2011); Stein (2009a, 2009b). For the psychological conception of trauma and PTSD, see Lifton ([1973] 2005); J. L. Herman ([1981] 2000; 1992); APA (1994, p. 428).

133. Plummer (1995, pp. 57–58, 66–73); J. E. Davis (2002, 2005a); Whittier (2009).

134. Alexander (2004a).

135. Cline (1997; emphasis added).

136. J. E. Davis (2005a, p. 105). See also Plummer (1995, pp. 68–75).

137. This popular adage was first used as the title of a paper published by second-wave feminist activist Carol Hanisch in the 1970 magazine *Notes from the Second Year: Women's Liberation—Major Writings of the Radical Feminists*. The phrase captures the movement from "personal troubles" to "public issues" at the heart of C. Wright Mills's ([1959] 2000) notion of the sociological imagination. Mills was an influence on the New Left in general. Notably, *The Sociological Imagination* is itself a guidebook for a certain type of awakening.

138. Illouz (2008). Illouz suggests that therapeutic culture involves "an extraordinary paradox" in that, while "the primary vocation of which is to heal," it "must generate a narrative structure in which suffering and victimhood actually define the self" (p. 173). See also Irvine (1999, p. 19–31) on "the therapeutic ethos" and Stein (2011) on "therapeutic politics."

139. Bass and Davis (1988, p. 16; emphasis added).

140. See J. E. Davis (2005a) on the moral work of the movement to define child sexual abuse as trauma. See Alexander (2004a) on the Holocaust as a "moral universal."

141. Plummer (1995, p. 49). For a critical discussion of modern sexual discovery stories, see Butler (1991); Phelan (1993).

142. Plummer (1995, pp. 49–61, 82–96, and esp. pp. 83, 143 on discovering "truth").

143. Bayer (1981, pp. 101–54). Bayer presents an illuminating analysis of American psychiatry's evolving position on homosexuality. In my treatment of this issue, I draw heavily from Bayer's work.

144. Ibid., p. 13.
145. Ibid., p. 49.
146. See Gould (2009, p. 214) on how the social movement ACT UP affected this emotional code inversion. See also Plummer (1995, p. 28).
147. See Stein (1997, pp. 154–83); Erzen (2006).
148. Brown (2002, p. 101). See also G. Harvey ([1997] 2000).
149. See, for example, the Zen Center of New York City, retrieved June 2012, www.mro.org/firelotus/. Concerning retreats associated with the human potential movement, see the Landmark Forum, retrieved June 2012, www .landmarkeducation.com. On *est* as an early example of the human potential movement, see Tipton (1982). On Pagan festivals, see Pike (2001). On contemporary Paganism and Pagan conversions, see Gallagher (1994); G. Harvey ([1997] 2000); Ezzy and Berger (2007); E. F. Johnston (2013).
150. "New Age of Aquarius: The Beginning to Spiritual Awakening," retrieved May 2012, http://www.new-age-of-aquarius.com/spiritual-awakening.html. On the post-1960s character of such movements, see Tipton (1982). See also Armstrong (2006a, p. xvii) on turning back to the Axial Age. Take as another example of a blending of the late modern with the ancient the conveners of one program using contemporary Internet technology to convey what they define to be an ancient shamanic wisdom that is much needed in this turbulent late modern era. Titling the series "Awakening the Cosmic Serpent: Shamanism and Plant Teachers in this Transformative Time," they use "state-of-the-art video streaming technology" to share information about ancient "indigenous shamanic ceremonies using psychedelic plants to open a path to deep personal insights and high spiritual truths." "Reality Sandwich," retrieved March 2013, http://realitysandwich .com/72276/cosmic_serpent/.
151. Gallagher (1994, p. 864).
152. Neopaganism is an umbrella category that includes a decentralized and very diverse set of organizations, ideas, and practices. Here, I provide an ideal-typical sketch that captures some of the most salient and overarching aspects of this community's worldview while ignoring nuanced, inter- and intracommunity distinctions. See M. Adler ([1979] 2006, pp. 1–21). On the connection between polytheism and the embrace of diversity, see p. 21.
153. Brown (2002, p. 103).
154. Ibid, p. 107. Alder ([1979] 2006, p. 4) writes that practitioners are "empowered by a sense of planetary crisis" and driven to address what they see as "an ecocidal nightmare."
155. M. Adler ([1979] 2006, pp. 13–21). See also G. Harvey (1999). See Ezzy and Berger (2007) on "individual seekership." Cf. Brown (2002, p. 119) on "like-minded seekers." See E. F. Johnston (2013) for an illuminating discussion of the structural continuity of Pagan conversion narratives.
156. For an example of atheists sharing stories about discovering and/or revealing their common worldview and shared cultural orientation, see the

forum titled "Coming Out Godless: What's Your Story?" at the website of Think Atheist, retrieved November 2012, http://www.thinkatheist.com /group/yourstory/forum.

157. Gallagher (1994, p. 857). Gallagher directly challenges M. Adler's ([1979] 2006) claim that there are no converts to Paganism.

158. Brown (2002, pp. 109–10).

159. Marion Zimmer Bradley depicts this historical perspective in her 1982 novel *The Mists of Avalon*. Bradley portrays the rise of Christianity to coincide with an increasing retreat of Avalon, the fictional center of pagan spiritualism, into the "mists." Paganism is symbolically both present and increasingly obscured with the development of Christian feudal Europe.

160. See Pike (2001, pp. 19–26) on the Pagan festival as the antithesis to "mundania."

161. I am broadening this point made by Weil (1975, p. 23) when discussing Axial Age breakthroughs.

CHAPTER THREE

1. Mills ([1959] 2000, p. 3).

2. Doe (1991). "Jane Doe," it was later revealed publicly, was a pseudonym for Jennifer Freyd's mother, Pamela.

3. Freyd (1996, p. 197).

4. J. E. Davis (2005a). I rely heavily on Davis's constructionist analysis of this phenomenon throughout. See also Whittier (2009).

5. Bedrock publications include Judith L. Herman's ([1981] 2000) *Father-Daughter Incest* and, later, the controversial survivor manual *The Courage to Heal* (Bass and Davis 1988). Many of these activists criticized core psychoanalytic ideas that root psychological distress in idiosyncratic internal conflicts. Very early in his career, Freud attributed "hysteria" in his female patients to premature sexual experiences, but he soon rejected this idea in favor of his oedipal theory, a principle that shifts the cause of a woman's psychological distress from the real activity of sexual abuse to her fantasies of seduction. According to his feminist critics, when Freud advanced his oedipal theory, he laid the groundwork for psychiatric professionals to question the reality of sexual abuse experiences that need to be acknowledged in order for victims of such abuse to heal. By focusing on unresolved internal conflicts and seduction fantasies, they argued, psychoanalysts are strengthening the socially ingrained failure of a patriarchal culture to acknowledge abuse as a widespread social problem. Moving away from psychoanalysis, these feminists began to emphasize a model that more closely resembles Pierre Janet's notion of dissociation where, as Jospeh E. Davis (2005a, p. 135) notes, "dissociated memories are relatively intact and recoverable, not mediated in the unconscious as with repression." For Freud's seduction theory, see Freud ([1896] 1984). On this conflict more generally,

see Masson (1984); J. L. Herman (1992, pp. 13–18); Zaretsky (2004, p. 29); J. E. Davis (2005a, p. 90).

6. See "Take Back the Night: Shatter the Silence, Stop the Violence," retrieved March 2012, http://www.takebackthenight.org/net.html.

7. DeGloma (2007).

8. Plummer (1995, p. 49–61). See also Best (1997); Stein (2011).

9. J. E. Davis (2005a) argues, "Thus, with their public stories, these early survivor-activists also validated the collective story by working to persuade other women of the personal benefits of mapping their experience in light of this general narrative framework and taking action accordingly" (p. 106). There was an implication "that speaking out by victims, even if done anonymously, would help bring an end to abuse. This belief in effect created a moral responsibility for victims to come forward" (p. 107).

10. Referring to the impact of the movement to define domestic abuse, Loseke (1992, p. 156) notes that this movement called into question the most extreme aspects of "the patriarchal scheme of interpretation and interpretations positively evaluating family privacy and stability." The challenge mounted by the recovered memory movement was fundamentally similar in this regard.

11. Website of the False Memory Syndrome Foundation, retrieved July 2009, http://fmsfonline.org/about.html.

12. M. B. Scott and Lyman (1968, p. 46) show this to be a characteristic of all actions that demand accounts. See also Orbuch (1997).

13. Berger and Luckmann (1966, p. 160); see also Berger (1963, pp. 56–58); Snow and Machalek (1983, pp. 266–69).

14. On historical discontinuity, see E. Zerubavel (2003, pp. 82–100). Such a historical discontinuity differs from the process that Teeger and Vinitzky-Seroussi (2007, pp. 64–67) call "divorcing the past." While awakeners make a sharp distinction between their past and present mindsets, the past is continually relevant to their personal accounts.

15. E. Zerubavel (1997, pp. 17–18, 96–101; 2003, pp. 18–19, 28–30).

16. E. Zerubavel (1997, pp. 87–92). See also Lewis (1975); Y. Zerubavel (1995).

17. Halbwachs ([1950] 1980, p. 26). See also E. Zerubavel (2003, p. 3) for a discussion of the way one experiences "a remarkable *existential fusion* of one's personal history with that of the communities to which one belongs" (emphasis added). See also Plummer (1995, pp. 40–41).

18. The process that Erving Goffman describes as "keying" ([1974] 1986, pp. 40–82) is generally relevant to my notion of mnemonic transformation. Goffman introduces the concept of keying to describe "the set of conventions by which a given activity, one already meaningful in terms of some primary framework, is transformed into something patterned on this activity but seen by participants to be something quite else" (pp. 43–44). David A. Snow and colleagues (1986) develop this notion with their concept of "frame transformation." However, while "keying intendedly leads all participants

to have the same view of what is going on" (Goffman [1974] 1986, p. 84), awakeners' mnemonic transformations are typically quite contentious. Awakeners who transform their definition of past experiences would claim that they are discrediting what Goffman calls a fabrication (pp. 83–86, 103–16). Those who oppose them would claim that the awakeners are miskeying (pp. 311–21) those past experiences, transforming the meaning of the past incorrectly and that such a transformation is not justified or credible.

19. On the cultural significance of the creation narrative, see Bamyeh (2001).

20. Awakening narratives convey what Alfred Schutz ([1932] 1967, pp. 86–96) calls "because-motives" (which provide an explanation "in terms of an actor's past experiences") and "in-order-to motives" (which provide an explanation in terms of future-oriented objectives). On future oriented projects, see pp. 57–63. For various takes on future projection, see also Giddens (1991, p. 72); Kerby (1991, pp. 19–20, 83); Emirbayer and Mische (1998); Loseke (2001, pp. 118–20); Mische (2008, 2009); Cerulo (2009).

21. To say, for example, in the words of John Newton, "I *once* [. . .] was *blind*, but *now* I *see*" is to make a distinction between one's past mindset (constrained or limited by one's metaphoric "blindness") and one's future-oriented outlook (emancipated by a newly acquired "sight"). Notably, the second half of Newton's phrase is redundant. One cannot (re)define one's past by asserting one's once-suffered "blindness" without implying one's current and ongoing ability to "see."

22. On the rerouting of collective timelines, see Benford (2002, p. 55), who argues that social "movement actors seek to insert themselves, individually and collectively, into an extant narrative . . . to bring about change, to create a new narrative." See also Robin Wagner-Pacifici (2005, p. 14), who shows how performative acts of surrendering "interrupt and reroute specific historical timelines and alter identities and fealties."

23. Rodgers (1995, p. 4). See also Boellstorff (2009, p. 355).

24. Frank (1995, p. 132).

25. Melissa's story (2005). Note that I use bracketed ellipses to indicate omissions in excerpts from awakening narratives.

26. In Goffman's ([1974] 1986) terms, Melissa is claiming that the perpetrator strategically created a fabrication (pp. 83–123), which caused her to "upkey" (pp. 312–14) the activity.

27. Ronn Cantu's story (2007a).

28. Ronn Cantu's story (2007b).

29. Scott Anderson's story (2008).

30. Giddens (1991, p. 72).

31. J. E. Davis (2005a, p. 192).

32. Berger (1963, p. 58).

33. Kristi's story (2009).

34. O'Rourke (1989).

35. Augustine ([397–398] 1961, pp. 49–51).

36. Anonymous survivor(1) (2008; emphasis added). Note that I use pseudonyms when discussing anonymously published personal stories to preserve the flow of the text.

37. On the politics of denial, as well as on the ways interpersonal interaction can create an imperative to social silence, see E. Zerubavel (2006, pp. 33–45). J. E. Davis (2005a, p. 135) writes, "The concept of a society-wide silence and denial, for example, had its analogue in the amnesia and defenses of the victim," and the "disorder was conceptualized to reflect the collective story already worked out by movement activists."

38. Christie Hubbard's story (2007; emphasis added).

39. Ronn Cantu's story (2007a).

40. Terr (1994, pp. 1–60).

41. Chopin ([1899] 2004).

42. Feinberg (1996).

43. Martin Briseno's story (2007).

44. Ibid.

45. Fritz Williams's story (2004).

46. Murdoch ([2003] 2008, pp. 23–36).

47. M. Adler ([1979] 2006, p. 9), for example, refers to the now-defunct Neopagan journal *The Julian Review*.

48. Murdoch ([2003] 2008, p. 11).

49. Ibid.

50. Wuthnow (1987, p. 161) also notes that Constantine's official recognition of Christianity allowed it "to expand beyond the relatively narrow niche it had previously occupied among the urban merchant class. As Christianity diffused among the population at large, which consisted mainly of the rural poor, it encountered a different type of family structure—a structure that had supported local goddess cults for several centuries."

51. Charles's story (2003).

52. Parker (2012).

53. See Wieland (2000).

54. Examples abound of different public actors who announce particular moral, political, or scientific objectives in opposition to the objectives they previously advocated. Mark Lynas (2013), for example, once a strong vocal opponent of the genetically modified (GM) food industry reinterpreted his prior anti-GM campaign and community as "an anti-science movement" and "anti-science environmentalism." Claiming he has now "discovered science," he asserts that "[w]hat we didn't realize at the time was that the real Frankenstein's monster was not GM technology, but our reaction against it," and "my cherished beliefs about GM turned out to be little more than green urban myths." David Blankenhorn (2012), founder of the conservative Institute for American Values and longtime opponent of gay marriage, expressed a similar reversal of public position when he embraced gay marriage. Likewise, Jason Childs (2011), a self-described

former "right-wing" Evangelical pastor who now directs the liberal Center for Progress in Alabama, uses his awakening to establish a political claim about his former sociomental community, writing, "I want you to know that the fundamentalist political movement is the beginning of a cultural revolution that will take our nation to a very dark place."

55. See Halbwachs ([1950] 1980, pp. 50–55). See also Halbwachs ([1925] 1992b); Olick and Robbins (1998, p. 111); Olick (1999a, p. 335).

56. Halbwachs ([1950] 1980, p. 72).

57. Olick (1999a, p. 335). See also B. Schwartz (1982, p. 375).

58. Halbwachs ([1925] 1992a, p. 224); Halbwachs ([1950] 1980, p. 51).

59. Scholars working within the broad symbolic interactionist tradition have explored how group-level processes and pressures shape the way individuals adopt particular ways of remembering that are rooted in a particular community or institution. Many have illuminated the ways that individuals reconstruct their autobiographies and redefine the past to conform to group-level autobiographical norms. See, for example, Goffman (1961; [1974] 1986, p. 521); Garfinkel ([1967] 1996); Hankiss (1981); Denzin (1989a, 1989b); Frank (1993, 2000); Fivush, Haden, and Reese (1996); Mason-Schrock (1996); Gergen and Gergen (1997); Vinitzky-Seroussi (1998); Irvine (1999, 2000); Ezzy (2000); Loseke (2001); J. E. Davis (2005a, 2005b); Kidron (2004); Howard (2006, 2008); LaRossa and Sinha (2006); DeGloma (2007); E. F. Johnston (2013); Meanwell (2013). On the impact of the group on individual remembering, see also Pillemer (1998).

60. On anniversaries, see Olick (1999b); Mueller (2010). On the sociological significance of calendars, see E. Zerubavel (1977, 1981). On the significance of museums as spaces of collective memory, see Teeger and Vinitzky-Seroussi (2007). On the mnemonic significance of monuments, see Wagner-Pacifici and Schwartz (1991). On collective memory and commemoration more generally, see, for example, Olick and Levy (1997); Shils (1981); B. Schwartz (1982); Spillman (1998); Vinitzky-Seroussi (2001, 2002). On iconic or mythic stories, see, for example, Hay (1969); B. Schwartz (1987); Y. Zerubavel (1995); A. D. Smith (1999).

61. Aside from the symbolic interactionists who focus on group processes, those relatively few scholars who approach autobiography from a social memory studies perspective tend to treat personal memory as the constructed consequence of broader social or demographic variables. See, for example, Howard Schuman and Jacqueline Scott (1989, pp. 359, 378, 380), who, in an important study of "the intersection of personal and national history," argue that an individual's age and location within a generational cohort largely determine which national events take on particular meaning for that individual. When individuals name a socially shared event as important, they "show a strong tendency to explain their choice in terms of straightforward personal experience at that time." From this perspective, socially situated personal experience makes events more memorable. In

this vein, Barry Schwartz and Howard Schuman (2005, pp. 183, 200) argue that collective memory scholars should "bring individual men and women into our understanding of collective memory" by focusing on "individuals' beliefs about the past." These scholars take important steps to include autobiography (or personal experience) as an analytic domain in social memory studies. However, such a focus leaves open several questions, particularly those consistent with a strong program in cultural sociology. Absent are important discussions of how individuals use deeply ingrained cultural structures and formulas to remember, as well as how individuals use their personal memories to shape broader mnemonic norms. For a more general social theory of generations, see also Mannheim ([1928] 1952). For additional studies related to this general discussion, see F. Davis (1979); Lomsky-Feder (1995); Pillemer (1998); Schuman, Akiyama, and Knäuper (1998); Schuman, Vinitzky-Seroussi, and Vinokur (2003); Teeger (2014).

62. For an important statement about the uses of collective memory, see Zelizer (1995, p. 226), who writes, "At the heart of memory's study, then, is its usability, its invocation as a tool to defend different aims and agendas." For exceptional studies that treat autobiography and memory as creative cultural strategies, see Frank (1995); Vinitzky-Seroussi (1998); Ezzy (2000).

63. Vinitzky-Seroussi (2002).

64. B. Schwartz and Schuman (2005, p. 185).

65. H. S. Becker ([1963] 1997); Wagner-Pacifici and Schwartz (1991, pp. 389–92); Fine (2001, pp. 62–63). This view is consistent with Andrew Abbott's (2005, p. 1) argument "that we should reinstate individuals as an important force in history." Abbott is interested specifically in the structural "conditions that make particular individuals particularly important."

66. Olick (1999a, pp. 333, 336) calls for a "multidimensional rapprochement between individualist and collectivist approaches" and the development of "an integrated paradigm that identifies the unique structures involved in each of these [individual memory and collective memory] and shows how they are related." This multidimensional and multilayered view of social memory is also advanced by E. Zerubavel (1997, 2003), who weaves back and forth between individual and collective cases to show that mnemonic norms, traditions, and battles manifest in formally similar and patterned ways at various levels of analysis. In addition, a multidimensional approach to social memory studies is also strengthened by Gary Alan Fine and Aaron Beim (2007, p. 2), who suggest that "a fusion of interactionism and collective memory research is conducive to interpreting memory as both process and product." Their call to bridge process- and product-oriented approaches to social memory studies emphasizes, among other things, the analytic need to consider the connection between the microlevel agentic construction of memory and the macrolevel collective mnemonic order.

67. Olick and Robins (1998, p. 112). See also Zelizer (1995, pp. 223–24).

68. P. Smith (2005, p. 33).

69. E. Zerubavel (1997, pp. 97–99; 2003, pp. 99–100, 105–10).
70. The term *memory war* is commonly used to refer to the ongoing dispute in the field of psychology over the veracity of recovered memories of child sexual abuse.
71. Foucault (1977, p. 160); Y. Zerubavel (1995, pp. 10–12, 197–213); Olick and Robbins (1998, pp. 126–28); Lorek (2012).
72. Collective memory scholars have illustrated the multivocal (Wagner-Pacifici and Schwarz 1991) and fragmented (Vinitzky-Seroussi 2002) character of commemorative activities. In highlighting the polysemic character of events, I build on these studies to elucidate the ways an event's public meaning depends on the position one holds in relation to deep-seated intercommunity conflicts over the nature of that event.
73. Olick (1999a, pp. 338–39). See also Levy (1999, p. 51).
74. Halbwachs ([1925] 1992b, p. 40).
75. Mills ([1959] 2000, p. 8).
76. B. Schwartz and Schuman (2005, p. 200).
77. Smelser (2004, p. 272).
78. Polletta (2006, p. viii).
79. Loseke (2009, pp. 499, 504, and 516).
80. See, for example, the website of the organization Vets for Freedom, retrieved June 2008, http://www.vetsforfreedom.org/default.aspx.
81. Anuradha Bhagwati's story (2008; emphasis added). Expressing a similar connection between personal and collective discovery, one IVAW newsletter describes the group's *"collective* experiences of *personal* transformation from warriors to fighters for peace and justice" (*Iraq Veterans Against the War Newsletter*, December 10, 2012, p. 1; emphasis added).
82. Kerby (1991, pp. 49 and 50). See also C. Taylor (1985, pp. 45–76).
83. On historical analogies, see E. Zerubavel (2003, pp. 48–52). See also May (1973); Khong (1992). Snow and Machalek (1983) argue that the "suspension of analogical reasoning" is a defining feature of "the convert as a social type." However, I have not found this to be the case with awakening stories. In fact, awakeners of all types commonly reason with analogies (both synchronic and diachronic) to redefine the past.
84. Victor Blazier's story (2008b).
85. For the concept of "frame alignment," see Snow et. al. (1986). On the notion of a temporal frame bridging strategy, see DeGloma (2009, p. 115).
86. See P. Smith (2005, p. 17).
87. Gross (2005, pp. 295–96).
88. Loseke (2009, p. 517).
89. Crossman (1950).
90. Horowitz (1989, pp. 55–56).
91. Website of the Church of Jesus Christ of Latter-Day Saints, retrieved July 2009, http://www.mormon.org/mormonorg/eng/basic-beliefs /the-restoration-of-truth/the-restoration-of-truth.

92. Richard Gaines's story (2008; emphasis added).
93. Deborah Wright's story (2008).
94. Halbwachs ([1950] 1980, p. 68).
95. Doctrine and Covenants 93:29. As articulated by Brigham Young, an iconic cognitive and mnemonic authority figure to Mormons, this faith-based collective memory means that "[t]here is not a person here to-day but what is a son or daughter of that Being [God]. In the spirit world [heaven] their spirits were first begotten and brought forth, and they lived with their parents for ages before they came here [to earth]. This, perhaps, is hard for many to believe, but it is the greatest nonsense in the world not to believe it. If you do not believe it, cease to call Him Father; and when you pray, pray to some other character" (Young 1857, p. 289).
96. See Ostler (1982).
97. Exmo #2 (2007).
98. Koestler (1950, pp. 17, 34–35, 55–56; emphasis added).
99. Cierra's story (2004).
100. On reconversion, see Menon (2003). Menon details "the politics of conversion" in this study of Hindus who convert to Christianity and then back to Hinduism, showing that such conversions and reconversions reveal the work of competing religious authorities. See also Glazier (2003) on "Spiritual Baptists who become Rastafarians and then become Spiritual Baptists again."
101. Reawakening stories follow a pattern that is even more generally reflected in what Christopher Booker (2004, pp. 193–214) calls "rebirth" tales such as "Sleeping Beauty." In such stories, Booker writes, "A hero or heroine falls under a dark spell which eventually traps them in some wintry state, akin to living death: physical or spiritual imprisonment, sleep, sickness, or some other form of enchantment. For a long time they languish in this frozen condition. Then a miraculous act of redemption takes place, focused on a particular figure who helps to liberate the hero or heroine from imprisonment. From the depths of darkness they are brought up into glorious light" (p. 194).
102. Olick and Robbins (1998, p. 126).
103. Nicolosi (1993, p. 7; emphasis added).
104. Ibid., p. 10 (emphasis added).
105. Ibid., p. 12 (emphasis in original). In a related point, Nicolosi tells his patient Father John, "Most homosexuals overfocus on the penis. So much of homosexual behavior is like two little boys playing *show me yours, I'll so you mine*. It's fetishistic behavior. The penis has an important symbolic power. It's a symbol of masculinity that you feel you need but don't have. Some trauma, some gap in your development seeks fulfillment in phallic fixation. That's part of the homosexuality" (p. 47; emphasis in original).
106. Although reparative therapists have put forth various ideas about the exact causes of homosexuality, their approach typically involves looking to what

they deem to be abnormalities (often directly or indirectly pertaining to Freud's theories of oedipal development) in a patient's early childhood relationships. See also, for example, Bieber et. al. (1962); Socarides (1968); Nicolosi (1991, 2009); Van Den Aardweg (1997); Cohen (2006).

107. Alan Medinger's story (2008; emphasis added).

108. Jerry A. Armelli's story (2000).

109. Frank's story (2000).

110. Rob's story (2004).

111. Richard Cohen's story (2000). Cohen (2006, pp. 3–15).

112. As reported in Nicolosi (1993, p. 86).

113. Chuck's story (2012).

114. Spillman and Conway (2007). See also Connerton (1989).

115. This foundational tenet of the gay pride movement is literally inverted by Richard Cohen, who titles his 2006 reparative manual, as well as his personal story (pp. 3–15), *Coming Out Straight*.

116. On the term *ex-ex-gay*, see Ford (2009).

117. Brian Mahieu's story (2006; emphasis in original).

118. Paul Williams's story (2000).

119. Tracey St. Pierre's story (2000).

120. Bass and Davis (1988, p. 22).

121. See J. E. Davis (2005a, pp. 151, 179–80). DeGloma (2007).

122. Linda's story (2006).

123. Ann's story (2006).

124. Michele's story (2008).

125. Desi ([1983] 1991, pp. 139–41).

126. This point is central to J. E. Davis's (2005b) constructionist analysis of such "accounts of innocence." See also Alexander (2004b) on the coding of trauma narratives more generally.

127. Beth Rutherford's story (1998a).

128. See also DeGloma (2007, p. 554).

129. See also J. E. Davis (2005b).

130. Anonymous retractor(1) (1996).

131. Trish's story (1996).

132. Diana Halbrooks's story (2007).

133. Ofshe and Watters (1994); Nathan and Snedeker (1995).

134. Shils (1981); Olick and Robbins (1998, p. 123).

CHAPTER FOUR

1. L. Davis (1990, p. 205). Note that I use bracketed ellipses to indicate omissions in excerpts from awakening narratives.

2. This quotation is widely attributed to Mahatma Ghandi.

3. V. Turner ([1964] 1970, pp. 93–111). Turner is building on Arnold Van Gennep's (1960) *The Rites of Passage*.

4. V. Turner ([1964] 1970, pp. 96, 98–99, 105, 106, 108).
5. Durkheim ([1912] 1995, pp. 303–29).
6. V. Turner ([1964] 1970, p. 93).
7. See also Patterson (2002); Germana (2003). Cf. McAdams (1993) on "pivotal scenes." See also G. Becker (1997, pp. 119–35).
8. E. Zerubavel (1991, p. 21–32).
9. On the social logic of periodization, see E. Zerubavel (1998). See also Berger (1963, p. 61); Strauss (1997); Lieblich, Tuval-Mashiach, and Zilber (1998, p. 106).
10. On the notion of sociomental lumping, see E. Zerubavel (1991, pp. 21–32). See also Brekhus (1996); Simpson (1996).
11. E. Zerubavel (1991, p. 27).
12. Brekhus (1996, 1998). See also B. Schwartz (1981, p. 39).
13. V. Turner ([1964] 1970).
14. Simmel ([1922] 1955). See also Gergen (1991).
15. As Mary Douglas ([1966] 2002, pp. 199, 141–72) has shown more generally, the boundaries or margins between polluted and pure groupings can be more highly marked than the contents they separate. See also Wuthnow (1987, p. 58); E. Zerubavel (1991, pp. 117–19). On managing boundaries between home and work, see Nippert-Eng (1996).
16. With regard to religious conversion, Stromberg (1993, p. 15) notes, "The conversion story manifests the same emotional themes and transformations that are said to have characterized the original conversion event."
17. E. Zerubavel (1991, pp. 21–32). Zerubavel uses the term *mental quantum leap* to describe the experience of traversing socially constructed boundaries. See Plummer (1995, p. 55) on "establishing a home."
18. Referring to Achilles, Plato indirectly compares the cave to Hades. See Francis MacDonald Cornford's comments in Plato ([ca. 380 BCE] 1941, p. 230).
19. Malcolm X (1964, p. 183). Malcolm X (who previously went by the name Malcolm Little) was convicted of larceny in 1946 and sentenced to ten years in prison. He began his sentence in Charlestown State Prison in Boston, Massachusetts. He was later transferred to Norfolk Prison, where he remained until his parole in 1952.
20. Koestler (1950, p. 67).
21. Prison serves the same purpose for Derek Vinyard, the fictional neo-Nazi turned antiracist in Tony Kaye's 1998 film *American History X*.
22. Lifton ([1973] 2005); Shay (1994).
23. See Simmel (1950c, pp. 402, 404).
24. Mills (1940); Burke ([1945] 1969).
25. In *The Varieties of Religious Experience*, William James ([1902] 1987, pp. 177–238) notes that religious conversions can be sudden or gradual and, citing Edwin Diller Starbuck ([1899] 1911), involuntary or voluntary. In these seminal works, both James and Starbuck reinterpret religious conversion

from a psychological perspective. From a sociological perspective, their theories exemplify a historical heightening of the cultural tension between psychological and religious realms of meaning. Analyzing the development of scientific knowledge, Thomas Kuhn ([1962] 1996) makes a similar distinction between sharp, sudden "paradigm shifts" and a more protracted, incremental accumulation of knowledge. Similarly, Murray S. Davis (1983, pp. 45–85) contrasts the "shock" that occurs with an immediate imposition of a sexual reality with the mental "slide" that occurs with a gradual easing into a sexual mindset. I build on these observations to show more generally how "sudden" and "gradual" awakenings are characteristic of two ideal-typical vocabularies of liminality that occur in different combinations in myriad stories across various realms of social life. See also Schutz (1945, pp. 552–53). For a discussion of the various types of religious conversion experiences, see Austin-Broos (2003). On the depictions of agency in self-stories about job loss, see Ezzy (2000).

26. Burke ([1945] 1969, p. 3).
27. Here, I combine Burke's ([1945] 1969) pentad schema (which includes awareness of the act, the scene, the agent, the attribution of agency, and the purpose behind the action) with Goffman's (1959) dramaturgical concepts (including props and other characters that make up the scenic front or setting of any performance) to depict the ways awakeners use rich vocabularies of liminality to convey major changes of mind.
28. B. Schwartz (1981).
29. Martin Briseno's story (2007).
30. Fiona's story (2005).
31. Stromberg (1993, p. 97).
32. Shadow's story (2003).
33. Robin's story (2005).
34. McAdams (1993, p. 296).
35. Sagha's story (2003).
36. Anonymous survivor(2) (2003; emphasis added). Note that I use pseudonyms when discussing anonymously published material to preserve the flow of the text.
37. George Franklin was tried and convicted in 1990 based on Eileen's testimony and sentenced to life in prison. He was released without retrial in 1996 after, among other factors, the veracity of Eileen's account was called into question. See Denzel (2014).
38. Terr (1994, pp. 2–3; emphasis added).
39. Debbie David's story (1996).
40. In a related observation, Loseke (2001, p. 117) notes that the narrative plot that positions domestic abusers in control of the abusive dynamic "also can be used to construct women as out of control of their own *emotions*" (emphasis in original).
41. Gerilena Spillios's story (1993, p. 341; emphasis in original).

42. Frank (1995, p. 115).

43. In this sense these figures serve as narrative manifestations of what George Herbert Mead ([1934] 1967, p. 154) calls the "generalized other," though at the level of the autobiographical community. They represent the moral voice of the new collective "which gives to the individual his [or her] unity of self."

44. Hobbes ([1651] 1962). Hobbes describes both the moment and the forfeiture of agency necessary to the rise of an enlightened state when he writes, "The only way to erect such a common power [commonwealth] [. . .] is [for the people] to confer all their power and strength upon one man, or upon one assembly of men, that may reduce all their wills, by plurality of voices, unto one will" (p. 132). For Hobbes, civic enlightenment required a forfeiture of will in a single collective act. Other modern philosophers, as we will see in the next section, used a different narrative model.

45. Dustin Fadale's story (2008).

46. Cothran (2008). See also Hart (2007). Charlene's story illustrates what Max Weber ([1915] 1946, p. 325) describes as an "active asceticism that is a God-willed *action* of the devout who are God's tools" (emphasis in original).

47. Rod Manney's story (2008; emphasis in original).

48. Anna Buttimore's story (2008).

49. Richard Johnson's story (2008).

50. Mountaingirl's story (2007).

51. See Tipton (1982, p. 237) on this phenomenon as experienced by adherents of new religious movements of the 1970s.

52. C. L. Hanson's story (2008; emphasis added).

53. Kim's story (2010; emphasis in original).

54. Arnold Steiber's story (2003; emphasis added).

55. Adam Charles Kokesh's story (2007).

56. Collier (1989, pp. 61–62; emphasis added).

57. David Fettke's story (2000).

58. For a discussion of "body memories" related to child sexual abuse, see Bass and Davis (1988, pp. 74–75).

59. On nonbiological actors, see Cerulo (2009).

60. See E. Zerubavel (2003, pp. 34–35).

61. Burke ([1945] 1969, p. 3).

62. V. Turner ([1964] 1970, p. 96).

63. Fritz Williams's story (2004).

64. Ben Newman's story (2007).

65. I use the term *reason* very generally here to refer to the process of actively thinking through a situation or problem. Those who contrast reason and religion are expressing a cultural tension that emerged between political and religious realms of meaning during the age of Western Enlightenment. Using a more general conception—i.e., "the mental powers concerned with forming conclusions, judgments, or inferences" (Dictionary.com

Unabridged, s.v. "reason," accessed March 26, 2014)—one can stress the process of reasoning within the religious realm of cultural life as well.

66. See Rousseau ([1755] 1994).
67. Bill Kempton's story (2006).
68. Charles's story (2003).
69. Moonshine (2008; emphasis in original).
70. Dbradhud's story (2008).
71. RuneWolf's story (2012).
72. Ibid.
73. Rob's story (2004).
74. Nicolosi (1993, p. 50). In 1962, thirty years before the publication of Nicolosi's book and the founding of the National Association for Research and Therapy of Homosexuality, Irving Beiber and colleagues (1962, p. 278) stressed the necessity of such a commitment when they suggested that reparative therapeutic success often requires more than 350 hours of treatment. In Ronald Bayer's (1981, p. 33) words, these psychiatrists were arguing that successful sexual reconversion required "a willingness to embark on the long, difficult, and often frustrating course of analytic therapy."
75. Bayer (1981, p. 56).
76. Scott Anderson's story (2008; emphasis added).
77. Frank (1995, p. 115). On quest stories, see also Booker (2004, pp. 69–86).
78. Dan's story (2008).
79. Bashō ([1694] 1991, p. 1).
80. Anonymous survivor(3) (2003).
81. Anonymous survivor(4) (2003).
82. Lilita's story (2003).
83. Beth Rutherford's story (1998a, 1998b).
84. On turning points, see Gergen and Gergen (1997); Abbott (2001); E. Zerubavel (2003); LaRossa and Sinha (2006).
85. Douglass Eckhoff's story (2008; emphasis added).
86. Stephen Merritt's story (2008; emphasis in original). For a discussion of conversion and reconversion as a process of spiritual journey or drift though the lifecourse, see Glazier (2003).
87. Stephen Merritt's story (2008). Similarly, Jean, a Christian convert analyzed by Stromberg (1993, pp. 44–45), describes searching for, and falling short of finding, a feeling of connection at work and with communities of gay men before finding her salvation in evangelical Christianity.
88. Jerry A. Armelli's story (2000).
89. Sweeney (2005, pp. 47–55).
90. Bellah (2011, p. 579). See also Nightingale (2004, pp. 105–6).
91. MacIntyre (1981, p. 219). See Plummer (1995, pp. 54–56, 83–86) on the "journey" plot.
92. See Lempert (1996, p. 25). See also Loseke (2001, p. 109).
93. Cheryl Johnson's story (2000; emphasis added).

94. Kathryn's story (2009; emphasis added).
95. On legato and staccato structures of time, see E. Zerubavel (2003, pp. 34–35).
96. Reverend Jerry Stephenson's story (2000).
97. Armstrong (2004). See especially pp. 55–59 for her elaboration on the metaphor of the spiral staircase.
98. Kristi's story (2009).
99. Arguello (1989, p. 111).
100. Ifshin (1989, pp. 81–88).
101. Christie Hubbard's story (2007).
102. See Jacobs (2007).
103. See Burke ([1945] 1969, pp. 3–20). These two ideal-typical vocabularies of liminality can also be seen in Buddhist and Christian architecture. For example, the Buddhist Borobudur Temple (Java, Indonesia) requires visitors to journey some distance, through various stages, to arrive at the top. In contrast, the Catholic Sistine Chapel places the visitor immediately under a magnificent depiction of God. Thanks to my student, Bradley Kingston, for bringing this to my attention.
104. Koestler ([1964] 1976, p. 211). Taking a somewhat similar position with regard to recovered memories of child sexual abuse, Schooler (2001, p. 118; emphasis in original) argues that the feeling of personal shock or surprise that accompanies newly recovered memories does not necessarily mean that the memories themselves are "new." Rather, individuals' "marked sense of 'aha' or surprise when they recall an event," according to Schooler, is often reflective of their "immediate *phenomenology at the time of recollection*," which often influences their "deliberative ruminations about the prior degree of forgetting."
105. Koestler (1950, p. 23).
106. Kuhn ([1962] 1996).
107. Ibid, pp. 52–53.
108. Weber ([1903–1917] 1949, p. 90; emphasis in original).
109. Coser (1971, p. 223).
110. Conway and Siegelman ([1978] 2005).
111. Gladwell ([2000] 2002).
112. This transformative moment in the film has become a more widely used metaphor. For example, an ex-Mormon who goes by the name "Astarte Moonsilver" (2007) compares her awakening to Neo's when she writes, "If I had stayed in my place and avoided the Internet, I wouldn't have woke up from the Matrix." In this case, Astarte Moonsilver describes a direct contradiction of her will and intention. Whereas she sought information to defend her Mormon worldview, she was thwarted and thrown into an awakening experience. Astarte Moonsilver's reference to Neo's awakening spurred several comments from other ex-Mormons who identified with the metaphor she built into her vocabulary of liminality. Dave, a site administrator, writes, "Welcome Astartemoonsilver—You are not alone in

feeling like you woke up from the Matrix. It ain't always pretty here outside the Matrix, but it is real" (Dave's story 2007). Tthom writes, "Like
Astartemoonsilver, my waking from Mormonism was a real Matrix moment" (Tthom's story 2007). As Loseke (2001, p. 114) argues with regard
to domestic violence treatment centers, such responses from more-
established group members prompt newer members to conform to storytelling norms. See also Kidron (2004).

113. This tension between the predetermined world of destiny and the agentic
world of choice is highlighted by the character of The Oracle, who in the
second film of the trilogy tells Neo, "You didn't come here to make the
choice, you already made it. You are here to understand why you made it."
On the distinction between the inevitable and the intentional as a fundamental aspect of culture, see Wuthnow (1987, p. 74). J. E. Davis (2005a,
p. 11) notes that our contemporary understanding of the self involves both
a view "of the self as (1) externally determined and as (2) autonomous, free
of external constraints."

114. Ronn Cantu's story (2007a).

115. APA (1994, pp. 424–29).

116. See Wieland (2000).

117. Anonymous Ex-Mormon(1) (2008).

118. Jerry A. Armelli's story (2000).

119. Likewise, Jim, the evangelical Christian convert described by Stromberg
(1993, p. 71), conveys a similar pivotal moment in his protracted conversion as a "very important dream in his 'spiritual quest.'"

120. Richard Cohen's story (2000).

121. Augustine ([397–398] 1961, pp. 177–78; emphasis added). Providing an
account that is remarkably similar to Augustine's, Dan P. McAdams's (1993,
p. 178) subject Shirley recounts, "[. . .] I couldn't find anything biblically to
undergird confirmation, and so I opened a book on church practice. And,
as I held the book, it just sort of fell open by itself and it went to the prerequisites for the ordained clergy. And I said, okay, you know, if this is what
you want, you've got it, and all of a sudden it was as if I could float. Every
care, everything went off of my shoulders and out of my body, and my
head was clear and the room was bright white. I mean it was just luminous,
and I sat awestruck. I have never felt like that before, and I have never
felt like that since, and from what I understand, I will never feel that way
again. But I know exactly what had happened, and I knew that I had been
touched and that I was in the presence of God."

122. Fischer ([1949] 1950, p. 222).

CHAPTER FIVE

1. Malcolm X (1964, p. 173).

2. Ibid., pp. 87–128.

3. In a similar statement, Eldridge Cleaver (1968, p. 16) writes, "I was very familiar with the Eldridge who came to prison, but that Eldridge no longer exists."

4. Nowhere in the New Testament is it reported that God changed Paul's name upon his conversion even though it is conventionally said to mark the difference between his pre- and postconversion selves. Acts 13:9 (New International Version) simply says, "Saul, who was also called Paul." The different versions of his name reflect the differing linguistic conventions of, on the one hand, the Hebrew-speaking Pharisees (and other Jewish sects based in Jerusalem) and, on the other hand, the Latin-speaking Roman ruling class (and Greek-speaking Hellenist-Jewish diaspora). However, the popular view that Paul's name was changed upon conversion underscores the way we associate such major changes of mindset with the adoption of an entirely new identity.

5. James Carroll (2001, p. 133) notes that the "slander of the Pharisees originates not in Jesus's contest with them but in the conflict of the second generation [Paul's generation] of his followers with the Pharisees." Highlighting the moral-coding in the Christian theological project, Jeffrey Alexander (2003, p. 113) notes that "the Christian devil was a means of separating the 'good religion' of Jesus from the evil (primarily Jewish) forces from which it had emerged."

6. Acts 22:3–5 (NIV). Note that I use bracketed ellipses in excerpts from awakening narratives to indicate omissions. It is written that "[w]hen they heard him speak to them in Aramaic [or, as noted, possibly Hebrew], they became very quiet" (Acts 22:2 [NIV]). His Semitic tongue, as implied by the account, marked his cultural upbringing as a Pharisee, which allowed him to gain a temporary respect from the crowd.

7. Acts 26:5, 9–11 (NIV).

8. On the dark and sinful nature of Paul's previous life, see also his well-known Epistle to the Romans, also known as the book of Romans, as well as Corinthians in which Paul writes, "For I am the least of the apostles and do not even deserve to be called an apostle, because I persecuted the church of God. But by the grace of God I am what I am" (Corinthians 15:9–10 [NIV]). Before becoming a Christian apostle, Paul took part in the stoning to death of Saint Stephen, the "first martyr" of Christianity. See Acts 7:54–59 (NIV). Some argue that it was Paul who agitated the crowd and thus condemned Stephen to die.

9. Generally speaking, *identity negations*—accounting for who one *is* by describing who one *is not*—take a variety of forms. For example, in the United States many individuals often consider themselves "white" by virtue of the fact that they do not fit into any of the more highly marked racial/ethnic categories (such as "black" or "Hispanic"). As Jamie L. Mullaney (2006) shows, vegans, virgins, nonsmokers, and straight-edge punks define their identities in negational contrast to those who eat meat, have sexual

intercourse, smoke cigarettes, and consume alcohol and drugs, respectively. Such identity negations also exist as durable cultural ascriptions. Thus, individuals who abandon or exit a long-held identity label like "nun" (see Ebaugh 1988) or "addict" (see Howard 2008, pp. 184, 187) typically must work hard to leave these labels behind precisely because their current identities are culturally perceived in light of their rejection of their former roles ("ex-nuns" or "recovering addicts"). On identity marking, see also Brekhus (1996, 1998).

10. Denzin (1989b, p. 73).

11. Herbert Blumer (1969, p. 62) uses the term *self-interaction* to refer to George Herbert Mead's ([1934] 1967) more elaborate description of inner dialogue.

12. Mead ([1934] 1967, pp. 155–56). See also Athens (1994); Perinbanayagam (2000).

13. Cooley (1922, p. 184).

14. Mead ([1934] 1967, p. 175).

15. Ibid., pp. 175–209.

16. Perinbanayagam (2000, p. 46). See also Bruner (1986, pp. 57–69) on the self as "transactional" in character.

17. Mead ([1934] 1967, p. 171). See also Athens (1994, p. 522).

18. Mead ([1934] 1967, p. 174); see also Mead (1932, pp. 68–90). See also Wiley (1994, pp. 40–73). Wiley elaborates on Mead's attention to temporality to theorize the self as a trialogic entity in which present self (the "I") engages with the past ("me") and, building on the pragmatism of Charles Sanders Peirce, a projected future self ("you"). As Ann Mische (2008, p. 371, n. 21) notes, "Mead's core idea of 'sociality' refers to the capacity of individuals to be both temporally and relationally in multiple systems at once. He argues that the human experience of temporality is based in the social character of 'emergence,' that is, in interrelated changes occurring throughout the multiple levels of organization within which human beings are embedded. The problematic experience of these intersecting changes leads to reflective evaluation of the past and deliberation over the future." See also Denzin (1989a, 1989b); Emirbayer and Mische (1998, p. 968); Cerulo (2009, pp. 537–39).

19. Athens (1994, p. 527).

20. Douglas Ezzy's (1998) cogent and compelling theory of narrative identity was influential here. Ezzy synthesizes Mead's conception of the self with Paul Ricoeur's (1984) theory of narrative identity and Erving Goffman's (1961) arguments about the institutional (contextual) impact on our autobiographical accounts.

21. From this perspective, our self-stories give form and meaning to what we understand as "lifestyle," and cultural contention often involves what Anthony Giddens (1991, p. 214) calls "a politics of lifestyle."

22. Giddens (1991, pp. 4–5).

23. Kerby (1991, p. 7).

24. Propp (1968, pp. 25–65).
25. As Anthony Paul Kerby (1991, p. 1) argues, "The self is perhaps best construed as a character not unlike those we encounter almost every day in novels, plays, and other story media. Such a self arises out of signifying practices rather than existing prior to them as an autonomous or Cartesian agent." From this perspective, the self is "a social and linguistic construct, a nexus of meaning rather than an unchanging entity" (p. 34).
26. MacIntyre (1981, p. 28).
27. Frank (1995, p. 128). Kerby (1991, p. 37) notes, "It is no accident that the word *person* derives from the Latin *persona*," which has explicit literary connotations.
28. On heroes and villains, see Wagner-Pacifici (1986, pp. 284–86). See also Alexander (2003, p. 110); P. Smith (2005, p. 22).
29. McAdams (1993, p. 315, n. 9).
30. Wuthnow (1989, p. 330). Wuthnow is describing the "*figural actors* who model appropriate ways of behaving" in the literature of the Enlightenment.
31. See Garfinkel ([1967] 1996); Mason-Schrock (1996); Rubin (2003); E. F. Johnston (2013).
32. Brekhus (2003, p. 29). See also Simmel ([1922] 1955, pp. 141–42) on the individual as the intersection of multiple social circles. Building on Simmel, Mische (2008, p. 43) argues that we can "consider individuals as the intersection of the set of groups through which they pass over time, that is, their trajectory of overlapping affiliations."
33. Stromberg (1993, p. 31). While Stromberg is referring to internal, emotional conflicts, I emphasize the ways that dueling characters represent broadly relevant moral and cultural tensions. See also Frank (1993) on a "rhetoric of self-change"; Wiley (1994, pp. 108–9) on "internal solidarity."
34. By using the term *moral career*, Goffman (1961, p. 128) is concerned with "the regular sequence of changes . . . in the person's self and in his framework of imagery for judging himself and others." As Anthony Giddens (1991, p. 79) argues, "disentangling . . . the true from the false self" allows one to act authentically in the world. One must achieve some sort of biographical continuity to achieve this sense of self-authenticity.
35. Gross (2005, p. 296). On the notion of the cultural "tool kit," see Swidler (1986).
36. Markus and Nurius (1986). As these authors note, "Some possible selves stand as symbols of hope, whereas others are reminders of bleak, sad, or tragic futures that are to be avoided" (p. 960).
37. MacIntyre (1981, p. 27).
38. Erikson (1966, p. 11). See also Wagner-Pacifici (1994, p. 45), who comments, "Melodrama can flatten the picture of social life, pitting the good against the bad rather than looking for possible points of interaction between parties."

39. Swartz (1997, p. 106). With my emphasis on autobiographical work, I take a narrative approach to the phenomenon that Pierre Bourdieu refers to as *habitus*. As with Bourdieu's concept, these narratives "generate and organize practices and representations" (Bourdieu 1990, p. 53). However, my notion of self-character schemes does not require relying on objective, structurally situated class positions as organizational/structuring categories. Further, viewing autobiographical storytelling as a speech act, I do not make a distinction between practical activity and discourse. See also Bourdieu (1984). For a critique of Bourdieu from the perspective of a strong program in cultural sociology, see Alexander and Smith (2003, p. 18). See also Tipton (1982, p. 236) on religious "conversion as a change of heart, mind, and way of life."

40. Gubrium and Holstein (1994, p. 694). While Gubrium and Holstein are contrasting two different family counseling programs, their argument applies to "local cultures" (p. 691) more generally.

41. Stromberg (1993, p. 76).

42. On this process of "othering," see Schwalbe et al. (2000, pp. 422–26).

43. Kerby (1991, p. 105).

44. Anonymous survivor(5) (2005). Note that I use pseudonyms when discussing anonymously published personal stories to preserve the flow of the text.

45. Goffman ([1974] 1986, p. 520).

46. See J. E. Davis (2005a, p. 145), who writes, "The term *survivor* has a more specific meaning. It connotes a present state of being and of understanding. To be an 'adult survivor' is to be a victim but one who has come to understand her childhood experience as sexual abuse. . . . The survivor rationale provides the interpretive framework of new understandings and accompanying emotion norms that define this identity change and its requirements." See also Loseke (2009, p. 505), who writes, "The cultural code of victim and the emotion code of sympathy are inextricably related." See also Plummer (1995, pp. 56, 75–77).

47. Elizabeth Godley's story (1994).

48. Anonymous Christian's story (2013; emphasis added).

49. Exmo #2 (2007; italics added, capital letters in original).

50. Horowitz (1989, p. 56).

51. Goffman ([1974] 1986, p. 521). As Wuthnow (1987, p. 73) points out, to repudiate a past version of self is to say that self is somehow not who one really is, not one's "true" self.

52. Tinkling Brass's story (2006).

53. Hamar's story (2007).

54. Charles's story (2003).

55. Kim's story (2010).

56. Crossman (1950, p. 11).

57. For critical discussions of this point, see Berman ([1970] 1980); C. Talyor (1991). See also J. E. Davis (2005a, pp. 259–62).

58. Cf. Plummer (1995, pp. 28, 154). Such a tension defines the character Jake Sully, the protagonist of James Cameron's 2009 film *Avatar*. As Jake transforms from a marine on an imperialist mission to one of the indigenous Na'vi tribe, he rediscovers his sense of pride and honor, commenting, "I barely remember my old life and it stuns me to think that I lived it."

59. Anonymous Ex-Mormon(1) (2008).

60. Brian Mahieu's story (2006).

61. Christine Bakke's story (2007).

62. Warmfuzzylogic's story (2008).

63. Rick's story (2009).

64. On the concepts of "appearance" and "manner," see Goffman's (1959) discussion of the personal front.

65. Brooke's story (2008, 2012).

66. Frank (2000, p. 138).

67. Malcolm X (1964, pp. 56–57).

68. Du Bois ([1903] 1995, pp. 45–46). Notably, Du Bois opens up this book with his own awakening story. After describing an incident from his childhood in which a white classmate rejected a card he offered, he writes, "Then it dawned on me with a certain suddenness that I was different from the others; or like, mayhap, in heart and life and longing, but shut out from their world by a vast veil" (p. 44). For Du Bois, to suffer from double consciousness is to be one who experiences a "contradiction of double aims" (p. 46) in that the self is composed of "two unreconciled strivings; two warring ideals," (p. 45) a socially situated conflict manifest in one's being.

69. Rod Manney's story (2008).

70. Bourdieu (1984, pp. 169–74). See also Swartz (1997, p. 109).

71. Rod Manney's story (2008).

72. On the adoption of new embodied practices by religious converts, see Norris (2003); Winchester (2008).

73. Luke 15:11–32 (NIV).

74. Sean's story (2007).

75. Daniel Blain's story (2008).

76. Victor Blazier's story (2008a).

77. Wagner-Pacifici (2005, p. 144). See also pp. 13–14, 135.

78. Ibid., p. 144.

79. Anonymous retractor(2) (1994; emphasis in original).

80. Ofshe and Watters (1994).

81. Jon Turner's story (2008).

82. Stieber and McCord (2012; emphasis added).

83. Markus and Nurius (1986, p. 958).

84. On this characteristic of dialogical others, see Frank (2000, p. 147).

85. Gayatri's story (2005).
86. If we revisit an account initially analyzed by Dan P. McAdams (1993, p. 181), we can see how the young man offering that account uses a passive voice to distance his present narrating self from his past doubting self. He switches to an active voice to portray the act of reembracing his religion (the bracketed comments and italics are mine). "[Active voice, present frame] I search for what is real. [passive voice, to articulate the transition to a past frame] At Saint Olaf College, my previous assumptions concerning the Bible, the nature of God, and my personal beliefs and experiences *were questioned* and—as I perceived it—threatened. This Bible *was said to be* non-authoritative. [. . .] God *was more a concept.* [. . .] My personal experience of conversion and of sensing God *was considered to be* a subjective emotional experience. [active voice, to begin the reawakening and mark the temporal division] I prayed and prayed and read a variety of books [. . .]."
87. Christine's story (1998).
88. Mary Ellen's story (2003).
89. Stromberg (1993, pp. 60–61), referring to a subject who recounts a dream, writes, "Jim consistently separates himself as narrator from himself as experiencer. . . . The adoption of the dreamer's voice is a means to separate the person talking in the interview from the dreamer." In such cases, he writes, "two separate voices are involved" (p. 70).
90. McAdams (1993, p. 274).
91. Dan's story (2008; emphasis added).
92. Ibid.
93. Yvonne's story (2005).
94. On rebirth stories, see Booker (2004, pp. 193–228). On the metaphor of the phoenix and rebirth, see Frank (1995, pp. 122–26). Such a narrative splitting strategy is also evident in Peter G. Stromberg's (1993, pp. 105–7) case of Jan, a religious convert who claims that she was a "real person [. . .] hidden in this fat person," portraying, in Stromberg's words, "her own birth out of the midst of her former overweight self."
95. Brian Mahieu's story (2006).
96. Ronn Cantu's story (2007a). Awakeners often capture the tension between temporally divided self-characters in the titles of their stories, such as when Kristi (2009) boastfully titles her account "Evangelical Creationist Turned Godless Evolutionist" or when Mike Thelnfidel (2011) titles his story "From Bible-Literalist Fundie to Outspoken Atheist."
97. Bellah (2011, p. 246). See also Hornung ([1995] 1999, pp. 3–4).
98. Cierra's story (2004).
99. Stromberg (1993, p. 101).
100. IVAW called this particular campaign "Operation First Casualty," arguing that the first casualty of war is truth and their duty, as veterans, is to expose this truth to public audiences.
101. On keying, see Goffman ([1974] 1986, pp. 40–82).

102. Paul Abernathy's story (2007).
103. Wacquant (2004, pp. 59–60). Building on Bourdieu's thinking about the body, Wacquant uses these words to describe the way professional prize fighters are "kinetically remodeled" (p. 60) and subject to "a particular (re)socialization of physiology" (p. 59). By portraying his past soldier self in a street theater reenactment, Paul describes his slip back into the socialized embodiment of that self that he most likely began to acquire as he was "kinetically remodeled" in boot camp and, later, at war.
104. Paul Abernathy's story (2007; emphasis added).
105. Frank's story (2000).
106. S. Fraser (1987, p. 7).
107. Pillemer (1998, p. 157).
108. Jared Hood's story (2007).
109. Anonymous Ex-Mormon(2) (2007; emphasis in original).
110. Erikson (1966, pp. 10–11). Cf. Plummer (1995, p. 178).
111. Such major changes of mind often occur independently of any change in physical, structural, or geographic location. Some awakeners remain tied to, or find themselves stuck in, their former communities after they have already mentally abandoned them. Such a situation is exemplified by the character Cuiqiao, the young Chinese peasant girl in Chen Kaige's 1984 film *Yellow Earth* (set in 1939). Cuiqiao experiences an awakening after an educated communist soldier (Gu) visits her isolated rural village in northern Shaanxi Province. After spending time with the young man and learning that communist women to the south, unlike herself, choose their own romantic partners, Cuiqiao comes to see her village to be, like Plato's cave, a space of darkness and confinement. Well before she attempts to physically leave her village (which presumably results in her drowning in the Yellow River), she experiences a sociomental migration. Her personal dissatisfaction transforms into a cognitive shift when she realizes another world is possible. Cuiqiao left her community and lifeworld in a subjective sense, despite her physical presence. Likewise, Edna Pontellier, the protagonist in Kate Chopin's *The Awakening*, suffers a fate similar to Cuiqiao's when, at the end of the novel, she ultimately swims into the Gulf of Mexico and drowns. Both characters drown (a death by actual suffocation to symbolize their social suffocation) after they awaken to discover their confinement but remain unable to transcend the physical and sociostructural boundaries that contain them.
112. Fabian (1983).
113. Mead ([1934] 1967, p. 154).

CHAPTER SIX

1. Dass (1978, opening and closing words to chapter 1). Note that I use bracketed ellipses in excerpts from awakening narratives to indicate omissions.

2. Das (1997, p. 3).

3. The first chapter of Ram Dass's book is titled "The Transformation: Dr. Richard Alpert, Ph.D., into Baba Ram Dass."

4. Herman Hesse's novel *Siddhartha* was first published in the United States in 1951 but only became widely popular during the 1960s and 1970s. The renowned Beat poet Allen Ginsberg, a friend of both Ram Dass and Bhagavan Das, published a poem titled "Ah, Bhagavan Das Singing" in 1972. Eastern spirituality continues to be widely influential today.

5. Karen Armstrong (2006b, p. xvii) argues, "In [later] times of spiritual and social crisis, men and women have constantly turned back to this [Axial] period for guidance." On this point, see also Dass ([1978] 1990, pp. xi–xii); Tipton (1982, p. 232).

6. See Buckser (2003).

7. Bellah (2011, p. 574).

8. Alexander (2007, p. 28).

9. In other words, awakening stories often implicitly disallow the type of communicative action Habermas (1987) advocates.

10. See also Wuthnow (1987, p. 160), who argues that "competing movements themselves add to the environmental uncertainty that ideologies attempt to restructure." See also Plummer (1995, pp. 161–64).

11. E. Zerubavel (1997, pp. 24–25).

12. See also Irvine (1999, p. 165), who argues that "people who, when faced with the loss of institutional anchors in their lives, hurried to restore structure and regain affiliation," and Austin-Broos (2003, p. 2) on religious conversion as "a quest for human belonging" and "a quest to be at home in a world experienced as turbulent or constraining or, in some particular way, as wanting in value."

13. Alexander (2004b, p. 12).

14. See Booker (2004, pp. 51–68). On progressive narratives, see also Gergen and Gergen (1997); Eyerman (2001); E. Zerubavel (2003); LaRossa and Sinha (2006).

15. See Washington (1901).

16. Halbwachs ([1950] 1980, p. 51).

17. On the sociology of time, see E. Zerubavel (1979, 1985, 2003); Flaherty (2011).

18. See Ricoeur (1984); Somers (1994); E. Zerubavel (2003).

19. E. Zerubavel (1998); see also Lieblich, Tuval-Mashiach, and Zilber (1998).

20. Such a strategy is extended and strikingly evident in the case of the transmission of trauma across generations. See Kidron (2004); DeGloma (2009); Stein (2009a, 2009b).

21. E. Zerubavel (2003, pp. 37–54).

22. Fleck ([1935] 1979); Mannheim (1936); Kuhn ([1962] 1996).

23. Mannheim (1936, p. 268).

24. Ibid., p. 269.

25. One exception to the latter point is Patricia Hill Collins (2000, pp. 102, 116, 147), who considers the published autobiographies of prominent African American women as evidence of the experiences typically shared by African American women in general, experiences that, according to Collins, provide a social standpoint that serves as a basis for their unique knowledge of the world. However, Collins limits her analysis to a socio-political evaluation of these accounts. She does not consider the common strategic use or deeper cultural significance of autobiography in the broader cultural field.
26. Fuller ([1998] 2002, p. x).
27. Mannheim (1936, p. 188).
28. See Stromberg (1993, p. 11) on religious conversion narratives as ritual activity.
29. Burke ([1945] 1969).
30. Goffman (1959).
31. Austin (1962); Searle ([1969] 1999). See also Kerby (1991); Frank (1995); Plummer (1995, pp. 20–24). Vinitzky-Seroussi (1998, pp. 59–77); Alexander (2004b, pp. 11–12); Wagner-Pacifici (2005, p. 144).
32. Tipton (1982, p. 243; emphasis in original).
33. Alexander (2004a, p. 202). See also Olick (1999a, pp. 338–39); Vinitzky-Seroussi (2002, pp. 32, 46–47).

References

Abbott, Andrew. 2001. *Time Matters: On Theory and Method*. Chicago: University of Chicago Press.

———. 2005. "The Historicity of Individuals." *Social Science History* 29 (1): 13–29.

Adam Charles Kokesh's story. 2007. "The Humanity Shield." Retrieved June 2007. http://www.ivaw.org/node/772.

Adler, Margot. (1979) 2006. *Drawing Down the Moon: Witches, Druids, Goddess-Worshippers and Other Pagans in America*. New York: Penguin Books.

Adler, Patricia A., and Peter Adler. 2008. "The Cyber Worlds of Self-Injurers: Deviant Communities, Relationships, and Selves." *Symbolic Interaction* 31:33–56.

Alan Medinger's story. 2008. "Reflections on 25 Years of Healing." Retrieved August 2008. http://www.peoplecanchange.com /About_Us_Medinger.htm.

Alexander, Jeffrey C. 2003. "A Cultural Sociology of Evil." In *The Meanings of Social Life: A Cultural Sociology*, pp. 109–19. Oxford: Oxford University Press.

———. 2004a. "On the Social Construction of Moral Universals: The 'Holocaust' from War Crime to Trauma Drama." In *Cultural Trauma and Collective Identity*, edited by Jeffrey C. Alexander, Ron Eyerman, Bernhard Giesen, Neil J. Smelser, and Piotr Sztompka, pp. 196–63. Berkeley: University of California Press.

———. 2004b. "Toward a Theory of Cultural Trauma." In *Cultural Trauma and Collective Identity*, edited by Jeffrey C. Alexander, Ron Eyerman, Bernhard Giesen, Neil J. Smelser, and Piotr Sztompka, pp. 1–30. Berkeley: University of California Press.

———. 2006. *The Civil Sphere*. New York: Oxford University Press.

———. 2007. "The Meaningful Construction of Inequality and the Struggles against It: A 'Strong Program' Approach to How Social Boundaries Change." *Cultural Sociology* 1:23–30.

———. 2008. "Clifford Geertz and the Strong Program: The Human Sciences and Cultural Sociology." *Cultural Sociology* 2 (2): 157–68.

Alexander, Jeffrey C., and Philip Smith. 1993. "The Discourse of American Civil Society: A New Proposal for Cultural Studies." *Theory and Society* 22 (2): 151–207.

———. 2003. "The Strong Program in Cultural Sociology: Elements of a Structural Hermeneutics." In *The Meanings of Social Life: A Cultural Sociology*, pp. 11–26. Oxford: Oxford University Press.

Anna Buttimore's story. 2008."It Was as Though Scales Fell from My Eyes." Retrieved July 2008. http://mormonconverts.com/anglican/scales-fell.htm.

Ann's story. 2006. Retrieved May 2006. http://susansmiles.com/stories5.html.

Anonymous Christian's story. 2013. "Set Free from the Lies of Roman Catholicism." Retrieved January 2013. http://www.precious-testimonies.com/Born Again/a-c/CaguladaVP.htm.

Anonymous ex-Mormon(1). 2008. "My Awakening." Retrieved January 2012. http://www.postmormon.org/exp_e/index.php/pomopedia/My_Awakening/.

Anonymous ex-Mormon(2). 2007. Retrieved August 2007. http://www.exmormon.org/mormon/mormon258.htm.

Anonymous retractor(1). 1996. *FMSF Newsletter* 5, no. 5. Retrieved May 2009. http://www.fmsonline.org/fmsf96.501.html.

Anonymous retractor(2). 1994. "The Guilt I Feel." Retrieved June 2008. http://www.fmsonline.org/retract2.html.

Anonymous survivor(1). 2008. "Terrible Truths." Retrieved June 2008. http://lowcountrysurvivors.com/?p=31.

Anonymous survivor(2). 2003. Retrieved September 2003. http://www.escapinghades.com/Survivors133.html.

Anonymous survivor(3). 2003. Retrieved March 2003. http://www.susansmiles.com/stories.html.

Anonymous survivor(4). 2003. Retrieved March 2003. http://www.susansmiles.com/stories4.html.

Anonymous survivor(5). 2005. Retrieved May 2005. http://www.susansmiles.com/anon7.html.

Anuradha Bhagwati's story. Retrieved June 2008. http://www.ivaw.org/user/90.

Anzaldúa, Gloria.1987. *Borderlands/La Frontera: The New Mestiza*. San Francisco, CA: Aunt Lute Books.

APA. 1994. *Diagnostic and Statistical Manual of Mental Disorders*. 4th ed. Washington, DC: American Psychiatric Association.

Arguello, Xavier. 1989. "Marxism Is Not Progress." In *Second Thoughts: Former Radicals Look Back at the Sixties*, edited by Peter Collier and David Horowitz, pp. 111–14. Lanham, MD: Madison Books.

Aristotle. 2006. *Poetics*. Translated by Joe Sachs. Newburyport, MA: Focus Publishing.

Armstrong, Karen. 1992. *Muhammad: A Biography of the Prophet*. San Francisco, CA: Harper.

———. 2004. *The Spiral Staircase: My Climb out of Darkness*. New York: Random House.

———. 2006a. *The Great Transformation: The Beginning of Our Religious Traditions*. New York: Random House.

———. 2006b. *Muhammad: A Prophet for Our Time*. New York: Atlas Books / Harper Collins.

Arnold Steiber's story. 2003."Waking Up to Peace." *Veteran* 33, no. 2. Retrieved February 2008. http://www.vvaw.org/veteran/article/?id=395.

Astarte Moonsilver's story. 2007. Retrieved July 2007. http://www.postmormon .org/exp_e/index.php/discussions/viewthread/16/P40/.

Athens, Lonnie. 1994. "The Self as a Soliloquy." *Sociological Quarterly* 35: 521–32.

Augustine (397–398) 1961. *Confessions*. London: Penguin Books.

Austin, John L. 1962. *How to Do Things with Words*. Oxford: Oxford University Press.

Austin-Broos, Diane. 2003. "The Anthropology of Conversion: An Introduction." In *The Anthropology of Religious Conversion*, edited by Andrew Buckser and Stephen D. Glazier, pp. 1–12. Lanham, MD: Rowman and Littlefield.

Bakhtin, M. M. 1981. *The Dialogic Imagination: Four Essays*. Austin: University of Texas Press.

———. 1986. *Speech Genres and Other Late Essays*. Edited by Caryl Emerson and Michael Holquist. Austin: University of Texas Press.

Bamyeh, Mohammed A. 2001. "Chaos and the Conduits of Understanding." *Social Semiotics* 11 (1): 5–21.

Bar-On, Dan. 1999. *The Indescribable and the Undiscussable: Reconstructing Human Discourse after Trauma*. Budapest, Hungary: Central European University Press.

Bashō, Matsuo. (1694) 1991. *The Narrow Road to the Interior*. Translated by Sam Hamill. Boston: Shambhala Publications.

Bass, Ellen, and Laura Davis. 1988. *The Courage to Heal: A Guide for Women Survivors of Child Sexual Abuse*. New York: Harper Perennial.

Bayer, Ronald. 1981. *Homosexuality and American Psychiatry: The Politics of Diagnosis*. New York: Basic Books.

BBC. 2005. "How Art Made the World." Episode 5, "To Death and Back." Retrieved May 2012. http://www.pbs.org/howartmadetheworld/episodes/death/.

Becker, Gay. 1997 *Disrupted Lives: How People Create Meaning in a Chaotic World*. Berkeley: University of California Press.

Becker, Howard S. (1963) 1997. *Outsiders: Studies in the Sociology of Deviance*. New York: Free Press.

Bellah, Robert N. 2011. *Religion in Human Evolution: From the Paleolithic to the Axial Age*. Cambridge, MA: Harvard University Press.

Bellah, Robert N., Richard Madsen, William M. Sullivan, Ann Swidler, and Steven M. Tipton. 1985. *Habits of the Heart: Individualism and Commitment in American Life*. New York: Perennial Library.

Benford, Robert D. 2002. "Controlling Narratives and Narratives as Control within Social Movements." In *Stories of Change: Narratives and Social Movements*, edited by Joseph E. Davis, pp. 53–75. Albany: State University of New York Press.

Benford, Robert D., and David A. Snow. 2000. "Framing Processes and Social Movements: An Overview and Assessment." *Annual Review of Sociology* 26:611–39.

Ben Newman's story. 2007. "A Change of Heart: My Two Years in Reparative Therapy." Retrieved December 2007. http://www.peoplecanchange.com /About_Us_Ben2.htm.

Berger, Peter L. 1963. *Invitation to Sociology: A Humanist Perspective*. Garden City, NY: Anchor Books.

Berger, Peter L., and Thomas Luckmann. 1966. *The Social Construction of Reality: A Treatise in the Sociology of Knowledge*. New York: Doubleday.

Berman, Marshall. (1970) 1980. *The Politics of Authenticity: Radical Individualism and the Emergence of Modern Society*. New York: Atheneum.

Best, Joel, 1997. "Victimization and the Victim Industry." *Society* 34 (4): 9–17.

Beth Rutherford's story. 1998a. "My Journey Home and Back to Truth." Retrieved December 2006. http://fmsfonline.org/retract2.html#apr98.

———. 1998b. "A Retractor Speaks: The Process." Retrieved December 2006. http://www.fmsfonline.org/fmsf98.128.html.

Bieber, Irving, Harvey J. Dain, Paul R. Dince, Marvin G. Drellich, Henry G. Grand, Ralph H. Gundlach, Malvina W. Kremer, Alfred H. Rifkin, Cornelia B. Wilbur, Toby B. Bieber. 1962. *Homosexuality: A Psychoanalytic Study*. New York: Basic Books.

Bill Kempton's story. 2006. "Dear Bishop, I'm Leaving the Fold." Retrieved June 2008. http://www.postmormon.org/exp_e/index.php/pomopedia/Dear _Bishop_Im_Leaving_the_Fold/.

Blankenhorn, David. 2012. "How My View on Gay Marriage Changed." Editorial, *New York Times*, June 22. Retrieved January 2013. http://www.nytimes .com/2012/06/23/opinion/how-my-view-on-gay-marriage-changed.html ?_r=0.

Blumer, Herbert. 1969. *Symbolic Interaction as Perspective and Method*. Berkeley: University of California Press.

Boellstorff, Tom. 2009. "Nuri's Testimony: HIV/AIDS in Indonesia and Bare Knowledge." *American Ethnologist* 36:351–63.

Booker, Christopher. 2004. *The Seven Basic Plots: Why We Tell Stories*. London: Continuum.

Bourdieu, Pierre. 1984. *Distinction: A Social Critique of the Judgement of Taste*. Cambridge, MA: Harvard University Press.

———. 1990. *The Logic of Practice*. Stanford, CA: Stanford University Press.

Boyce, Mary. (1979) 2001. *Zoroastrians: Their Religious Beliefs and Practices*. London: Routledge.

Brekhus, Wayne H. 1996. "Social Marking and the Mental Coloring of Identity: Sexual Identity Construction and Maintenance in the United States." *Sociological Forum* 11:497–522.

———. 1998. "A Sociology of the Unmarked: Redirecting Our Focus." *Sociological Theory* 16:34–51.

———. 2003. *Peacocks, Chameleons, Centaurs: Gay Suburbia and the Grammar of Social Identity*. Chicago: University of Chicago Press.

———. 2007. "The Rutgers School: A Zerubavelian Culturalist Cognitive Sociology." *European Journal of Social Theory* 10:453–70.

Brian Mahieu's story. 2006. "My Story: A Journey toward Living an Authentic and Integrated Life." Retrieved June 2009. http://www.brianmahieu.com/my_story.html.

Brooke's story. 2008. "Brooke's Testimony." Retrieved April 2008. http://www.faith-travels.org/web/pageid/65420/pages.asp.

———. 2012. "Deliverance from Darkness." Retrieved October 2012. http://www.answers2prayer.org/answered_prayers/prayers/deliverance/deliverance_from_darkness.htm.

Brown, Michael F. 2002. "Moving toward the Light: Self, Other, and the Politics of Experience in New Age Narratives." In *Stories of Change: Narrative and Social Movements*, edited by Joseph E. Davis, pp. 101–22. Albany: SUNY Press.

Bruner, Jerome. 1986. *Actual Minds, Possible Worlds*. Cambridge, MA: Harvard University Press.

———. 1987. "Life as Narrative." *Social Research* 54:11–32.

———. 1990. *Acts of Meaning*. Cambridge, MA: Harvard University Press.

Buckle, Stephen. 2007. "Descartes, Plato and the Cave." *Philosophy* 82:301–37.

Buckser, Andrew. 2003. "Social Conversion and Group Definition in Jewish Copenhagen." In *The Anthropology of Religious Conversion*, edited by Andrew Buckser and Stephen D. Glazier, pp. 69–84. Lanham, MD: Rowman and Littlefield.

Buckser, Andrew, and Stephen D. Glazier, eds. 2003. *The Anthropology of Religious Conversion*. Lanham, MD: Rowman and Littlefield.

Burke, Kenneth. (1945) 1969. *A Grammar of Motives*. Berkeley: University of California Press.

Bushman, Richard L. 1984. *Joseph Smith and the Beginnings of Mormonism*. Urbana: University of Illinois Press.

———. 2005. *Joseph Smith: Rough Stone Rolling*. New York: Alfred A. Knopf.

Butler, Judith. 1991. "Imitation and Gender Insubordination." In *Inside/Out: Lesbian Theories, Gay Theories*, edited by Diana Fuss, pp. 13–31. New York: Routledge.

Cadge, Wendy, and Lynn Davidman. 2006. "Ascription, Choice and the Construction of Religious Identities in the Contemporary United States." *Journal for the Scientific Study of Religion* 45 (1): 23–38.

Carroll, James. 2001. *Constantine's Sword: The Church and the Jews*. Boston: Houghton Mifflin.

Cerulo, Karen A. 1997. "Reframing Sociological Concepts for a Brave New (Virtual?) World." *Sociological Inquiry* 67:48–58.

———. 1998. *Deciphering Violence: The Cognitive Structure of Right and Wrong*. New York: Routledge.

————. 2009. "Non-Humans in Social Interaction." *Annual Review of Sociology* 35:531–52.

Charles's story. 2003. "A Crisis of Faith: An Ex-Creationist Speaks." Retrieved December 2012. http://www.talkorigins.org/origins/postmonth/oct03.html.

Chayko, Mary. 2002. *Connecting: How We Form Social Bonds and Communities in the Internet Age.* Albany: State University of New York Press.

————. 2008. *Portable Communities: The Social Dynamics of Online and Mobile Connectedness.* Albany: State University of New York Press.

Cheryl Johnson's story. 2000. In *Finally Free: Personal Stories: How Love and Self-Acceptance Saved Us from Ex-Gay Ministries,* p. 16. Washington, DC: Human Rights Campaign Foundation.

Childs, Jason. 2011. "I Was a Right-Wing Evangelical Pastor—until I Saw the Light." *Church and State Magazine.* Retrieved January 2012. http://www.alternet.org/story/151034/i_was_a_right-wing_evangelical_pastor_—_until_i_saw_the_light.

Chodorow, Nancy J. 1999. *The Power of Feelings: Personal Meaning in Psychoanalysis, Gender, and Culture.* New Haven, CT: Yale University Press.

Choksy, Jamsheed K. 2003. "To Cut Off, Purify, and Make Whole: Historiographical and Ecclesiastical Conceptions of Ritual Space." *Journal of the American Oriental Society* 123:21–41.

Chopin, Kate. (1899) 2004. *The Awakening.* New York: Pocket Books.

Chopra, Deepak. 2007. *Buddha: A Story of Enlightenment.* New York: HarperOne.

Christie Hubbard's story. 2007. "Member Profile" posted to the website of Iraq Veterans Against the War. Retrieved August 2007. http://www.ivaw.org/user/158.

Christine's story. 1998. Retrieved March 2003. http://www.soc-um.org/survivors/stories/christine2.html.

Christine Bakke's story. 2007. Retrieved March 2012. http://www.beyondexgay.com/who.

Chuck's story. 2012. Retrieved June 2012. http://www.peoplecanchange.com/jim/testimonials.php.

Cierra's story. 2004. "From Christian to Pagan to Christian and Back to Pagan Again." Retrieved November 2012. http://testimonials.exchristian.net/2004/07/from-christian-to-pagan-to-christian.html.

Clanchy, M. T. 1993. *From Memory to Written Record: England 1066–1307.* Oxford: Blackwell Publishing.

Cleaver, Eldridge. 1968. *Soul on Ice.* New York: Dell.

Cline, David. 1997. "Jersey City's Secret Memorial." *Veteran* 27, no. 2. Retrieved May 2005. http://www.vvaw.org/veteran/article/?id=256.

C. L. Hanson's story. 2008. "80s Teen Apostate." Retrieved July 2008. http://www.postmormon.org/exp_e/index.php/pomopedia/80s_teen_apostate/.

Cohen, Richard. 2006. *Coming Out Straight: Understanding and Healing Homosexuality.* Winchester, VA: Oakhill Press.

Coleman, Simon. 2003. "Continuous Conversion? The Rhetoric, Practice, and Rhetorical Practice of Charismatic Protestant Conversion." In *The Anthropology of Religious Conversion*, edited by Andrew Buckser and Stephen D. Glazier, pp. 15–27. Lanham, MD: Rowman and Littlefield.

Collier, Peter. 1989. "Coming Home." In *Second Thoughts: Former Radicals Look Back at the Sixties*, edited by Peter Collier and David Horowitz, pp. 59–65. Lanham, MD: Madison Books.

Collins, Patricia Hill. 2000. *Black Feminist Thought: Knowledge, Consciousness, and the Politics of Empowerment*. New York: Routledge.

Comte, Auguste. (1830–42) 1975. *Cours de Philosophie Positive*. In *Auguste Comte and Positivism: The Essential Writings*, edited by Gertrud Lenzer, pp. 71–306. New York: Harper and Row.

Condorcet, Nicolas Caritat de. 1796. *Outlines of an Historical View of the Progress of the Human Mind*. New York. Retrieved June 2009. http://oll.libertyfund.org /title/1669.

Connerton, Paul. 1989. *How Societies Remember*. Cambridge: Cambridge University Press.

Conway, Flo, and Jim Siegelman. (1978) 2005. *Snapping: America's Epidemic of Sudden Personality Change*. New York: Stillpoint Press.

Cooley, Charles Horton. 1922. *Human Nature and the Social Order (Revised edition.* New York: Charles Scribner's Sons.

Coser, Lewis A. 1956. *The Functions of Social Conflict: An Examination of the Concept of Social Conflict and Its Use in Empirical Sociological Research*. New York: Free Press.

———. 1971. *Masters of Sociological Thought: Ideas in Historical and Social Context*. New York: Harcourt Brace Jovanovich.

Cothran, Charlene. 2008. "Redeemed! 10 Ways to Get Out of the Gay Life, If You Want Out." Retrieved November 2008. http://www.venusmagazine.org /cover_story.html.

Crenshaw, Kimberle Williams. 1991. "Mapping the Margins: Intersectionality, Identity Politics, and Violence against Women of Color." *Stanford Law Review* 43:1241–99.

Crossman, Richard. 1950. "Introduction." In *The God That Failed*, edited by Richard H. Crossman, pp. 1–11. New York: Columbia University Press.

Daniel Blain's story. 2008. Retrieved December 2008. http://ivaw.org/member /daniel-blain.

Dan's story. 2008. "My Journey to Peace." Retrieved July 2008. http://peoplecan change.com/About_Us_Dan.htm.

Das, Bhagavan. 1997. *It's Here Now (Are You?): A Spiritual Memoir*. New York: Broadway Books.

Dass, Ram. (1978) 1990. *Journey of Awakening: A Meditator's Guidebook*. New York: Bantam Books.

———. 1978. *Remember: Be Here Now*. New York: Crown.

Dave's story. 2007. Retrieved July 2007. http://www.postmormon.org/exp_e/index .php/discussions/viewthread/16/P40/.

David Fettke's story. 2000. In *Finally Free: Personal Stories: How Love and*

Self-Acceptance Saved Us from Ex-Gay Ministries, pp. 14–15. Washington, DC: Human Rights Campaign Foundation.

Davis, Fred. 1979. *Yearning for Yesterday: A Sociology of Nostalgia*. New York: Free Press.

Davis, Joseph E. 2002. "Narrative and Social Movements." In *Stories of Change: Narrative and Social Movements*, edited by Joseph E. Davis, pp. 2–39. New York: State University of New York Press.

———. 2005a. *Accounts of Innocence: Sexual Abuse, Trauma, and the Self*. Chicago: University of Chicago Press.

———. 2005b. "Victim Narratives and Victim Selves: False Memory Syndrome and the Power of Accounts." *Social Problems* 52:529–48.

Davis, Laura. 1990. *The Courage to Heal Workbook: For Women and Men Survivors of Child Sexual Abuse*. New York: Harper & Row.

Davis, Murray S. 1983. *Smut: Erotic Reality/Obscene Ideology*. Chicago: University of Chicago Press.

Dbradhud's story. 2008. "Could Not Live a Lie." Retrieved July 2008. http://www .postmormon.org/exp_e/index.php/pomopedia/Could_Not_Live_A_Lie/.

Debbie David's story. 1996. "Retraction Is a Process." *FMS Foundation Newsletter* 5, no. 7. Retrieved June 2006. http://www.fmsfonline.org/fmsf96.701.html.

Deborah Wright's story. 2008. "Putting Together the Puzzle." Retrieved June 2008. http://www.mormonconverts.com/catholic/the-puzzle.htm.

DeGloma, Thomas. 2007. "The Social Logic of 'False Memories': Symbolic Awakenings and Symbolic Worlds in Survivor and Retractor Narratives." *Symbolic Interaction* 30:543–65.

———. 2009. "Expanding Trauma through Space and Time: Mapping the Rhetorical Strategies of Trauma Carrier Groups." *Social Psychology Quarterly* 72:105–22.

———. 2011. "Defining Social Illness in a Diagnostic World: Trauma and the Cultural Logic of Posttraumatic Stress Disorder." In *Advances in Medical Sociology*, vol. 12, *Sociology of Diagnosis*, edited by P. J. McGann and David J. Hutson, pp. 59–82. Bingley, UK: Emerald.

DeGloma, Thomas, and Asia Friedman. 2005 "Thinking with Sociomental Filters: Exploring the Social Structuring of Attention and Significance." Paper presented at the Annual Meeting of the American Sociological Association, Philadelphia, PA.

Denzel, Stephanie. 2014. "George Franklin." The National Registry of Exonerations. Retrieved March 2014. http://www.law.umich.edu/special/exoneration /Pages/casedetail.aspx?caseid=3221.

Denzin, Norman K. 1987. *The Alcoholic Self*. Newbury Park, CA: Sage.

———. 1989a. *Applied Social Research Methods*. Vol. 16, *Interpretive Interactionism*. Newbury Park, CA: Sage.

———. 1989b. *Qualitative Research Methods*. Vol. 17, *Interpretive Biography*. Newbury Park, CA: Sage.

Desi. (1983) 1991. "Story of a Granddaughter." In *I Never Told Anyone: Writings by Woman Survivors of Child Sexual Abuse*, edited by Ellen Bass and Louise Thornton, pp. 139–41. New York: HarperPerennial.

Diana Halbrooks's story. 2007. Retrieved July 2007. http://www.fmsfonline.org/retract1.html.

DiMaggio, Paul. 1997. "Culture and Cognition." *Annual Review of Sociology* 23: 263–87.

Doe, Jane. 1991. "How Could This Happen? Coping with a False Accusation of Incest and Rape." *Issues in Child Abuse Accusations* 3:154–65. Retrieved March 2012. http://www.ipt-forensics.com/journal/volume3/j3_3_3.htm.

Douglas, Mary. (1966) 2005. *Purity and Danger*. London: Routledge.

Douglass Eckhoff's story. 2008. "I Found My Direction Home." Retrieved July 2007. http://mormonconverts.com/catholic/found-my-direction-home.htm.

Du Bois, W. E. B. (1903) 1995. *The Souls of Black Folk*. New York: Penguin Books.

Durkheim, Emile. (1893) 1984. *The Division of Labor in Society*. New York: Free Press.

———. (1912) 1995. *The Elementary Forms of Religious Life*. New York: Free Press.

———. (1914) 1960. "The Dualism of Human Nature and Its Social Conditions." In *Essays on Sociology and Philosophy*, edited by Kurt H. Wolff, pp. 325–39. New York: Harper and Row.

Dustin Fadale's story. 2008. "I Had Never Heard Something So Amazing." Retrieved June 2008. http://www.mormonconverts.com/catholic/something-so-amazing.htm.

Ebaugh, Helen R. F. 1988. *Becoming an Ex: The Process of Role Exit*. Chicago: University of Chicago Press.

Eisenstadt, S. N. 1986. "The Axial Age Breakthroughs—Their Characteristics and Origins." In *The Origins and Diversity of Axial Age Civilizations*, edited by S. N. Eisenstadt, pp. 1–25. Albany: State University of New York Press.

Eliasoph, Nina, and Paul Lichterman. 2003. "Culture in Interaction." *American Journal of Sociology* 108:735–94.

Elizabeth Godley's story. 1994. "My Mother Abused Me, Didn't She?" Retrieved December 2006. http://fmsfonline.org/retract1.html#feb94.

Elkana, Yehuda. 1986. "The Emergence of Second-Order Thinking in Classical Greece." In *The Origins and Diversity of Axial Age Civilizations*, edited by S. N. Eisenstadt, pp. 40–64. Albany: State University of New York Press.

Emerson, Joan P. 1970. "Behavior in Private Places: Sustaining Definitions of Reality in Gynecological Examinations." In *Recent Sociology No. 2: Patterns of Communicative Behavior*, edited by Hans-Peter Dreitzel, pp. 74–93. London: Macmillan.

Emirbayer, Mustafa, and Ann Mische. 1998. "What Is Agency?" *American Journal of Sociology* 103:962–1023.

Engels, Friedrich. (1893) 1970. "Engels to F. Mehring in Berlin." In *Karl Marx and Friedrich Engels: Selected Works*, pp. 689–92. Moscow: Progress Publishers.

Engerman, David C. 2001. "Forward to the 2001 Edition." In *The God That Failed*, edited by Richard H. Crossman, pp. vii–xxxiv. New York: Columbia University Press.

Epstein, Steven. 2008. "Culture and Science/Technology: Rethinking Knowledge, Power, Materiality, and Nature." *Annals of the American Academy of Political and Social Science* 619:165–82.

Erikson, Kai T. 1966. *Wayward Puritans: A Study in the Sociology of Deviance*. New York: John Wiley & Sons.

Erzen, Tanya. 2006. *Straight to Jesus: Sexual and Christian Conversions in the Ex-Gay Movement*. Berkeley: University of California Press.

Exmo #2. 2007. Retrieved August 2007. http://www.exmormon.org/mormon/mormon052.htm.

Eyerman, Ron. 2001. *Cultural Trauma: Slavery and the Formation of African American Identity*. Cambridge: Cambridge University Press.

Ezzy, Douglas. 1998. "Theorizing Narrative Identity: Symbolic Interaction and Hermeneutics." *Sociological Quarterly* 39 (2): 239–52.

———. 2000. "Fate and Agency in Job Loss Narratives." *Qualitative Sociology* 23:121–34.

Ezzy, Douglas, and Helen A. Berger. 2007. "Becoming a Witch: Changing Paths of Conversion in Contemporary Witchcraft." In *The New Generation Witches: Teenage Witchcraft in Contemporary Culture*, edited by Hannah E. Johnston and Peg Aloi, pp. 41–55. Aldershot, UK: Ashgate.

Fabian, Johannes. 1983. *Time and the Other: How Anthropology Makes Its Object*. New York: Columbia University Press.

Feinberg, Leslie. 1996. *Transgender Warriors: Making History from Joan of Arc to Ru-Paul*. Boston, MA: Beacon Press.

Fichter, Joseph H. 1987. *Autobiographies of Conversion*. Lewiston, NY: Edwin Mellen Press.

Fine, Gary Alan. 2001. *Difficult Reputations: Collective Memories of the Evil, Inept, and Controversial*. Chicago: University of Chicago Press.

Fine, Gary Alan, and Aaron Beim. 2007. "Introduction: Interactionist Approaches to Collective Memory." *Symbolic Interaction* 30:1–5.

Fiona's story. 2005. Retrieved May 2005. http://www.susansmiles.com/stories2.html.

Fischer, Louis. (1949) 1950. In *The God That Failed*, edited by Richard H. Crossman, pp. 196–228. New York: Columbia University Press.

Fish, Stanley. 1980. *Is There a Text in This Class? The Authority of Interpretive Communities*. Cambridge, MA: Harvard University Press.

Fivush, Robyn, Catherine Haden, and Elaine Reese. 1996. "Remembering, Recounting, and Reminiscing: The Development of Autobiographical Memory in Social Context." In *Remembering Our Past: Studies in Autobiographical Memory*, edited by David C. Rubin, pp. 341–58. New York: Cambridge University Press.

Flaherty, Michael G. 2011. *The Textures of Time: Agency and Temporal Experience*. Philadelphia, PA: Temple University Press.

Fleck, Ludwik. (1935) 1979. *Genesis and Development of a Scientific Fact*. Chicago: University of Chicago Press.

Ford, Jeffrey G. 2009. "Reparative Therapy: A Pseudoscience." Retrieved June 2009. http://jgford.homestead.com/index.html.

Foucault, Michel. (1969) 1972. *The Archeology of Knowledge*. New York: Pantheon Books.

———. 1977. *Language, Counter-Memory, Practice: Selected Essays and Interviews*. Ithaca, NY: Cornell University Press.

———. (1978) 1990. *The History of Sexuality*. Vol. 1, *An Introduction*. New York: Random House.

Frank, Arthur W. 1993. "The Rhetoric of Self-Change: Illness Experience as Narrative." *Sociological Quarterly* 34:39–52.

———. 1995. *The Wounded Storyteller: Body, Illness, and Ethics*. Chicago: University of Chicago Press.

———. 2000. "Illness as Autobiographical Work: Dialogue as Narrative Destabilization." *Qualitative Sociology* 23:135–56.

Frank's story. 2000. "Transformed." Retrieved January 2012. http://www.peoplecanchange.com/stories/frank.php.

Fraser, Nancy. 1995. "From Redistribution to Recognition? Dilemmas of Justice in a 'Post-Socialist' Age." *New Left Review* I (212): 68–93.

Fraser, Sylvia. 1987. *My Father's House: A Memoir of Incest and of Healing*. New York: Ticknor and Fields.

Freud, Sigmund. (1896) 1984. "The Aetiology of Hysteria." In *The Assault on Truth: Freud's Suppression of the Seduction Theory*, by Jeffrey Moussaieff Masson, pp. 251–82. New York: Farrar, Straus and Giroux.

———. (1899) 1938. *The Interpretation of Dreams*. In *The Basic Writings of Sigmund Freud*, edited by A. A. Brill, pp. 181–549. New York: Modern Library.

———. (1901) 1938. *Psychopathology of Everyday Life*. In *The Basic Writings of Sigmund Freud*, edited by A. A. Brill, pp. 35–178. New York: Modern Library.

———. (1905) 1963. *Dora: An Analysis of a Case History*. New York: Touchstone.

———. (1909) 1963. "Notes upon a Case of Obsessional Neurosis." In *Three Case Histories: The "Wolf Man," The "Rat Man," and the Psychotic Doctor Schreber*, pp. 15–102. New York: Collier Books.

———. (1910) 1938. "The History of the Psychoanalytic Movement." In *The Basic Writings of Sigmund Freud*, edited by A. A. Brill, pp. 933–97. New York: Modern Library.

———. (1911) 1963. "Psychoanalytic Notes upon an Autobiographical Account of a Case of Paranoia (Dementia Paranoides)." In *Three Case Histories: The "Wolf Man," The "Rat Man," and the Psychotic Doctor Schreber*, pp. 103–86. New York: Collier Books.

———. (1912) 1963. "A Note on the Unconscious in Psychoanalysis." In *General Psychological Theory: Papers on Metapsychology*, pp. 49–82. New York: Collier Books.

———. (1918) 1963. "From the History of an Infantile Neurosis." In *Three Case*

Histories: The "Wolf Man," The "Rat Man," and the Psychotic Doctor Schreber, pp. 187–316. New York: Collier Books.

Freyd, Jennifer J. 1996. *Betrayal Trauma: The Logic of Forgetting Childhood Abuse.* Cambridge, MA: Harvard University Press.

Fritz Williams's story. 2004. "Born Again: A Conversion Story." Retrieved June 2007. http://baltimoreethicalsociety.org/Conversion.php.

Frye, Northrop. 1957. *Anatomy of Criticism.* Princeton, NJ: Princeton University Press.

Fuller, Steve. (1998) 2002. *Social Epistemology.* Bloomington: Indiana University Press.

———. 1991. "Disciplinary Boundaries and the Rhetoric of the Social Sciences." *Poetics Today* 12 (2): 301–25.

Gallagher, Eugene V. 1994. "A Religion without Converts? Becoming a Neo-Pagan." *Journal of the American Academy of Religion* 62 (3):851–67.

Gamson, William A. 1992. "The Social Psychology of Collective Action." In *Frontiers in Social Movement Theory,* edited by Aldon Morris and Carol Mueller, pp. 53–76. New Haven, CT: Yale University Press.

Garfinkel, Harold. (1967) 1996. "Passing and the Managed Achievement of Sex Status in an Intersexed Person." In *Studies in Ethnomethodology,* pp. 116–85. Cambridge, UK: Polity Press.

Gayatri's story. Retrieved June 2005. http://www.soc-um.org/.

Geertz, Clifford. 1973. *The Interpretation of Cultures.* New York: Basic Books.

———. 1998. *Works and Lives: The Anthropologist as Author.* Stanford, CA: Stanford University Press.

Gennette, Gérard, 1980. *Narrative Discourse: An Essay in Method.* Ithaca, NY: Cornell University Press.

Gergen, Kenneth J. 1991. *The Saturated Self: Dilemmas of Identity in Contemporary Life.* New York: Basic Books.

Gergen, Kenneth J., and Mary M. Gergen. 1997. "Narratives of the Self," In *Memory, Identity, Community: The Idea of Narrative in the Human Sciences,* edited by Lewis P. Hinchman and Sandra K. Hinchman, pp. 161–84. Albany: State University of New York Press.

Gerilena Spillios's story. 1993. "The Truth Set Me Free." In *True Stories of False Memories,* edited by Eleanor Goldstein and Kevin Farmer, pp. 333–45. Boca Raton, FL: SIRS Books.

Germana, Rachelle. 2003. "In-Between and Becoming: Victims, Survivors, and the Narrative of Transformation." Unpublished manuscript, Rutgers University.

Giddens, Anthony. 1991. *Modernity and Self-Identity: Self and Society in the Late Modern Age.* Stanford, CA: Stanford University Press.

Gillespie, V. Bailey. 1979. *Religious Conversion and Personal Identity.* Birmingham, AL: Religious Education Press.

Gladwell, Malcolm. (2000) 2002. *The Tipping Point: How Little Things Can Make a Big Difference.* New York: Back Bay Books.

Glaser, Barney G., and Anselm L. Strauss. (1967) 2008. *The Discovery of Grounded Theory: Strategies for Qualitative Research*. New Brunswick, NJ: AldineTransaction.

Glazier, Stephen D. 2003. "'Limin' wid Jah': Spiritual Baptists Who Become Rastafarians and Then Become Spiritual Baptists Again." In *The Anthropology of Religious Conversion*, pp. 149–70. Lanham, MD: Rowman and Littlefield Publishers.

Gocer, Asli. 2000. "The Puppet Theater in Plato's Parable of the Cave." *Classical Journal* 95:119–29.

Goffman, Erving. 1959. *The Presentation of Self in Everyday Life*. New York: Anchor Books, Doubleday.

———. 1961. *Asylums: Essays on the Social Situation of Mental Patients and Other Inmates*. New York: Anchor Books.

———. (1974) 1986. *Frame Analysis: An Essay on the Organization of Experience*. Boston, MA: Northeastern University Press.

Gould, Deborah B. 2009. *Moving Politics: Emotion and ACT UP's Fight against AIDS*. Chicago: University of Chicago Press.

Graham, Gordon. 1997. *The Shape of the Past: A Philosophical Approach to History*. Oxford: Oxford University Press.

Gramsci, Antonio. 1971. *Selections from the Prison Notebooks*. New York: International Publishers.

Gross, Neil. 2005. "The Detraditionalization of Intimacy Reconsidered." *Sociological Theory* 23 (3): 286–311.

Gubrium, Jaber F. 1992. *Out of Control: Family Therapy and Domestic Disorder*. Newbury Park, CA: Sage.

———. 2005. "Introduction: Narrative Environments and Social Problems." *Social Problems* 52:525–28. "Grounding the Postmodern Self."

Gubrium, Jaber F., and James A. Holstein. 1994. "Grounding the Postmodern Self." *Sociological Quarterly* 35 (4): 685–703.

———. 2000. "The Self in a World of Going Concerns." *Symbolic Interaction* 23:95–115.

———. 2009. *Analyzing Narrative Reality*. Thousand Oaks, CA: Sage.

Habermas, Jürgen. 1987. *The Theory of Communicative Action*. Vol. 2, *Lifeworld and System: A Critique of Functionalist Reason*. Boston, MA: Beacon Press.

Halbwachs, Maurice. (1925) 1992a. "The Legendary Topography of the Gospels in the Holy Land." In *On Collective Memory*, edited by Lewis A. Coser, pp. 193–235. Chicago: University of Chicago Press.

———. (1925) 1992b. "The Social Frameworks of Memory." In *On Collective Memory*, edited by Lewis A. Coser, pp. 37–189. Chicago: University of Chicago Press.

———. (1950) 1980. *The Collective Memory*. New York: Harper and Row.

Hamar's story. 2007. Retrieved July 2008. http://www.postmormon.org/exp_e/index.php/discussions/viewthread/16/P40/.

Hankiss, Agnes. 1981. "Ontologies of the Self: On the Mythological Rearranging of One's Life-History." In *Biography and Society: The Life History Approach in the Social Sciences*, edited by Daniel Bertaux, pp. 203–9. Beverly Hills, CA: Sage.

Hart, Joseph. 2007. "Queer Magazine Born Again: Founder of *Venus*, a Publication for Black Lesbians, Repudiates Lifestyle." *Utne Reader* 143:28–29.

Harvey, Graham. (1997) 2000. *Contemporary Paganism: Listening People, Speaking Earth*. New York: New York University Press.

———. 1999. "Coming Home and Coming Out Pagan but Not Converting." In *Religious Conversion: Contemporary Practices and Controversies*, edited by Christopher Lamb and Darrol Bryant, pp. 233–46. London: Cassell.

Harvey, Peter. 1990. *An Introduction to Buddhism: Teaching, History, Practice*. Cambridge: Cambridge University Press.

Hay, Robert P. 1969. "George Washington: American Moses." *American Quarterly* 21:780–91.

Herman, Edward S., and Noam Chomsky. (1988) 2002. *Manufacturing Consent: The Political Economy of the Mass Media*. New York: Pantheon Books.

Herman, Judith Lewis. (1981) 2000. *Father-Daughter Incest*. Cambridge, MA: Harvard University Press.

———. 1992. *Trauma and Recovery: The Aftermath of Violence—From Domestic Abuse to Political Terror*. New York: Basic Books.

Hertz, Robert. (1909) 1973. "The Preeminence of the Right Hand." In *Right and Left: Essays in Dual Symbolic Classification*, edited by Rodney Needham, pp. 3–31. Chicago: University of Chicago Press.

Hesse, Hermann. (1922) 1951. *Siddhartha*. New York: Bantam Books.

Hobbes, Thomas. (1651) 1962. *Leviathan*. New York: Macmillan.

Hochschild, Arlie R. 1979. "Emotion Work, Feeling Rules and Social Structure." *American Journal of Sociology* 85 (3): 551–75.

———. 1983. *The Managed Heart: The Commercialization of Human Feeling*. Berkeley: University of California Press.

Holstein, James A., and Jaber F. Gubrium. 2000. *The Self We Live By: Narrative Identity in a Postmodern World*. New York: Oxford University Press.

Hornung, Erik. (1995) 1999. *Akhenaten and the Religion of Light*. Ithaca, NY. Cornell University Press.

Horowitz, David. 1989. "Why I Am No Longer a Leftist." In *Second Thoughts: Former Radicals Look Back at the Sixties*, edited by Peter Collier and David Horowitz, pp. 53–57. Lanham, MD: Madison Books.

———. 1997. *Radical Son: A Generational Odyssey*. New York: Touchstone.

Horwitz, Allan V. 1990. *The Logic of Social Control*. New York: Plenum.

———. 2002. *Creating Mental Illness*. Chicago: University of Chicago Press.

Horwitz, Gordon J. 1990. *In the Shadow of Death: Living Outside the Gates of Mauthausen*. New York: Free Press.

Howard, Jenna. 2000. "Memory Reconstruction in Autobiographical Narrative Construction: Analysis of the Alcoholics Anonymous Recovery Narrative." Unpublished paper, Department of Sociology, Rutgers University, New Brunswick, NJ.

———. 2006. "Expecting and Accepting: The Temporal Ambiguity of Recovery Identities." *Social Psychology Quarterly* 69:307–24.

———. 2008. "Negotiating an Exit: Existential, Interactional, and Cultural Obstacles to Disorder Disidentification." *Social Psychology Quarterly* 71:177–92.

Hughes, Everett C. 1984. "Going Concerns: The Study of American Institutions." In *The Sociological Eye: Selected Papers*, pp. 52–64. New Brunswick, NJ: Transaction Books.

Hume, David. (1748) 1961. "An Enquiry Concerning Human Understanding." In *The Empiricists*, pp. 307–430. New York: Doubleday.

Hunt, Scott A., and Robert D. Benford. 1994. "Identity Talk in the Peace and Justice Movement." *Journal of Contemporary Ethnography* 22:488–517.

Ifshin, David. 1989. "A Political Journey." In *Second Thoughts: Former Radicals Look Back at the Sixties*, edited by Peter Collier and David Horowitz, pp. 81–88. Lanham, MD: Madison Books.

Illouz, Eva. 2008. *Saving the Modern Soul: Therapy, Emotions, and the Culture of Self-Help*. Berkeley: University of California Press.

Irvine, Leslie. 1999. *Codependent Forevermore: The Invention of Self in a Twelve Step Group*. Chicago: University of Chicago Press.

———. 2000. "'Even Better than the Real Thing': Narratives of the Self in Codependency." *Qualitative Sociology* 23:9–28.

Israel, Eleonai. 2007. "The Journey of a VIP Bodyguard, Sniper against the War." Retrieved November 2007. http://www.ivaw.org/node/1522.

Jackson, A. V. Williams. 1896. "The Moral and Ethical Teachings of the Ancient Zoroastrian Religion." *International Journal of Ethics* 7:55–62.

Jacobs, Ron. 2007. "A Conversation with Three Iraq Veterans against the War." *CounterPunch* April 14. Retrieved June 2007. http://www.vaiw.org/vet/modules.php?name=News&file=article%sid=3215.

James, William. (1902) 1987. *The Varieties of Religious Experience*. In *William James: Writings 1902–1910*, pp. 1–477. New York: Library of America.

Jared Hood's story. 2007. "Is the United States Military a Terrorist Organization?" and "A Family in IVAW." Retrieved August 2007. http://www.ivaw.org/user/159.

Jaspers, Karl. (1953) 2010. *The Origin and Goal of History*. New York: Routledge.

Jerry A. Armelli's story. 2000. "Coming Home." Retrieved January 2013. http://www.peoplecanchange.com/About_Us_Armelli.htm.

Johnston, Erin F. 2013. "'I Was Always This Way . . .': Rhetorics of Continuity in Narratives of Conversion." *Sociological Forum* 28 (3): 549–73.

Johnston, Hank. 2009. "Protest Cultures: Performance, Artifact, and Ideations." In *Culture, Social Movements, and Protest*, edited by Hank Johnston, pp. 3–29. Farnham, UK: Ashgate.

Johnston, Hank, Enrique Laraña, and Joseph R. Gusfield. 1994. "Identities, Grievances, and New Social Movements." In *New Social Movements: From Ideology to Identity*, edited by Enrique Laraña, Hank Johnston, and Joseph R. Gusfield, pp. 3–35. Philadelphia, PA: Temple University Press.

Jon Turner's story. 2008. Testimony reproduced in "This Is Where We Take Our Stand," video trailer. Retrieved July 2009. http://vimeo.com/5448532.

Jung, Carl. 1959. *The Undiscovered Self.* New York: Mentor Books.

Kant, Immanuel. (1781) 1993. *Critique of Pure Reason.* London: Orion.

———. (1785) 2008. *Groundwork of the Metaphysics of Morals.* Radford, VA: Wilder.

Kathryn's story. 2009. Retrieved July 2009. http://www.beyondexgay.com/narratives /kathryn.html.

Kerby, Anthony Paul. 1991. *Narrative and the Self.* Bloomington: Indiana University Press.

Khong, Yuen Foong. 1992. *Analogies at War: Korea, Munich, Dien Bien Phu, and the Vietnam Decisions of 1965.* Princeton, NJ: Princeton University Press.

Kidron, Carol A. 2004. "Surviving a Distant Past: A Case Study of the Cultural Construction of Trauma Descendant Identity." *Ethos* 31:513–44.

Kim's story. 2010. "How I Lost My Faith in One Month's Time." Retrieved December 2012. http://www.thinkatheist.com/group/yourstory/forum/topics /how-i-lost-my-faith-in-one.

Kippenberg, Hans G. 1986. "The Role of Christianity in the Depolitization of the Roman Empire." In *The Origins and Diversity of Axial Age Civilizations*, edited by S. N. Eisenstadt, pp. 261–79. Albany: State University of New York Press.

Knorr Cetina, Karin. 1999. *Epistemic Cultures: How the Sciences Make Knowledge.* Cambridge, MA: Harvard University Press.

Koestler, Arthur. 1950. "Arthur Koestler." In *The God That Failed*, edited by Richard H. Crossman, pp. 15–75. New York: Columbia University Press.

———. (1964) 1976. *The Act of Creation.* London: Hutchinson.

Kövecses, Zoltán. 2002. *Metaphor: A Practical Introduction.* Oxford: Oxford Univeristy Press.

———. 2005. *Metaphor in Culture: Universality and Variation.* Cambridge: Cambridge University Press.

Kristi's story. 2009. "Evangelical Creationist Turned Godless Evolutionist." Retrieved December 2012. http://www.thinkatheist.com/group/yourstory/forum /topics/evangelical-creationist-turned?xg_source=activity.

Kuhn, Thomas S. (1962) 1996. *The Structure of Scientific Revolutions.* Chicago: University of Chicago Press.

Lakoff, George, and Mark Johnson. 1980. *Metaphors We Live By.* Chicago: University of Chicago Press.

Lamont, Michèle, and Virág Molnár. 2002. "The Study of Boundaries in the Social Sciences." *Annual Review of Sociology* 28:167–95.

Lane, Michael. 1970. *Introduction to Structuralism.* New York: Basic Books.

LaRossa, Ralph, and Cynthia B. Sinha. 2006. "Constructing the Transition to Parenthood." *Sociological Inquiry* 76:433–57.

Lempert, Lora Bex. 1996. "Language Obstacles in the Narratives of Abused Women." *Mid-American Review of Sociology* 19 (1/2): 15–32.

Lenin, Vladimir Ilyich. (1913) 1996. "The Three Sources and Component Parts of Marxism." Originally published in *Lenin's Collected Works*, 19:21–28. 1977.

Moscow: Progress Publishers. Retrieved April 2009 from the Lenin Internet Archives. http://www.marxists.org/archive/lenin/works/1913/mar/x01.htm.

Lévi-Strauss, Claude. 1963. *Structural Anthropology*. New York: Basic Books.

Levy, Daniel. 1999. "The Future of the Past: Historiographical Disputes and Competing Memories in Germany and Israel." *History and Theory* 38 (1): 51–66.

Lewis, Bernard. 1975. *History: Remembered, Recovered, Invented*. Princeton, NJ: Princeton University Press.

Lieblich, Amia, Rivka Tuval-Mashiach, and Tamar Zilber. 1998. *Narrative Research: Reading, Analysis, and Interpretation*. Thousand Oaks, CA: Sage.

Lifton, Robert Jay. (1973) 2005. *Home From the War: Learning from Vietnam Veterans*. New York: Other Press.

Lilita's story. 2003. Retrieved March 2003. http://www.susansmiles.com/stories4.html.

Linda's story. 2006. Retrieved May 2006. http://www.susansmiles.com/linda2.html.

Locke, John. (1690) 1961. "An Essay Concerning Human Understanding." In *The Empiricists*, pp. 7–133. New York: Doubleday.

———. (1690) 1980. *Second Treatise of Government*. Indianapolis, IN: Hackett.

Lomsky-Feder, Edna. 1995. "The Meaning of War through Veterans' Eyes: A Phenomenological Analysis of Life Stories." *International Sociology* 10:463–82.

Lopez, Donald S. 2001. *The Story of Buddhism: A Concise Guide to Its History and Teachings*. New York: HarperCollins.

Lorek, Melanie. 2012. "Two Sides of a Coin: The Interplay between Autobiographical and Collective Memory of the German Democratic Republic." Paper presented at the Annual Meeting of the Eastern Sociological Society, New York, February.

Loseke, Donileen R. 1992. *The Battered Women and Shelters: The Social Construction of Wife Abuse*. Albany: State University of New York Press.

———. 2001. "Lived Realities and Formula Stories of 'Battered Women.'" In *Institutional Selves: Troubled Identities in a Postmodern World*, edited by Jaber F. Gubrium and James A. Holstein, pp. 107–26. New York: Oxford University Press.

———. 2009. "Examining Emotion as Discourse: Emotion Codes and Presidential Speeches Justifying War." *Sociological Quarterly*, 50:497–524.

Lukács, Georg. (1920) 1971. *History and Class Consciousness*. London: Merlin Press.

Luker, Kristen. 1984. *Abortion and the Politics of Motherhood*. Berkeley: University of California Press.

Lukes, Steven. 1974. *Power: A Radical View*. London: Macmillan.

Lynas, Mark. 2013. Lecture to Oxford Farming Conference. Retrieved January 2013. http://www.marklynas.org/2013/01/lecture-to-oxford-farming-conference-3-january-2013/.

MacIntyre, Alasdair. 1981. *After Virtue: A Study in Moral Theory*. Notre Dame, IN: University of Notre Dame Press.

Malcolm X. 1964. *The Autobiography of Malcolm X (As Told to Alex Haley*. New York: Ballantine Books.

Mannheim, Karl. (1928) 1952. "The Problem of Generations." In *Essays on the Sociology of Knowledge*, pp. 276–322. London: Routledge.

———. 1936. *Ideology and Utopia: An Introduction to the Sociology of Knowledge*. San Diego, CA: Harcourt.

Maratea, Ray. 2008. "The e-Rise and Fall of Social Problems: The Blogosphere as a Public Arena." *Social Problems* 55:139–59.

Markus, Hazel, and Paul Nurius. 1986. "Possible Selves." *American Psychologist* 41 (9): 954–69.

Martin, John Levi. 2002. "Power, Authority, and the Constraint of Belief Systems." *American Journal of Sociology* 107:861–904.

Martin Briseno's story. 2007. "From Cocaine to Christ." Retrieved August 2007. http://www.precious-testimonies.com/BornAgain/a-c/Briseno.htm.

Marx, Karl. (1844) 1963. "Introduction to the Critique of Hegel's Philosophy of Right," In *Reader in Marxist Philosophy: From the Writings of Marx, Engels, and Lenin*, edited by Howard Selsam and Harry Martel, pp. 226–27. New York: International Publishers.

———. (1845) 1963. "The German Ideology: Part I." In *Reader in Marxist Philosophy: From the Writings of Marx, Engels, and Lenin*, edited by Howard Selsam and Harry Martel, pp. 199–201. New York: International Publishers.

———. (1845) 1978. "The German Ideology: Part I." In *The Marx-Engels Reader, Second Edition*, edited by Robert C. Tucker, pp. 146–200. New York: W. W. Norton.

———. (1867) 2010. *Capital*. Vol. 1, *A Critique of Political Economy*. Lawrence, KS. Digireads.com Publishing, Neeland Media.

Mary Ellen's story. 2003. Retrieved March 2003. http://www.susansmiles.com /stories4.html.

Marshall, Philip. 1994. "Philip's Story." In *Female Sexual Abuse of Children*, edited by Michele Elliot, pp. 176–77. New York: Guilford Press.

Mason-Schrock, Douglas. 1996. "Transsexuals' Narrative Construction of the 'True Self.'" *Social Psychology Quarterly* 59:176–92.

Masson, Jeffrey Moussaieff. 1984. *The Assault on Truth: Freud's Suppression of the Seduction Theory*. New York: Farrar, Straus and Giroux.

May, Ernest R. 1973. *"Lessons" of the Past: The Use and Misuse of History in American Foreign Policy*. New York: Oxford University Press.

McAdams, Dan P. 1993. *The Stories We Live By: Personal Myths and the Making of the Self*. New York: Guilford Press.

Mead, George Herbert. 1932. *The Philosophy of the Present*. LaSalle, IL: Open Court.

———. (1934) 1967. *Mind, Self, and Society: From the Standpoint of a Social Behaviorist*. Chicago: University of Chicago Press.

Meanwell, Emily. 2013. "Profaning the Past to Salvage the Present: The Symbolically Reconstructed Pasts of Homeless Shelter Residents." *Symbolic Interaction*. 36 (4): 439–56.

Melissa's story. 2005. Safeguarding Our Children—United Mothers. "Survivor Stories." Retrieved November 2005. http://pub46.bravenet.com/forum /3893375066/fetch/677925/5.

Melucci, Alberto. 1989. *Nomads of the Present: Social Movements and Individual Needs in Contemporary Society*. Philadelphia, PA: Temple University Press.

Menon, Kalyani Devaki. 2003. "Converted Innocents and Their Trickster Heroes: The Politics of Proselytizing in India." In *The Anthropology of Religious Conversion*, edited by Andrew Buckser and Stephen D. Glazier, pp. 43–53. Lanham, MD: Rowman and Littlefield.

Merton, Robert K. (1949) 1964. *Social Theory and Social Structure*. London: Free Press of Glencoe.

Michele's story. 2008. Retrieved August 2008. http://www.pandys.org/escaping hades/Survivors98.html.

Mike Thelnfidel's story 2011. "From Bible-Literalist Fundie to Outspoken Atheist." Retrieved December 2012. http://www.thinkatheist.com/group/yourstory /forum/topics/from-bibleliteralist-fundie-to.

Mills, C. Wright. 1940. "Situated Actions and Vocabularies of Motive." *American Sociological Review* 5:904–13.

———. (1959) 2000. *The Sociological Imagination*. Oxford: Oxford University Press.

Mische, Ann. 2008. *Partisan Publics: Communication and Contention across Brazilian Youth Activist Networks*. Princeton, NJ: Princeton University Press.

———. 2009. "Projects and Possibilities: Researching Futures in Action." *Sociological Forum* 24:694–704.

Moonshine's story. 2008. "A Tale of Two Cities and Two Towers." Retrieved June 2008. http://www.postmormon.org/exp_e/index.php/pomopedia/A_Tale _of_Two_Cities_and_Two_Towers/.

Mountaingirl's story. 2007. Retrieved July 2008. http://www.postmormon.org/exp _e/index.php/discussions/viewthread/16/.

Mueller, Andrea. 2010. "Negotiating Storied Continuities: Remembering in Berlin on the 20th Anniversary of the Fall of the Wall." Paper presented at the Annual Meeting of the Eastern Sociological Society, Boston, MA.

Mullaney, Jamie L. 2006. *Everyone Is NOT Doing It: Abstinence and Personal Identity*. Chicago: University of Chicago Press.

Murdoch, Adrian. (2003) 2008. *The Last Pagan: Julian the Apostate and the Death of the Ancient World*. Rochester, VT: Inner Traditions.

Nathan, Debbie, and Michael Snedeker. 1995. *Satan's Silence: Ritual Abuse and the Making of a Modern American Witch Hunt*. New York: Basic Books.

Newton, John. (1788) 2010. *Thoughts upon the African Slave Trade*. Digitized version of the 1788 London edition, Internet Archive, 2010. Retrieved March 2014. https://archive.org/details/thoughtsuponafri00newt.

———. 2003. *Out of the Depths*. Grand Rapids, MI: Kregel Publications.

Newton, Sir Isaac. 1687. *Philosophiae Naturalis Principia Mathematica*. Retrieved February 2009. http://www.archive.org/details/newtonspmathema00newtrich.

Nicolosi, Joseph. 1991. *Reparative Therapy of Male Homosexuality: A New Clinical Approach*. Lanham, MD: Rowman & Littlefield.

———. 1993. *Healing Homosexuality: Case Studies of Reparative Therapy*. Northvale, NJ: Jason Aronson.

———. 2009. *Shame and Attachment Loss: The Practical Work of Reparative Therapy.* Downers Grove, IL: InterVarsity Press.

Nietzsche, Friedrich. (1891) 1917. *Thus Spake Zarathustra.* New York: Modern Library.

Nightingale, Andrea Wilson. 2004. *Spectacles of Truth in Classical Greek Philosophy: Theoria in Its Cultural Context.* Cambridge: Cambridge University Press.

Nigosian, S. A. 1993. *The Zoroastrian Faith: Tradition and Modern Research.* Montreal: McGill-Queen's University Press.

Nippert-Eng, Christena. 1996. *Home and Work: Negotiating Boundaries through Everyday Life.* Chicago: University of Chicago Press.

Norris, Rebecca Sachs. 2003. "Converting to What? Embodied Culture and the Adoption of New Beliefs." In *The Anthropology of Religious Conversion,* edited by Andrew Buckser and Stephen D. Glazier, pp. 171–81. Lanham, MD: Rowman and Littlefield.

Ofshe, Richard, and Ethan Watters. 1994. *Making Monsters: False Memories, Psychotherapy, and Sexual Hysteria.* New York: Charles Scribner's Sons.

Olick, Jeffrey K. 1999a. "Collective Memory: The Two Cultures." *Sociological Theory* 17:333–48.

———. 1999b. "Genre Memories and Memory Genres: A Dialogical Analysis of May 8th, 1945 Commemorations in the Federal Republic of Germany." *American Sociological Review* 64:381–402.

Olick, Jeffrey K., and Daniel Levy. 1997. "Collective Memory and Cultural Constraint: Holocaust Myth and Rationality in German Politics." *American Sociological Review* 62:921–36.

Olick, Jeffrey K., and Joyce Robbins. 1998. "Social Memory Studies: From 'Collective Memory' to the Historical Sociology of Mnemonic Practices." *Annual Review of Sociology* 24:105–40.

Orbuch, Terri L. 1997. "People's Accounts Count: The Sociology of Accounts." *Annual Review of Sociology* 23:455–78.

O'Rourke, P. J. 1989. "The Awful Power of Make-Believe." In *Second Thoughts: Former Radicals Look Back at the Sixties,* edited by Peter Collier and David Horowitz, pp. 203–9. Lanham, MD: Madison Books.

Ostler, Blake. 1982. "The Idea of Pre-existence in the Development of Mormon Thought." *Dialogue* 15:59–78.

Parker, Gary. 2012. "From Evolution to Creation: A Personal Testimony." Institute for Creation Research. Retrieved December 2012. http://creation.com /recovery-from-evolution.

Parkin, David. 1996. "The Power of the Bizarre." In *The Politics of Cultural Performance,* edited by David Parkin, Lionel Caplan, and Humphrey Fisher, pp. xv–xl. Providence, RI: Berghahn Books.

Patterson, Wendy. 2002. "Narrative Imaginings: The Liminal Zone in Narratives of Trauma." In *Strategic Narrative: New Perspectives on the Power of Personal and Cultural Stories,* edited by Wendy Patterson, pp. 71–87. Lanham, MD: Lexington Books.

Paul Williams's story. 2000. In *Finally Free: Personal Stories: How Love and Self-Acceptance Saved Us from Ex-Gay Ministries*, pp. 18–19. Washington, DC: Human Rights Campaign Foundation.

Paul Abernathy's story. 2007. "Reliving the Nightmare." Retrieved June 2008. http://ivaw.org/membersspeak/ofc-ii-reliving-nightmare.

Perinbanayagam, R. S. 1991. *Discursive Acts*. New York: Aldine De Gruyter.

———. 2000. *The Presence of Self*. Lanham, MD: Roman and Littlefield.

Phelan, Shane. 1993. "(Be)Coming Out: Lesbian Identity and Politics." *Signs* 18:765–90.

Pike, Sarah M. 2001. *Earthly Bodies, Magical Selves: Contemporary Pagans and the Search for Community*. Berkeley: University of California Press.

Pillemer, David B. 1998. *Momentous Events, Vivid Memories: How Unforgettable Moments Help Us Understand the Meaning of Our Lives*. Cambridge, MA: Harvard University Press.

Plato. (ca. 380 BCE) 1941. *The Republic of Plato*. Translated by Francis MacDonald Cornford. London: Oxford University Press.

Plummer, Ken. 1995. *Telling Sexual Stories: Power, Change and Social Worlds*. London: Routledge.

Polletta, Francesca. 2006. *It Was Like a Fever: Storytelling in Protest and Politics*. Chicago: University of Chicago Press.

Polletta, Francesca, and John Lee. 2006. "Is Telling Stories Good for Democracy? Rhetoric in Public Deliberation after 9/11." *American Sociological Review* 71:699–723.

Prager, Jeffrey. 1998. *Presenting the Past: Psychoanalysis and the Sociology of Misremembering*. Cambridge, MA: Harvard University Press.

Propp, Vladimir. 1968. *Morphology of the Folktale*. Austin: University of Texas Press.

Prus, Robert. 1987. "Generic Social Processes: Maximizing Conceptual Development in Ethnographic Research." *Journal of Contemporary Ethnography* 16:250–93.

Rambo, Lewis R. 1982. "Current Research on Religious Conversion." *Religious Studies Review* 8 (2): 146–59.

———. 1993. *Understanding Religious Conversion*. New Haven, CT: Yale University Press.

Reed, Issac. 2008. "Maximal Interpretation in Clifford Geertz and the Strong Program in Cultural Sociology: Towards a New Epistemology." *Cultural Sociology* 2 (2): 187–200.

Remini, Robert. 2002. *Joseph Smith*. New York: Penguin Group.

Reverend Jerry Stephenson's story. 2000. In *Finally Free: Personal Stories: How Love and Self-Acceptance Saved Us from Ex-Gay Ministries*, p. 10. Washington, DC: Human Rights Campaign Foundation.

Richard Cohen's story. 2000. "Coming Out Straight." Retrieved January 2013. http://www.peoplecanchange.com/stories/richard.php.

Richard Gaines's story. 2008. "I Found the Truth." Retrieved June 2008. http://www.mormonconverts.com/catholic/I-Found-The-Truth.htm.

Richard Johnson's story. 2008. "A Quiet Whisper . . . 'This is True!'" Retrieved July 2008. http://mormonconverts.com/methodist/a-quiet-whisper.htm.

Rick's story. 2009. Retrieved July 2009. http://www.beyondexgay.com/Narratives /Rick.

Ricoeur, Paul. 1984. *Time and Narrative*. Vol. 1. Chicago: University of Chicago Press.

Rieff, Philip. (1962) 1963. "Introduction." In *Dora: An Analysis of a Case History*, pp. vii–xix. New York: Touchstone.

Robin's story. 2005. Retrieved November 2005. http://www.gentletouchsweb .com/Stories/Robin.html.

Rob's story. 2004. "A Hard-Work Miracle." Retrieved January 2013. http://www .peoplecanchange.com/stories/rob.php.

Rodgers, Susan. 1995. *Telling Lives, Telling History: Autobiography and Historical Imagination in Modern Indonesia*. Berkeley: University of California Press.

Rod Manney's story. 2008. "Drugs, Sex and Booze Just Don't Get It!" Retrieved September 2008. http://www.precious-testimonies.com/BornAgain/o-r /RManney.htm.

Ronn Cantu's story. 2007a. "The Death of a Pro-War Conservative -or- The Day I Got Away with Murder." Retrieved August 2007. http://ivaw.org/membersspeak /one-soldiers-musings.

———. 2007b. "What, Exactly, Are We Dying For?" Retrieved August 2007. http:// ivaw.org/membersspeak/what-exactly-are-we-dying.

Rousseau, Jean-Jacques. (1755) 1994. *Discourse on the Origin of Inequality*. Oxford: Oxford University Press.

———. (1762) 1968. *The Social Contract*. London: Penguin Books.

Rubin, Henry. 2003. *Self-Made Men: Identity and Embodiment among Transsexual Men*. Nashville, TN: Vanderbilt University Press.

RuneWolf's story. 2012. "Converting to Paganism." Retrieved December 2012. http://www.witchvox.com/va/dt_va.html?a=usva&c=words&id=4035.

Ryan, Dan. 2006. "Getting the Word Out: Notes on the Social Organization of Notification." *Sociological Theory* 24:228–54.

Sagha's story. 2003. Retrieved March 2003. http://www.susansmiles.com/stories4 .html.

Saito, Hiro. 2006. "Reiterated Commemoration: Hiroshima as National Trauma." *Sociological Theory* 24 (4): 353–76.

Saussure, Ferdinand de. (1915) 1992 *Course in General Linguistics*. La Salle, IL: Open Court.

Schooler, Jonathan W. 2001. "Discovering Memories of Abuse in the Light of Meta-awareness." In *Trauma and Cognitive Science: A Meeting of Minds, Science, and Human Experience*, edited by Jennifer J. Freyd and Anne P. DePrince, pp. 105–36. New York: Hawthorn Press.

Schuman, Howard, Hiroko Akiyama, and Bärbel Knäuper. 1998. "Collective Memories of Germans and Japanese about the Past Half-Century." *Memory* 6 (4): 427–54.

Schuman, Howard, and Jacqueline Scott. 1989. "Generations and Collective Memories." *American Sociological Review* 54:359–81.

Schuman, Howard, Vered Vinitzky-Seroussi, and Amiram D. Vinokur. 2003. "Keeping the Past Alive: Memories of Israeli Jews at the Turn of the Millennium." *Sociological Forum* 18 (1): 103–36.

Schutz, Alfred. (1932) 1967. *The Phenomenology of the Social World.* Evanston, IL: Northwestern University Press.

———. 1945. "On Multiple Realities." *Philosophy and Phenomenological Research* 5 (4): 533–76.

Schwalbe, Michael, Sandra Godwin, Daphne Holden, Douglas Schrock, Shealy Thompson, and Michele Wolkomir. 2000. "Generic Processes in the Reproduction of Inequality: An Interactionist Analysis." *Social Forces* 79 (2): 419–52.

Schwartz, Barry. 1981. *Vertical Classification: A Study in Structuralism and the Sociology of Knowledge.* Chicago: University of Chicago Press.

———. 1982. "The Social Context of Commemoration: A Study in Collective Memory." *Social Forces* 61:374–402.

———. 1987. *George Washington: The Making of an American Symbol.* New York: Free Press.

Schwartz, Barry, and Howard Schuman. 2005. "History, Commemoration, and Belief: Abraham Lincoln in American Memory, 1945–2001." *American Sociological Review* 70:183–203.

Schwartz, Benjamin I. 1975. "The Age of Transcendence." *Daedalus* 104 (2): 1–7.

Scott, Marvin B., and Stanford M. Lyman. 1968. "Accounts." *American Sociological Review* 33 (1): 46–62.

Scott, Wilbur J. 1990. "PTSD in DSM-III: A Case in the Politics of Diagnosis and Disease." *Social Problems* 37:294–310.

Scott Anderson's story. 2008. "Becoming the Man I Was Attracted To." Retrieved June 2008. http://www.peoplecanchange.com/About_Us_Andersen.htm.

Sean's story. 2007. Retrieved September 2007. http://ivaw.org/view/profiles?apage=M.

Searle, John R. (1969) 1999. *Speech Acts: An Essay in the Philosophy of Language.* Cambridge: Cambridge University Press.

Sewell, William H., Jr. 1999. "The Concept(s) of Culture." In *Beyond the Cultural Turn: New Directions in the Study of Society and Culture*, edited by Victoria E. Bonnell and Lynn Hunt, pp. 35–61. Berkeley: University of California Press.

Shadow's story. 2003. Retrieved March 2003. http://www.susansmiles.com/penpal.html.

Shahbazi, A. Shapur. 1977. "The 'Traditional Date of Zoroaster' Explained." *Bulletin of the School of Oriental and African Studies* 40:25–35.

Shay, Jonathan. 1994. *Achilles in Vietnam: Combat Trauma and the Undoing of Character.* New York: Scribner.

Shephard, Ben. 2001. *A War of Nerves: Soldiers and Psychiatrists in the Twentieth Century.* Cambridge, MA: Harvard University Press.

Shibutani, Tamotsu. 1955. "Reference Groups as Perspective." *American Journal of Sociology* 60:562–69.

Shils, Edward. 1981. *Tradition*. Chicago: University of Chicago Press.

Simmel, Georg. (1922) 1955. "The Web of Group Affiliations." In *Conflict and the Web of Group Affiliations*, pp. 125–95. New York: Free Press.

———. 1950a. "The Field of Sociology." In *The Sociology of Georg Simmel*, edited by Kurt H. Wolff, pp. 3–25. New York: Free Press.

———. 1950b. "Quantitative Aspects of the Group." In *The Sociology of Georg Simmel*, edited by Kurt H. Wolff, pp. 145–53. New York: Free Press.

———. 1950c. "The Stranger." In *The Sociology of Georg Simmel*, edited by Kurt H. Wolff, pp. 402–8. New York: Free Press.

———. 1957. "Fashion." *American Journal of Sociology* 62 (6): 541–58.

———. 1965. "The Poor." *Social Problems* 13 (2): 118–40.

Simpson, Ruth. 1994. ""I Was There: Establishing Presence at Events." Paper presented at the Annual Meeting of the American Sociological Association, Los Angeles, CA.

———. 1996. "Neither Clear nor Present: The Social Construction of Safety and Danger." *Sociological Forum* 11:549–62.

Smelser, Neil J. 2004. "Psychological Trauma and Cultural Trauma." In *Cultural Trauma and Collective Identity*, edited by Jeffrey C. Alexander, Ron Eyerman, Bernhard Giesen, Neil J. Smelser, and Piotr Sztompka, pp. 31–59. Berkeley: University of California Press.

Smilde, David, and Matthew May. 2010. "The Emerging Strong Program in the Sociology of Religion." Social Science Research Council Working Papers. Retrieved March 2012. http://blogs.ssrc.org/tif/wp-content/uploads/2010/02 /Emerging-Strong-Program-TIF.pdf.

Smith, Adam. (1776) 2003. *The Wealth of Nations*. New York: Bantam Classics.

Smith, Anthony D. 1999. *Myths and Memories of the Nation*. Oxford: Oxford University Press.

Smith, Philip. 2005. *Why War? The Cultural Logic of Iraq, the Gulf War, and Suez*. Chicago: University of Chicago Press.

———. 2008. "The Balinese Cockfight Decoded: Reflections on Geertz, the Strong Program and Structuralism." *Cultural Sociology* 2 (2): 169–86.

Snow, David A., and Robert D. Benford. 1992. "Master Frames and Cycles of Protest." In *Frontiers in Social Movement Theory*, edited by Aldon D. Morris and Carol McClurg Mueller, pp. 133–55. New Haven, CT: Yale University Press.

Snow, David A., and Richard Machalek. 1983. "The Convert as a Social Type." *Sociological Theory* 1:259–89.

———. 1984. "The Sociology of Conversion." *Annual Review of Sociology* 10:167–90.

Snow, David A., E. Burke Rochford Jr., Steven K. Worden, and Robert D. Benford. 1986. "Frame Alignment Processes, Micromobilization, and Movement Participation." *American Sociological Review* 51:464–81.

Socarides, Charles W. 1968. *The Overt Homosexual*. New York: Grune and Stratton.

Somers, Margaret R. 1994. "The Narrative Constitution of Identity: A Relational and Network Approach." *Theory and Society* 23:605–49.

Spillman, Lyn. 1995. "Culture, Social Structure, and Discursive Fields." *Current Perspectives in Social Theory* 15:129–54.

———. 1998. "When Do Collective Memories Last? Founding Moments in the United States and Australia." *Social Science History* 22 (4): 445–77.

Spillman, Lyn, and Brian Conway. 2007. "Texts, Bodies, and the Memory of Bloody Sunday." *Symbolic Interaction* 30:79–103.

Spinoza, Benedict de. (1670) 2007. *Theological-Political Treatise.* Cambridge: Cambridge University Press.

Starbuck, Edwin Diller. (1899) 1911. *The Psychology of Religion.* New York: Charles Scribner's Sons.

Stein, Arlene. 1997. *Sex and Sensibility: Stories of a Lesbian Generation.* Berkeley: University of California Press.

———. 2009a. "'As Far as They Knew, I Came from France': Stigma, Passing, and Not Speaking about the Holocaust." *Symbolic Interaction* 32:44–60.

———. 2009b. "Feminism, Therapeutic Culture, and the Holocaust in the United States: The Second-Generation Phenomenon." *Jewish Social Studies* 16 (1): 27–53.

———. 2011. "Therapeutic Politics: An Oxymoron?" *Sociological Forum* 26 (1): 187–93.

Steinberg, Marc W. 1999. "The Talk and Back Talk of Collective Action: A Dialogic Analysis of Repertoires of Discourse among Nineteenth-Century English Cotton Spinners." *American Journal of Sociology* 105:736–80.

Steinmetz, George. 1992. "Reflections of the Role of Social Narratives in Working-Class Formation: Narrative Theory in the Social Sciences." *Social Science History* 16 (3): 489–516.

Stephen Merritt's story. 2008. "Searching All the Wrong Doctrines." Retrieved August 2008. http://www.precious-testimonies.com/BornAgain/L-N/merritt .htm.

Stieber, Josh, and Ethan McCord. 2012. "An Open Letter of Reconciliation & Responsibility to the Iraqi People." Retrieved March 2014. http://www.warre sisters.org/letterofreconciliation.

Strauss, Barry S. 1997. "The Problem of Periodization: The Case of the Peloponnesian War." In *Inventing Ancient Culture: Historicism, Periodization, and the Ancient World*, edited by Mark Golden and Peter Toohey, pp. 165–75. London: Routledge.

Stromberg, Peter G. 1993. *Language and Self-Transformation: A Study of the Christian Conversion Narrative.* Cambridge: Cambridge University Press.

Swartz, David. 1997. *Culture and Power: The Sociology of Pierre Bourdieu.* Chicago: University of Chicago Press.

Sweeney, Julia. 2005. *Letting Go of God.* Transcript of the compact disc, Ars Nova Theater, New York, November 19.

Swidler, Ann. 1986. "Culture in Action: Symbols and Strategies." *American Sociological Review* 51:273–86.

Tal, Kali. 1996. *Worlds of Hurt: Reading the Literatures of Trauma.* Cambridge, UK: Cambridge University Press.

Taylor, Charles. 1985. *Philosophical Papers.* Vol. 1, *Human Agency and Language.* Cambridge: Cambridge University Press.

———. 1989. *Sources of the Self: The Making of Modern Identity.* Cambridge, MA: Harvard University Press.

———. 1991. *The Ethics of Authenticity.* Cambridge, MA: Harvard University Press.

———. 2004. *Modern Social Imaginaries.* Durham, NC: Duke University Press.

Taylor, Verta, and Nancy E. Whittier. 1992. "Collective Identity in Social Movement Communities: Lesbian Feminist Mobilization." In *Frontiers in Social Movement Theory,* edited by Aldon D. Morris and Carol McClurg Mueller, pp. 104–29. New Haven, CT: Yale University Press.

Teeger, Chana. 2014. "Collective Memory and Collective Fear: How South Africans Use the Past to Explain Crime." Qualitative Sociology 37:69–92.

Teeger, Chana, and Vered Vinitzky-Seroussi. 2007. "Controlling for Consensus: Commemorating Apartheid in South Africa." *Symbolic Interaction* 30:57–78.

Terr, Lenore. 1994. *Unchained Memories: True Stories of Traumatic Memories, Lost and Found.* New York: Basic Books.

Thomas, William I. 1923. *The Unadjusted Girl with Cases and Standpoint for Behavior Analysis.* Boston: Little Brown. Retrieved May 2012. http://www.brocku .ca/MeadProject/Thomas/Thomas_1923/Thomas_1923_toc.html.

Thomassen, Bjørn. 2010. "Anthropology, Multiple Modernities and the Axial Age Debate." *Anthropological Theory* 10 (4): 321–42.

Thumma, Scott. 1991. "Seeking to Be Converted: An Examination of Recent Conversion Studies and Theories." *Pastoral Psychology* 39 (3): 185–94.

Tinkling Brass's story. 2006. Retrieved July 2008. http://www.postmormon.org /exp_e/index.php/discussions/viewthread/16/.

Tipton, Steven M. 1982. *Getting Saved from the Sixties: Moral Meaning in Conversion and Cultural Change.* Berkeley: University of California Press.

Tracey St. Pierre's story. 2000. In *Finally Free: Personal Stories: How Love and Self-Acceptance Saved Us from Ex-Gay Ministries,* p. 20. Washington, DC: Human Rights Campaign Foundation.

Trish's story. 1996. "The Accuser's Life." Retrieved November 2006. http://fmsfon line.org/fmsf96.n01.html.

Tthom's story. 2007. Retrieved July 2007. http://www.postmormon.org/exp_e /index.php/discussions/viewthread/16/P40/.

Turner, Steve. 2002, *Amazing Grace: The Story of America's Most Beloved Song.* New York: HarperCollins.

Turner, Victor. (1964) 1970. *The Forest of Symbols: Aspects of Ndembu Ritual.* Ithaca, NY: Cornell University Press.

Van Den Aardweg, Gerard J. M. 1997. *The Battle for Normality: A Guide for (Self-) Therapy for Homosexuality.* San Francisco: Ignatus Press

Van Gennep, Arnold. 1960. *The Rites of Passage*. Chicago: University of Chicago Press.

Vaughan, Diane. 2002. "Signals and Interpretive Work: The Role of Culture in a Theory of Practical Action." In *Culture in Mind: Toward a Sociology of Culture and Cognition*, edited by Karen A. Cerulo, pp. 28–54. New York: Routledge.

Victor Blazier's story. 2008a. Untitled. Retrieved June 2008. http://www.ivaw.org /user/85.

———. 2008b. "What Have We Become?" Retrieved June 2008. http://ivaw.org /membersspeak/what-have-we-become.

Vinitzky-Seroussi, Vered. 1998. *After Pomp and Circumstance: High School Reunion as an Autobiographical Occasion*. Chicago: University of Chicago Press.

———. 2000. "'My God, What Am I Gonna Say?': Class Reunions as Social Control." *Qualitative Sociology* 23:57–75.

———. 2001. "Commemorating Narratives of Violence: The Yitzhak Rabin Memorial Day in Israeli Schools." *Qualitative Sociology* 24:245–68.

———. 2002. "Commemorating a Difficult Past: Yitzhak Rabin's Memorials." *American Sociological Review* 67:30–51.

Wacquant, Loïc. 2004. *Body and Soul: Notebooks of an Apprentice Boxer*. Oxford: Oxford University Press.

Wagner-Pacifici, Robin. 1986. *The Moro Morality Play: Terrorism as Social Drama*. Chicago: University of Chicago Press.

———. 1994. *Discourse and Destruction: The City of Philadelphia versus MOVE*. Chicago: University of Chicago Press.

———. 2005. *The Art of Surrender: Decomposing Sovereignty at Conflict's End*. Chicago: University of Chicago Press.

Wagner-Pacifici, Robin, and Barry Schwartz. 1991. "The Vietnam Veterans Memorial: Commemorating a Difficult Past." *American Journal of Sociology* 97:376–420.

Walker, Katherine. 2000. "'It's Difficult to Hide It': The Presentation of Self on Internet Home Pages." *Qualitative Sociology* 23:99–120.

Warmfuzzylogic. 2008. "My Story, My Therapy." Retrieved June 2008. http://www .postmormon.org/exp_e/index.php/pomopedia/My_Story_My_Therapy/.

Washington, Booker T. 1901. *Up from Slavery*. Retrieved October 2012. http:// xroads.virginia.edu/~hyper/washington/toc.html.

Waskul, Dennis D. 2003. *Self-Games and Body-Play: Personhood in Online Chat and Cyberspace*. New York: Peter Lang.

Weber, Max. (1903–1917) 1949. *The Methodology of the Social Sciences*. New York: Free Press.

———. (1915) 1946. "Religious Rejections of the World and Their Directions." In *From Max Weber: Essays in Sociology*, edited by H. H. Gerth and C. Wright Mills, pp. 323–59. New York: Oxford University Press.

———. (1930) 1992. *The Protestant Ethic and the Spirit of Capitalism*. London: Harper Collins Academic.

———. 1968. *Economy and Society*. Berkeley: University of California Press.

Weil, Eric. 1975. "What Is a Breakthrough in History?" *Daedalus* 104 (2): 21–36.

Wells, H. G. 1904. "The Country of the Blind." Retrieved January 2008. http://www.online-literature.com/wellshg/3/.

White, Hayden. (1974) 1978. "The Historical Text as Literary Artifact." In *Tropics of Discourse: Essays in Cultural Criticism*, pp. 81–100. Baltimore, MD: Johns Hopkins University Press.

———. 1987. *The Content of the Form: Narrative Discourse and Historical Representation.* Baltimore, MD: Johns Hopkins University Press.

Whittier, Nancy. 2009. *The Politics of Child Sexual Abuse Emotion, Social Movements, and the State.* New York: Oxford University Press.

Wieland, Carl. 2000. "Recovery from Evolution: A Chat with Hydo-scientist Alan Galbriath." *Creation Ex Nihilo* 22 (2): 16–17. Retrieved December 2012. http://creation.com/recovery-from-evolution.

Wiley, Norbert. 1994. *The Semiotic Self.* Chicago: University of Chicago Press.

Winchester, Daniel. 2008. "Embodying the Faith: Religious Practice and the Making of a Muslim Moral Habitus." *Social Forces* 86 (4): 1753–80.

Wuthnow, Robert. 1987. *Meaning and Moral Order: Explorations in Cultural Analysis.* Berkeley: University of California Press.

———. 1989. *Communities of Discourse: Ideology and Social Structure in the Reformation, the Enlightenment, and European Socialism.* Cambridge, MA: Harvard University Press.

———. 2011. "Taking Talk Seriously: Religious Discourse as Social Practice."

Young, Allan. 1995. *The Harmony of Illusions: Inventing Post-Traumatic Stress Disorder.* Princeton, NJ: Princeton University Press.

Young, Brigham. 1857. *Journal of Discourses.* Vol. 4. Retrieved July 2009. http://www.journalofdiscourses.org/volume-04/.

Yvonne's story. 2005. "Becoming Yvonne." Retrieved October 2005. http://susansmiles.com/yvonne.html.

Zaretsky, Eli. 2004. *Secrets of the Soul: A Social and Cultural History of Psychoanalysis.* New York: Alfred A. Knopf.

Zelizer, Barbie. 1995. "Reading the Past against the Grain: The Shape of Memory Studies." *Critical Studies in Mass Communication* 12 (2):214–39.

Zerubavel, Eviatar. 1977. "The French Republican Calendar: A Case Study in the Sociology of Time." *American Sociological Review* 42:868–77.

———. 1979. *Patterns of Time in Hospital Life: A Sociological Perspective.* Chicago: University of Chicago Press.

———. 1981. *Hidden Rhythms: Schedules and Calendars in Social Life.* Chicago: University of Chicago Press.

———. 1985. *The Seven-Day Circle: The History and Meaning of the Week.* New York: Free Press.

———. 1991. *The Fine Line: Making Distinctions in Everyday Life.* Chicago: University of Chicago Press.

———. 1997. *Social Mindscapes: An Invitation to Cognitive Sociology.* Cambridge, MA: Harvard University Press.

———. 1998. "Language and Memory: 'Pre-Columbian' America and the Social Logic of Periodization." *Social Research* 65:315–30.

———. 2003. *Time Maps: Collective Memory and the Social Shape of the Past*. Chicago: University of Chicago Press.

———. 2006. *The Elephant in the Room: Silence and Denial in Everyday Life*. Oxford: Oxford University Press.

———. 2007. "Generally Speaking: The Logic and Mechanics of Social Pattern Analysis." *Sociological Forum* 22:1–15.

Zerubavel, Yael. 1995. *Recovered Roots: Collective Memory and the Making of Israeli National Tradition*. Chicago: University of Chicago Press.

Zussman, Robert. 1996. "Review: Autobiographical Occasions." *Contemporary Sociology* 25:143–48.

———. 2000. "Autobiographical Occasions: Introduction to the Special Issue." *Qualitative Sociology* 23:5–8.

Index

Made in the USA
Middletown, DE
11 May 2023

30361330R00151